Such Stuff as Dreams

The Psychology of Fiction

Keith Oatley

A John Wiley & Sons, Ltd., Publication

This edition first published 2011
© 2011 Keith Oatley

Wiley-Blackwell is an imprint of John Wiley & Sons, formed by the merger of Wiley's global Scientific, Technical and Medical business with Blackwell Publishing.

Registered Office
John Wiley & Sons Ltd, The Atrium, Southern Gate, Chichester, West Sussex, PO19 8SQ, United Kingdom

Editorial Offices
350 Main Street, Malden, MA 02148-5020, USA
9600 Garsington Road, Oxford, OX4 2DQ, UK
The Atrium, Southern Gate, Chichester, West Sussex, PO19 8SQ, UK

For details of our global editorial offices, for customer services, and for information about how to apply for permission to reuse the copyright material in this book please see our website at www.wiley.com/wiley-blackwell.

The right of Keith Oatley to be identified as the author of this work has been asserted in accordance with the UK Copyright, Designs and Patents Act 1988.

Wiley also publishes its books in a variety of electronic formats. Some content that appears in print may not be available in electronic books.

Designations used by companies to distinguish their products are often claimed as trademarks. All brand names and product names used in this book are trade names, service marks, trademarks or registered trademarks of their respective owners. The publisher is not associated with any product or vendor mentioned in this book. This publication is designed to provide accurate and authoritative information in regard to the subject matter covered. It is sold on the understanding that the publisher is not engaged in rendering professional services. If professional advice or other expert assistance is required, the services of a competent professional should be sought.

Library of Congress Cataloging-in-Publication Data
Oatley, Keith.
  Such stuff as dreams : the psychology of fiction / Keith Oatley.
      p. cm.
    Includes bibliographical references and index.
    ISBN 978-0-470-97457-5 (pbk.)
    1. Fiction–History and criticism–Theory, etc.   2. Fiction–Psychological
aspects.   3. Psychology and literature.   4. Literature–Psychology. I. Title.
    PN3352.P7O28 2011
    808.3–dc22

                                        2011002207

A catalogue record for this book is available from the British Library.

This book is published in the following electronic formats: ePDFs 9781119970927; Wiley Online Library 9781119970910; ePub 9781119973539

Set in 10.5 on 13 pt Minion by Toppan Best-set Premedia Limited
Printed and bound in Singapore by Fabulous Printers Pte Ltd

1   2011

For Simon, Susan, Grant, & Hannah
and
Daisy, Amber, Ewan, & Kaya

Contents

Preface

This book is about how fiction works in the minds and brains of readers, audience members, and authors, about how – from mere words or images – we create experiences of stories that are enjoyable, sometimes profound.

The book draws on an idea developed by William Shakespeare, Samuel Taylor Coleridge, Robert Louis Stevenson, and others, that fiction is not just a slice of life, not just entertainment, not just escape from the everyday. It often includes these but, at its center, it is a guided dream, a model that we readers and viewers construct in collaboration with the writer, which can enable us to see others and ourselves more clearly. The dream can offer us glimpses beneath the surface of the everyday world.

A piece of fiction is a model of the world, but not of the whole world. It focuses on human intentions and plans. That is why it has a narrative structure of actions and of incidents that occur as a result of those actions. It tells of the vicissitudes of our lives, of the emotions we experience, of our selves and our relationships as we pursue our projects. We humans are intensely social and – because our own motives are often mixed and because others can be difficult to know – our attempts to understand ourselves and others are always incomplete. Fiction is a means by which we can increase our understanding.

In the last 20 years or so, several groups of researchers have worked on finding out how fiction works in the mind, and why people enjoy reading novels and going to the movies. At the same time research on brain imaging has started to show how the brain represents emotions, actions, and thinking about other people, about which one reads in fiction. In the research group in which I work, we have started to show how identification with fictional characters occurs, how literary art can improve social abilities, how it can move us emotionally, and can prompt changes of selfhood. You can read opinion, reviews, and research, etc., by our group in our on-line magazine on the psychology of fiction, *OnFiction,* at http://www.onfiction.ca/

I am both a psychologist and a novelist. Although, until recently, it has not been much studied in psychology, fiction turns out to be of great psychological interest. The idea behind this book was first published in *Best Laid Schemes.* In it I put forward the cognitive-psychological hypothesis that fiction is a kind of simulation, one that runs not on computers but on minds: a simulation of selves in their interactions with others in the social world. This is what Shakespeare and others called a dream.

In this book, I cover a field that has been laid out for fiction by writers from Henry James and E.M. Forster onwards, but I approach the field from a psychological direction. Among traditional themes, I deal mainly with four: character, action, incident, and emotion. Among techniques, I deal with metaphor, metonymy, defamiliarization, and cues (which Elaine Scarry calls instructions to the reader). Among traditional contents, I concentrate on dialogue and people's presentations of themselves to each other.

The book is intended for general readers, psychologists, literary theorists, and students. I have preferred it to be brief rather than a tome, though it does contain pointers to research in a way that indicates the range of the field. In the book, I offer literary evidence in the form of quotations, and psychological evidence in the form of studies designed to move beyond mere opinion. But I have also imagined the book as having some of the qualities of fiction. That is to say I have designed it to have a narrative flow, and with some earlier parts leading to realizations that only come later. Within the narrative, I invite you to fill in some of the gaps between the paragraphs and sections in your own way.

The main text is designed for the general reader. There is also a parallel text in the numbered endnotes, in which I give the provenance of ideas and evidence from psychological studies, as well as more technical pieces of discussion.

In the book I cite a number of literary works, but some I refer to several times, and these are integral to the discussion. For them, I cite the relevant sections in the text, but the works as a whole can also be read alongside this book. For each of the reiterated works I give in an endnote, when it is first introduced, an internet address to a text available in the public domain.

The book's cover shows a detail from Johannes Vermeer's "The art of painting." I chose it because to me Vermeer's paintings, including this one, are theatrical events, instants suspended in time, dreamlike in that they include meaningful elements chosen to set off associations in the viewer in the same kind of way that objects and events set off mental associations in works of fiction. In this painting the central character is the muse Clio. She wears a laurel wreath and she carries a book and a musical instrument. Her eyelids are shyly lowered. Behind her is a map. On a stout table near her are an open manuscript and a mask. What might such elements suggest? It's from settings like this that stories can be born.

I shall sometimes address you – dear reader – as "you." And sometimes I shall talk of "we" (or "us"), meaning you and me.

I hope you enjoy the book.

Acknowledgments

The book arises from thinking a lot, reading a lot, discussing a lot, and from a series of psychological studies undertaken in the last 20 years in collaboration with people who started working with me as graduate students. These people are (in alphabetical order). Alisha Ali, Elise Axelrad, Angela Biason, Valentine Cadieux, Maja Djikic, Allan Eng, Mitra Gholamain, Alison Kerr, Laurette Larocque, Gerald Lazare, Raymond Mar, Maria Medved, Seema Nundy, Janet Sinclair, Patricia Steckley, and Rebecca Wells-Jopling. They have gone on to other things, including being professors, school psychologists, and psychotherapists. With two of them, Maja Djikic and Raymond Mar, who have stayed in Toronto, I continue to work closely. I thank also the members of a reading group that has met in Toronto, usually in the house of my partner (Jenny Jenkins) and me, for nearly 20 years (in alphabetical order this group is: Pat Baranek, Alina Gildiner, Sholom Glouberman, Susan Glouberman, Debbie Kirshner, Jenny Jenkins, Morris Moscovich, Berl Schiff [and me]). I also thank those in the community of researchers on the psychology of fiction and related matters with whom I have had enlightening discussions. Some I have known fondly for many years, others I have met for a few days at conferences, still others I have corresponded with by e-mail, but all have contributed to my thinking on the topics about which I write in this book: Lynne Angus, Jan Auracher, Bill Benzon, Nicholas Bielby, Brian Boyd, Jens Brockmeier, Jerry Bruner, Michael Burke, Nöel Carroll, Andy Clark, the late Max Clowes, Gerry Cupchik, Greg Currie, Ellen Dissanayake, Stevie Draper, Robin Dunbar, Judy Dunn, Charles Fernyhough, Jackie Ford, Fabia Franco, Don Freeman, Margaret Freeman, Nico Frijda, Simon Garrod, Melanie Green, Les Greenberg, Frank Hakemulder, Paul Harris, Jeannette Haviland-Jones, Geoff Hinton, Patrick Hogan, Norm Holland, Frank Kermode, David Konstan, Don Kuiken, Ian Lancashire, David Lodge, Carol Magai, Tony Marcel, Stephen Metcalf,

David Miall, Jonathan Miller, Martha Nussbaum, the late Tony Nuttall, David Olson, Jaak Panksepp, Joan Peskin, Jordan Peterson, Paul Rozin, Tom Scheff, Jacob Schiff, Murray Smith, Ronnie de Sousa, Keith Stanovich, Gerard Steen, Brian Stock, Ed Tan, Michael Tomasello, Michael Toolan, the late Tom Trabasso, Reuven Tsur, Peter Vorderer, Willie van Peer, Sonia Zyngier, Lisa Zunshine, Rolf Zwann.

Valentine Cadieux, Frank Hakemulder, Jeannette Haviland-Jones, Patrick Hogan, David Miall, Dan Perlitz, Joan Peskin, Martin Peskin, Willie van Peer, and Ed Tan, all read two draft chapters; Brian Boyd, Maja Djikic, Jenny Jenkins, and Raymond Mar, read drafts of the whole book. Each of them has offered comments that let me know where I was going in worthwhile directions, and that identified places in which I needed to think some more. I very much appreciate their kindness and thoughtfulness; their suggestions have been extraordinarily helpful.

I warmly thank the excellent editorial staff at Wiley-Blackwell, Andy Peart, Annie Rose, Karen Shield, and Suchitra Srinivasan, as well as the assiduous picture researcher, Kitty Bocking. In addition, I would like to thank the ever helpful project manager Aileen Castell and Kathy Syplywczak for her skillful copy-editing. My profound gratitude goes to my spouse and principal editor, Jenny Jenkins, who – as always – has been kind, encouraging, and insightful.

1

Fiction as Dream

Figure 1.1 Frontispiece of the 1600 edition of *A midsummer night's dream*.
Source: The Huntington Library, San Marino, California.

Such Stuff as Dreams: The Psychology of Fiction, First Edition. K. Oatley.
© 2011 K. Oatley. Published 2011 by John Wiley & Sons, Ltd.

Fiction as Dream: Models, World-Building, Simulation

Shakespeare and dream

"Dream" was an important word for William Shakespeare. In his earliest plays he used it with its most common meaning, of a sequence of actions, visual scenes, and emotions that we imagine during sleep and that we sometimes remember when we awake, as well as with its second most common meaning of a waking fantasy (day-dream) of a wishful kind. Two or three years into his playwriting career, he started to use it in a subtly new way, to mean an alternative view of the world, with some aspects like those of the ordinary world, but with others unlike.[1] In the dream view, things look different from usual.

In or about December 1594, something changed for Shakespeare.[2] What changed was his conception of fiction. He started to believe, I think, that fiction should contain both visible human action and a view of what goes on beneath the surface. His plays moved beyond dramatizations of history as in the three *Henry VI* plays, beyond entertainments such as *The taming of the shrew.*[3] They came to include aspects of dreams. Just as two eyes, one beside the other, help us to see in three dimensions so, with our ordinary view of the world and an extra view (a dream view), Shakespeare allows us to see our world with another dimension. The plays that he first wrote when he had achieved his idea were *A midsummer night's dream* and *Romeo and Juliet.*

In *A midsummer night's dream* it is as if Shakespeare says: imagine a world a bit different from our own, a model world, in which, while we are asleep, some mischievous being might drip into our eyes the juice of "a little western flower" so that, when we awake, we fall in love with the person we first see. This is what happens to Titania, Queen of the Fairies. Puck drips the juice into her eyes. When she wakes, she sees Bottom the weaver, who – in the dream world – has been turned into an ass, and has been singing.

> *Titania:* I pray thee, gentle mortal, sing again:
>   Mine ear is much enamour'd of thy note;
>   So is mine eye enthralled to thy shape;
>   And thy fair virtue's force perforce doth move me
>   On the first view to say, to swear, I love thee (1, 3, 959)

Could it be that, rather than considering what kind of person we could commit ourselves to, we first love and then discover in ourselves the words and thoughts and actions that derive from our love?[4]

A midsummer night's dream helped Shakespeare, I think, to articulate his idea of theater as model-of-the-world. Although perhaps not as obviously, *Romeo and Juliet,* which was written at about the same time, comes from the same idea. It starts with a Prologue, which begins like this.

> Two households, both alike in dignity,
> In fair Verona, where we lay our scene,
> From ancient grudge break to new mutiny,
> Where civil blood makes civil hands unclean.
> From forth the fatal loins of these two foes
> A pair of star-cross'd lovers take their life;
> Whose misadventured piteous overthrows
> Do with their death bury their parents' strife (Prologue, 1).

A model is an artificial thing.[5] So Shakespeare doesn't start *Romeo and Juliet* with anything you might see in ordinary life. He starts it with someone who is clearly an actor coming on to the stage and addressing the audience in a sonnet. The sonnet form has 14 lines, each having ten syllables with the emphasis on the second syllable of each pair. So this sonnet reads: "Two **house**-holds **both** a-**like** . . ." This makes for a certain attention-attracting difference, because if you pronounce the verse in this iambic way, and make sure also to emphasize slightly the rhymes at the end of each line, it sounds different from colloquial English.[6] The iambic meter seems almost to echo the human heart-beat: te-tum, te-tum, te-tum.

The sonnet at the beginning of *Romeo and Juliet* tells us the play's theme. As with *A midsummer night's dream,* the play is about the effects of an emotion, once again love. In the what-if world of this play, the threat by the civil authority of punishing public fighting by death is futile. The only thing that will temper hatred is love: in this case the love between the children of the two households, and the love of the parents for their children. This, says the actor who recites the prologue-sonnet, "Is now the two-hour's traffic of our stage." Once a different view than usual has been suggested by means of the model world of what-if, each of us in the audience can wonder: "What do we think?"

Shakespeare's idea of dream had at its center the idea of model, or imagination, that could be compared with the visible aspects of the world.

It was extended to include two features that he continued to develop throughout his writing.

One of these features was the relation of surface actions to that which is within. Shakespeare uses a range of words that include: "shadow," "action," "show," "form," and "play," to indicate outwardly visible behavior. (Shadow meant what it does today, as well as reflection as in a mirror.)[7] To indicate what is deeper and externally invisible in a person, Shakespeare uses another range of words that include: "substance," "heart," "mettle," and "that within." It's not that outer behavior is deceptive as compared with that within which is real. That would be banal. Shakespeare typically depicts relations between shadow and substance. This idea of shadow and substance – of actions that are easily visible accompanied by glimpses of what goes on beneath the surface – enables us to compare actions and their meanings.

The second further feature in Shakespeare's idea of dream is recognition. One form it takes is of a character thinking someone to be whom he or she seems to be on the surface, and then finding this person to be someone else. It's an extension of the idea of shadow and substance, but with emphasis coming to fall on implications of the recognition. It is the story-outcome of the idea that some aspects of others (and ourselves) are hidden.

Rather than offering quotations that can be tantalizingly insufficient, let me offer a whole piece by Shakespeare that is quite brief. With it we shall be able to see, I hope, how the idea of dream (with its idea of model-in-the imagination, and its features of substance-and-shadow and of recognition) can work together. This piece is Shakespeare's Sonnet 27, which is as follows.

Sonnet 27: A story in sonnet form

Weary with toil I haste me to my bed,
The dear repose for limbs with travel tired;
But then begins a journey in my head
To work my mind when body's work's expired;
For then my thoughts, from far where I abide,
Intend a zealous pilgrimage to thee,
And keep my drooping eyelids open wide
Looking on darkness which the blind do see:
Save that my soul's imaginary sight
Presents thy shadow to my sightless view,
Which like a jewel hung in ghastly night

Makes black night beauteous and her old face new.
  Lo! thus by day my limbs, by night my mind,
  For thee, and for myself, no quietness find.

The poet is away. Tired with his work and his travel, he goes to bed. In line 3, there is a metaphor, "journey in my head." Just as on a journey one visits a series of places so, in one's mind, one visits a series of thoughts. At the same time, the whole sonnet is a model, a metaphor in the large, and a wide-awake dream, in which the poet thinks of his loved one with urgent feelings.

Although it has only 14 lines, a sonnet is often a story. Or one can think of it as a compression of a story into its turning point. The sonnet form includes an expectation that there will be at least one such turning point. There is also the expectation that the sonnet will reach a conclusion.[8]

In the sonnet form, the first turning point is expected between lines 8 and 9. This kind of change derives from the earliest kind of sonnet, which is called Petrarchan, after the Italian poet Petrarch. In this form, the first eight lines comprise what is known as the octave. It's followed at line 9 by the last six lines or sestet – in a way that is like a change of key in music – in which the skilled poet takes us through an important juncture in the story, or enables us to see first part of the poem in a different way. In the slightly different, Elizabethan, form of the sonnet, the change occurs at line 13. In his Sonnet 27, Shakespeare arranges two changes: at line 9 and at line 13.

The octave of Sonnet 27 is a description, as if in a letter: "Weary with toil I haste me to my bed . . ." Once a reader has worked out that the poet is away from home and that the poem is addressed to the poet's beloved, the meaning seems clear. The poet goes to bed tired, wanting to sleep and, as he lies in bed, he thinks of his loved one, far away. Perhaps the journey in his head retraces the physical journey away from his loved one. But as the reader starts to think about it, this idea doesn't quite make sense. If the poet were merely missing his beloved, there would be longing, perhaps memories of being together. There's nothing of the sort. So the reader has to think harder. The poet has already complained that his daytime work is wearying. Now, in bed, the act of thinking about his beloved is work (another metaphor). These are not fond thoughts of the loved one. The metaphor implies that these thoughts, too, are wearying.

Shakespeare chooses words carefully. He doesn't write "eager pilgrimage to thee." He writes "zealous pilgrimage to thee" with "zealous" perhaps having the word "jealous" hiding behind it.[9] We might also think that a connotation of "zealous" is "slightly crazy." Why is the poet lying with "eyelids open wide," although they are "drooping?" He stares into the darkness, unable to see. "Looking on darkness which the blind do see." He's like a blind person, a person blinded by – what?

When line 9 is reached a change, or turning point, occurs to the last six lines, the sestet. It offers a different view:[10] "Save that my soul's imaginary sight." In other words, the poet says: "What has gone before is right, it's dark and I can't see, except that . . ." suddenly the poet can see his loved one – all too clearly – in his imagination. That's what's keeping him awake. In the poet's imaginary sight comes Shakespeare's use of "shadow" (meaning externally visible actions), with its implicit contrast with substance (meaning who the loved one really is).

The beloved is beautiful, and therefore "like a jewel." But what a juxtaposition: "hung in ghastly night." The poet lies in bed, and imagines what his beautiful beloved might be up to. It's ghastly! The poet imagines that his beloved is not lying quietly in bed, not asleep. The beloved is doing something else. What?

The poet tries to wrench his mind around, to counter this distressing idea. In the twelfth line he offers the poem's only positive thought of the loved one, who makes the "night beauteous," and makes ancient darkness new.

But the moment is fleeting, because now comes a further turning point. In the Elizabethan sonnet form the rhyming couplet of the last two lines sometimes provide a pithy summary of what has gone before. There is some of this here, with: "Lo! thus by day my limbs, by night my mind." But now we see the final couplet is not just a summary. It holds a shocking conclusion. "For thee, and for myself, no quietness find." Despite thinking of the beloved as a jewel that makes night beautiful and renews it, the poet can't reach quiet contentment with the night-time journey of his thoughts. Why? "For thee" is ambiguous. It can be joined to the previous line to make: "by night my mind, for thee," which would be a more-or-less simple summary of a mental journey. But the last line is stark. "For thee, and for myself, no quietness find." There is no quietness for the beloved, nor for the poet, nor between them.

We know – not just from this sonnet but from others that follow it in the sequence – that the poet fears his love is not fully reciprocated. The lack of quiet is because the beloved may perhaps be in bed, though not quietly asleep but with someone else. Or perhaps the beloved is out, being a jewel to another admirer. That is why the night in which the jewel hangs would be ghastly.

We can regard fiction as a description of people's actions and interactions. So, in this sonnet, Shakespeare offers the octave in terms of actions. At the same time the best fiction is, or includes, something like a dream-model, which enables us to see the substance beneath the surface. In this sonnet the sestet shows the poet, in the dream of his imagination, wondering what the loved one may be up to.

This is a poem about the actions of a journey and an accompanying model world of the imagination, a poem of shadow and substance, a poem of recognition of whom the beloved might be. In this miniature form, with an extraordinary density of thought, Shakespeare offers us a moving and recognizable dream of a world we can understand, of being in love but of being sleeplessly anxious about whether the love is recognized or reciprocated.

This is one possible meaning for the poet in his relationship with his beloved, and it's also one meaning for us, the readers of this sonnet-story. This is my suggestion. I wonder what you think.

Approach by the dream

In this book, I propose that Shakespeare's idea of dream (model with its aspects of shadow-and-substance and of recognition) allows us to understand important aspects of the psychology of fiction. I have presented Sonnet 27, because, in miniature it shows how this approach can work. In the rest of the book, I hope to show further aspects, how fiction enters the mind, how it prompts us towards emotions, how it affords insights into ourselves and others, how it is enjoyable, how it has been shown to have worthwhile effects on readers.

People often think the word "fiction" means untrue, but this is not true. The word derives from the Latin *fingere*, which means "to make." In the same way the word "poetry" comes from the Greek word *poesis*, which also means "to make." Fiction and poetry are constructed in the imagination, and are different from something discovered as in physics, or from something that happened as in the news. Fiction and poetry are not false; they are about what could happen.[11]

I take fiction to be theater, narrative poetry, novels, short stories, and fiction films. It's about selves, about intentions and the vicissitudes they meet, about the social world.[12] I take it, too, that fiction is based in narrative, which is a distinct mode of thought and feeling about us human beings.

Victorian views

Shakespeare's idea of fiction-as-dream is not the only one that circulates about the nature of fiction. It is not even the most popular. Indeed, I think, it is not widely known.

Let us look at how things stood in 1884, when Henry James published an article in *Longman's Magazine* called "The art of fiction." He put a theory that was very different from Shakespeare's. He said that a novel is "a direct impression of life." Robert Louis Stevenson disagreed. He was for something more like Shakespeare's view and, a few months after he read James's article, he published a reply in the same magazine. He called his reply "A humble remonstrance." His title makes one think that he was apologizing. Perhaps he needed to, because he (known mainly for his children's stories like *Treasure Island*) was right, and Henry James (one of the world's great novelists) was wrong. Despite this, James's essay has remained famous, and Stevenson's reply relatively obscure. It's by grasping Shakespeare's and Stevenson's idea that we can come closer to understanding the psychology of fiction.

A novel, says Stevenson, is not a direct impression of life. It's a work of art.

> Life is monstrous, infinite, illogical, abrupt and poignant; a work of art in comparison is neat, finite, self-contained, rational, flowing, and emasculate. Life imposes by brute energy, like inarticulate thunder; art catches the ear, among the far louder noises of experience, like an air artificially made by a discreet musician (p. 182).

Life, says Stevenson, includes huge forces "whose sun we cannot look upon, whose passions and diseases waste and slay us" (p. 181). Art is different.[13] It is abstract, like mathematics. Straight lines and circles do not exist in the physical world, but now they have been invented we cannot do without them. They are abstract. They exist in model worlds. But in the practical activities of engineering in which bridges are designed and cars are constructed, they are essential. Straightish tracks and serviceable wheels were, of course, invented before straight lines and circles. The purpose of lines and circles in mathematics is to allow us to understand the deeper properties, the essence of straightness and the way in which wheels take their being from circularity, to allow calculations that are essential in the design of technologies. Similarly, and perhaps for millions of years, everyone could understand certain aspects of other people's behavior. They saw that sometimes individuals behaved with their own kind of consistency but that, at other times, something from outside them seemed to affect them, when they became fond of someone, or were angry. We now talk of character and emotion. The deepest developments of our ideas about character and emotion – abstract ideas – occur in fiction. Or, rather, the ideas are depicted in fiction so that we can develop them in ourselves and in our lives.

Why do we need models? Why don't we just observe what goes on in the real world, perhaps notice some regularities? A good deal of narrative fiction is of this kind. In the *Iliad*, Homer offers something like the following: this is how it was in the Trojan War, Achilles had an argument with Agamemnon, and then went into a sulk, because of it the Greeks were nearly defeated by the Trojans. Among the first plays Shakespeare wrote were histories. He implies something similar. If we had been there, we would have seen something like this. After he had his idea of theater-as-a-model-of-the world, Shakespeare offers something different. He says: could this be what goes on beneath the surface of things?

The idea of dream
From around 1594 onwards, Shakespeare moves towards making the more abstract aspect the center of what he writes. The something-beneath-the surface that he depicts is an underlying pattern of how people are and what they're up to. It's a reaching towards understandings of people's inner being. One can't always achieve these understandings from surface actions, but if you start to see the deeper kind of movement, glimpsed by means of models, you can start to understand better how things work.

Shakespeare did not invent the idea of theater-as-a-model-of-the-world, but when he saw its significance, it became strong for him. He may have been prompted towards it by Erasmus, whose influence on him was considerable. In Erasmus's most famous book, *Praise of Folly*, Folly, a woman, stands up and gives a speech in praise of herself, a very foolish thing to do. Folly is emotion. In her speech she explains how, although on the surface many serious people such as politicians, teachers, and the learned, present themselves as guided only by reason, really they often act from emotion, sometimes emotion that is rather self-interested, for instance the prideful urge to make themselves superior by being right in comparison to other people who are wrong, or the needy insistence on being the center of attention. Such emotions don't seem very creditable. People often think they are best kept beneath the surface. Folly says:

> It's confessed on all sides that the emotions are the province of folly.
> Indeed, this is the way we distinguish the wise man from the fool, that
> the one is governed by his reason, the other by his emotions . . . Yet these
> emotions not only serve as guides to those who press towards the gates
> of wisdom, they also act as spurs and incitements to the practice of every
> virtue (p. 29).

In part, Folly satirizes Erasmus's own scholarly pursuits. But Erasmus also
writes his satire as a way of pursuing the deeper idea that people who recognize their own emotions, and understand them, enable themselves to
avoid being puffed up with the self-importance of their learning, with the
self-confirming logic of their opinion about how things ought to be. Such
people have often been able to live lives of kindness or piety. In an echo of
this, George Eliot wrote in *Middlemarch:* "Our good depends on the quality
and breadth of our emotion" (p. 510).

In his reading of *Praise of folly,* Shakespeare may have seen the idea that
something artificial – a satire – could be a pointer to what is real, beneath
the surface.

Four years after his reply to Henry James, Robert Louis Stevenson was
still thinking about the nature of fiction, and wrote an essay on dreams. In
it he says this:

> The past is all of one texture – whether feigned or suffered – whether
> acted out in three dimensions, or only witnessed in that small theater
> of the brain which we keep brightly lighted all night long, after the jets
> are down, and darkness and sleep reign undisturbed in the remainder
> of the body (p. 189).

Stevenson went on to say that he had always been a dreamer, and that all
his best ideas for stories came to him as dreams.[14] So rather than a direct
impression, this was what literary art was, a kind of dream.

Not far into *Romeo and Juliet*, Shakespeare depicts Romeo as seeing,
across a room, a girl about whom he knows nothing, Juliet. Romeo crosses
the room and – rather forwardly, one might think – he touches her. Then
he speaks. The lines Romeo and Juliet speak between them take the form
of the play's second sonnet, this time using the sonnet form for its traditional purpose, to depict love. It begins like this.

> *Romeo:* If I profane with my unworthiest hand
>   This holy shrine, the gentler sin is this:
>   My lips, two blushing pilgrims, ready stand
>   To smooth that rough touch with a tender kiss (I, 5, 719).

Romeo tells Juliet that he sees her as a statue of a saint, to which he can come as a pilgrim, to worship, and be allowed to touch, and to kiss.

As in *A midsummer night's dream*, here is the idea that an emotion works by prompting us towards a certain kind of relationship with a certain person. In Romeo's case, the emotion is adoration. Might model worlds enable us to see beneath the surface to how emotions work? And might not this idea allow us to understand how fiction works, how it really works?

Shakespeare often also lets us know something of the way in which he is thinking. In *A midsummer night's dream*, he has Theseus use the term "fantasies" (that is to say "dreams"), and then to say:

The poet's eye, in a fine frenzy rolling,
Doth glance from heaven to earth, from earth to heaven;
And as imagination bodies forth
The forms of things unknown, the poet's pen
Turns them to shapes and gives to airy nothing
A local habitation and a name (5, 1, 1843).

The idea of theater-as-a-model-of-the-world prompted the name of the playhouse of which Shakespeare was co-owner, The Globe. Its Latin motto was *Totus mundus agit histrionem*, which can be translated as "All the world's a stage" (*As you like it*, 2, 7, 1037).

These ideas – theater-as-a-model-of-the-world, with its features of shadow-and-substance and of recognition – continue throughout Shakespeare's career. They give structure, for instance to *Hamlet*, which was written around 1600 and performed at The Globe not long after it was built. Not only is the play itself a model but, perhaps by way of explaining to us how it works, Shakespeare embeds within it a play-within-the-play, the dramatic purpose of which is for Hamlet to show publicly for himself and for others, and for Claudius, what has been going on beneath the surface.[15]

The feature of shadow and substance is the key to the first extended speech of Hamlet, in which he replies to his mother who has asked him why he "seems" so sad, and why he continues so obdurately in mourning for his dead father. Hamlet replies that he knows not "seems." Wearing black, sighing, and weeping are mere outward forms. These he says are:

. . . actions that a man can play;
But I have that within which passeth show –
These but the trappings and the suits of woe (1, 2, 279).

Figure 1.2   Shakespeare's company's theatre The Globe, from an engraving by Visscher. Source: British Library, London, UK/© British Library Board. All Rights Reserved/The Bridgeman Art Library.

Recognition pervades *Hamlet*. Hamlet comes to recognize who Claudius is, and then more movingly who his mother is, who his friends are, who he is. Most importantly, by means of the counterpoint between Hamlet's actions and his inwardness we in the audience come to recognize something of who we are, ourselves.

Mimesis
The idea of fiction as involving models started long before Shakespeare. The core idea is already present in the book that is seen, in the West, as the foundation of both the theory and psychology of imaginative literature: Aristotle's *Poetics*. The term around which Aristotle's book revolves is *mimesis:* the relation of a piece of literature to the world. Aristotle took up

the issue of *mimesis* from his teacher Plato, who discusses it extensively in *The Republic*. Nearly always, in English, the Greek *mimesis* is translated as imitation, copying, representation, and the like. This is the sense that Henry James had in mind in his essay "The art of fiction," with his term, "direct impression." This is the aspect of narrative that Homer employed to depict what happened in the Trojan War, and Shakespeare used to depict political events in his early history plays in the *Henry VI* series.

There is a whole category of representational art. Fiction can imitate, or represent, somewhat as a mirror can. Perhaps Hamlet had this idea in mind when he enjoined the travelling players who visited the court at Elsinore to "hold the mirror up to nature" (3, 3, 1896). Perhaps, at the same time, he was interested in holding up the mirror so that Claudius could see himself as others saw him.

More recently, of course, photographs and video recordings have become emblematic of accurate copying and representation of events. A writer of realist fiction, too, can offer correspondences of things, events, and people in the fictional world with things, events, and people in the real world, just as a scientist can study correspondences or absences of correspondence with predictions made from a theory and careful observations of the real world. And when we see a film adapted from one of Jane Austen's novels we may ask: "Did people really dress like that 200 years ago?"

There is nothing wrong with the idea that poetry or fiction can be representational or imitative – well, nothing very wrong with it. It's just that it's only half the issue, maybe less than half. As Stephen Halliwell has shown, the Greek word, *mimesis* also had a second family of meanings that are less widely discussed, and sometimes even ignored. We might imagine that it was this second set in which William Shakespeare and Robert Louis Stevenson were most interested. They were right to be so, because this second idea is more far-reaching. This second set of meanings – of *mimesis-as-dream* – has to do with world-making, with model-building, with imagination, with recognizing what goes on beneath the surface. As Halliwell puts it:

> Reduced to a schematic but nonetheless instructive dichotomy, these varieties of mimetic theory and attitude can be described as encapsulating a difference between a "world-reflecting" [conception] (for which the mirror has been a common though far from straightforward metaphorical emblem), and, on the other side, a "world simulating" or "world creating" conception of artistic representation (p. 22).

The book you are reading now, like many on the theory of literature, has Aristotle's idea of *mimesis* at its center. I concentrate on the "world-simulating" or "world-creating" aspect[16] because I think it needs to be considered first, and because I think it offers the deeper insights into the psychology of fiction.

The world-reflecting idea of art is that there is correspondence between elements of a work of art and elements of the ordinary world. To an extent this is true, so people in a play might correspond to people you know. But in *A midsummer night's dream*, there is no correspondence between the juice of the little western flower and any pharmacological agent of Shakespeare's time or ours. You will not read in the newspapers about anyone like Titania, Queen of the Fairies. Nor is there any possibility for any of us to be turned, suddenly, into an ass. The dream world does not depend on detailed correspondences between a thing in the model and a thing in the ordinary world. The second idea of *mimesis* – the idea of "world-simulating" or "world-creating" – works with larger structures. It depends more on coherence among its elements than on correspondences between specific elements of the model and elements of the ordinary world. It works because certain relationships among things in the model world correspond to certain relationships among things in the ordinary world (world-creating is perhaps not exactly the right term for this). It works because a certain relational structure is made salient in the model world so that we can see its correspondence to a relational structure of the real world. The relation between people when they are in love in the dream world points to a possible relation between people in love in the ordinary world.

Well, you may say, the idea of a theatrical play as a model is all very well, but in what way does the juice of a little western flower dropped into someone's eyes differ from cupid's arrow? One difference, I think, is that in Shakespeare's time, Cupid's arrow was already a cliché. The flower-juice and the idea of falling in love with whom you first see when you awake, in *A midsummer-night's dream,* makes the involuntariness of love surprising and striking all over again. It draws the attention. It makes the idea strange.[17]

In *Romeo and Juliet* Shakespeare continues to press unfamiliar ideas about emotions. It will have occurred to us that when we experience a strong emotion, we cannot stop ourselves. Shakespeare shows in *Romeo and Juliet* how not even an explicit command, on pain of death, by the ruler of Verona can enable the Capulets and Montagues and their retainers to stop hating each other. What Shakespeare makes of this is surprising and new. It remains still striking and new in psychotherapy. It is the suggestion that when one is in the grip of a strong emotion, it can be changed only by another emotion.[18] The hatred that the two families bear each other is only changed by something stronger, the love that parents bear towards their children. This is a profound idea, a surprising idea, which emerges as we tunnel down to what lies beneath the surface of external action.

You might also say that if theater is a dream, does this mean that it is merely fantasy? The answer is no. We live, now, in a period when a great deal of narrative art is in the mode of realism. When we go to the movies, most dramas and comedies depict people whose actions (on the surface) are much as we might recognize them in the lives of ourselves and those we know. There is, in them, a strong aspect of *mimesis*-as-imitation. *Romeo and Juliet*, also, is explicitly a depiction of the world of two families in Verona, not unlike the realism of modern film dramas. By comparison, *A midsummer night's dream* is explicitly a fantasy. The issue is one of emphasis. Every true artistic expression, I think, is not just about the surface of things. It always has some aspect of the abstract. The issue is whether, by a change of perspective or by a making the familiar strange, by means of an artistically depicted world, we can see our everyday world in a deeper way.

In *The winter's tale*, Shakespeare replays ideas of love and death that he treated in *Romeo and Juliet*, but with a happy ending: a scene of recognition in which a statue (a work of art) of Hermione (for whom King Leontes has spent 16 years in repentance that he condemned her to death), turns out to be the real Hermione, alive.

Once Shakespeare has had his idea about dreams (or models) with their workings in shadow-and-substance, and their outcomes in recognition, he visits them again and again, not just repeating them, but exploring them each time further than before.[19] In *The tempest*, a play he wrote towards the end of his literary career, Shakespeare was still extending these ideas.

Prospero: . . . These our actors,
As I foretold you, were all spirits, and
Are melted into air, into thin air:
And, like the baseless fabric of this vision,
The cloud-capp'd towers, the gorgeous palaces,
The solemn temples, the great globe itself,
Yea, all which it inherit, shall dissolve,
And, like this insubstantial pageant faded,
Leave not a rack behind. We are such stuff
As dreams are made on, and our little life
Is rounded with a sleep (4, 1, 1877).[20]

The idea of dream (model, shadow-and-substance, and recognition) that Shakespeare conceived is so good that it applies to fiction of every kind: poetry, plays, novels, short stories, films. Two hundred years after Shakespeare died, Samuel Taylor Coleridge reflected on the idea during a voyage to Malta. "Poetry" he wrote in his notebook is, "a rationalized Dream dealing . . . to manifold Forms our own Feelings" (p. 66).[21]

When Shakespeare had conceived his idea of drama as dream, he saw that he could create worlds on the stage which were interestingly different from the quotidian world, but which could parallel it in imagination. By transforming certain human matters, such as the emotion of love, into those of an imagined world that was somewhat unfamiliar, we the audience members are able to compare the dream world with the ordinary world. From such comparisons, we can focus on matters to which habit usually blinds us. Though some matters in the dream world, such as sonnets, fairies, and magic potions, are far from anything that occurs in the everyday world, other matters such as character and emotions pass readily through the membrane between the model world and the everyday world. As they pass, they undergo certain kinds of transformation of a kind that can afford us insight.

Language has many words for the imaginative function: dream, model, simulation, metaphor, simile, analogy, theory, allegory, fable, schema, game. All involve not just one-to-one correspondences, in the way indicated by the idea of copying and imitation, but whole imagined worlds.

Fiction and simulation

"Dream" is a good metaphor for fiction because most of us have experience of dreaming and know that dreams are somewhat apart from the ordinary world. We know, too, that they are constructed by ourselves. They are not direct impressions of the world, and they may be meaningful.

Shakespeare's principle of dream had forerunners in medieval times, when allegory was central to literature. Here is a medieval Latin verse that describes four aspects of a text:

Littera gesta docet;
Quid credas allegoria;
Moralia quid agas;
Quo tendas anagogia.

(The literal teaches what happened; The allegorical what to believe; The moral what to do; The anagogical where to go.)

Dante expounded this idea in his *Il convivio* (The banquet). In Dante's poetry, the love between a man and a woman is offered as an allegory of the love of God for his creation. By means of it we can understand a tiny bit of God's love for us his creatures from our own limited experience of human love in the day-to-day world.

Shakespeare's idea of dream was close to the medieval idea of allegory, which he would have known. But, whereas the medieval idea was typically used in the way Dante used it, to create a meditative system of religious and moral symbolism,[22] in his idea, Shakespeare turned towards explorations of shadow-and-substance, that lead to recognitions of others and oneself in this world.

If we want to talk about the dream idea in linguistic terms we might say "metaphor-in-the-large" or "extended metaphor." Or we might use a term that one sees often in literary theory: "imagination."

We can trace the idea from the world-making aspect of *mimesis*, through the medieval idea of allegory, to Shakespeare's idea of dream, to the present. For psychologists two suggestive metaphors for this function are "model" and "simulation." I have already used the idea of model, but simulation takes it further. Narrative stories are simulations that run not on computers but on minds. Simulation is a good metaphor in its sense of construction from parts. For complex matters we may know how each part works, but we may need something like a simulation to see how the parts fit together in combination.[23]

I know simulation is not such a good metaphor for people who are suspicious of computers. With apologies to these people, I am, however, going to use this metaphor in places because it enables us to see a continuity of concerns and intuitions from Aristotle, through Shakespeare, to modern psychology and brain research.

Often, we want to take both aspects of *mimesis* together, representational and world-creating. For this conjoined sense, we might need yet further metaphors. Or perhaps we might not do any better than Ingmar Bergman in his film, *Fanny and Alexander*, who has his character Oscar Ekdahl, manager of a theater company in a small town, give a speech at the company's Christmas party, to the inhabitants of the little world inside the playhouse walls. "Outside," he says, "is the big world, and sometimes the little world succeeds in reflecting the big one so that we can see it better."

I shall therefore use terms and phrases such as dream, fantasy, imagination, metaphor-in-the-large, allegory, simulation, and so on, appropriately to what I am saying.

With the idea of fiction as world-creating, and also world-reflecting, we can understand something of what happens psychologically when we engage with fiction as readers or audience members, and of what we are doing as writers and performers.

Fiction: one's own version

If we take on the idea of *mimesis* as world-creating alongside its meaning as world reflecting, our idea of what we do as readers and audience members can change. In this case, we don't just respond to fiction (as might be implied by the idea of reader response), or receive it (as might be implied by reception studies), or appreciate it (as in art appreciation), or seek its correct interpretation (as seems sometimes to be suggested by the New Critics). We create our own version of the piece of fiction, our own dream, our own enactment.[24] We run a simulation on our own minds. As partners with the writer, we create a version based on our own experience of how the world appears on the surface and of how we might understand its deeper properties.

Art does not generally drive people towards a particular conclusion. It enables thoughts and feelings around a shared object – the work of art – in a way that offers multiple possibilities of understanding.[25] Most of Shakespeare's plays put to the audience some circumstances, and ask what do *you* think?

An apt and elegant instantiation of the idea of literary simulation is by David Lodge who has offered twin pieces of writing: an academic one tending towards a conclusion, an essay called *Consciousness and the novel,* and one that is more open ended, a novel called *Thinks.* Both are about the relation of psychology and fiction. The essay allows a scholarly exposition of the issues while the novel allows the reader to identify with a cognitive psychologist in a simulation of conducting research on consciousness. What could be better?

For writers and performers the task is not only to be true to nature, or to imitate life, or to mirror the world accurately, although these aspects are nearly always important. It is to invite the reader or audience member to start up a dream. It is to offer the cues to the reader to consider an allegory, to offer the instructions to world-making that will help make the simulation run and sustain itself.

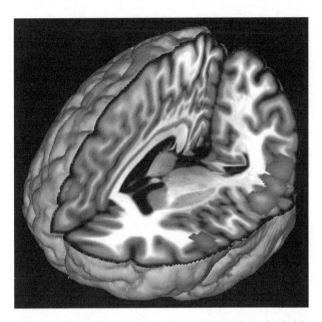

Figure 1.3 In a meta-analysis, Raymond Mar (2011) found reliable activation in the medial prefrontal cortex, left inferior frontal gyrus, and left temporal lobe, associated with studies of story comprehension. Mar, R. A. (2011). The neural bases of social cognition and story comprehension. *Annual Review of Psychology, 62,* in press.

memory, finding one's way around in the world, imaginative thinking about the future, knowing the perspectives of other people, and appear similar to the activity observed in the brain during undirected thought (e.g. daydreaming). As Raymond Mar has also shown in a recent review, this network has similarities to brain regions involved in story comprehension, which also overlap with those involved in perspective-taking. It may be that the various functions associated with the core network are drawn on in creating and sustaining mental simulations of the social world that are concerned both in the understanding of others and in engaging with narrative fiction.

In offering a piece of fiction to readers or viewers a writer needs to indicate characters' actions in a way that the reader imagines these actions into being. Imagination begins in childhood, and is expressed in play. It is to this activity that we now turn.

2

The Space-In-Between

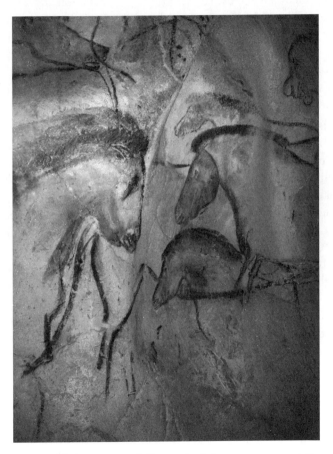

Figure 2.1 Detail from one of the earliest known cave paintings, from Chauvet. Photo Jean Clottes/Chauvet Cave scientific team.

Such Stuff as Dreams: The Psychology of Fiction, First Edition. K. Oatley.
© 2011 K. Oatley. Published 2011 by John Wiley & Sons, Ltd.

The Space-in-Between: Childhood Play
as the Entrance to Fiction

World-making and play

First they are pirates sailing on a search for treasure, then their ship is wrecked, and they are attacked by sharks; they reach the safety of an island, and build a house (under the table). What to eat and how to cook it are problems that are ingeniously solved. Their elaborate adventure, their quickly solved disputes (are they being attacked by sharks or by crocodiles?), their extended conversations about what happens next – all are captured by our video camera in the corner of the room.

This scene takes place in a room where there are some dressing up clothes, some toys, a table, and two four-year-old boys who have been friends for a year. Is it a game, or is it a story?

The scene comes at the beginning of *Children's friendships,* by Judy Dunn, who points out the children's "absorption in the shared narrative." She points out, too, that the "pirate adventure depends on both children," and that what is going on is "emotionally exciting and absorbing."

Here is another scene, one that I observed. My daughter was about five, and she sat with three friends in front of a television to watch a movie on a cassette.

"I'll be x," said my daughter, naming one of the characters in the movie, which the friends had watched before. "You can be y," she said to the girl who sat next to her. There was some discussion among the four girls, until each had chosen who would be who. Then they watched the film.

The two boys played a game that had many of the attributes of a children's story of pirates. The four girls transformed the watching of a film into a game with roles. Children can move effortlessly between modes of pretend play and story, different versions of the same activity. In one, the children take on roles, for instance of pirates and castaways, no doubt derived from pirate stories they have heard. In the other they can enter the world of imagination to inhabit a piece of fiction by identifying with characters in it.

In this chapter I discuss the experience of fiction. It's as enjoyable as play.[1] The imagination does not die as childhood ends. It is transformed into conversation, into sports, into the arts.

Childhood origins

In Aristotle's *Poetics,* the meaning of *mimesis* that concerns world-making seems curiously less obvious than that of imitation, but if we think about it properly, the meaning of world-making is not distant. It's the world of imagination, which starts with children's play. Aristotle talks about the childhood origins of *mimesis*. Here's some of what he says:

> . . . the habit of *mimesis* is congenital to human beings from childhood (actually man differs from the other animals in that he is the most *mimetic* and learns his first lessons by *mimesis*), and so is . . . the pleasure that all men take in works of *mimesis* (p. 20).[2]

The best book I know on the psychology of childhood imagination is by Paul Harris. In it he points out that in pretend play children create whole imaginary worlds. They can for instance, create the world of a tea party in which pretend tea is poured from a toy teapot into toy cups. If an adult knocks over a cup and says, "I'm terribly sorry," and makes a show of wiping up the pretend spillage, and then says "Can you fill it up again, please," the child knows to bring the teapot to pour pretend tea into just that cup that was pretend-spilled, and not into any of the other cups, all of which – in the real world – are also empty. It used to be said that children find it difficult to distinguish fantasy and reality, but this is not so. Children at the pretend tea party know that nothing will get actually wet when pretend tea is spilled. They can create whole self-consistent pretend worlds, which they know are different from the ordinary world, and they easily maintain boundaries between the worlds.[3]

The derivation of fiction from childhood play was proposed in an article of 1908 by Sigmund Freud, which starts like this:

> We laymen have always been intensely curious to know . . . from what sources that strange being, the creative writer, draws his material, and how he manages to make such an impression on us with it and to arouse in us emotions of which, perhaps, we had not even thought ourselves capable (p. 131).

The answer? It's that the writer draws on the play of childhood. Such play, Freud says, is the expression of wishes. In childhood, a frequent wish is to be grown-up. Day-dreaming, like night dreaming, is also an expression of wishes, and is one of the adult continuations of play. Writers – especially popular writers – offer such expressions of wishes which are either, as Freud puts it in his usual slightly fusty way, ambitious or erotic. He uses these terms to indicate what we now call action stories (liked mainly by men) and romances (liked mainly by women). He points out that in an action story a hero may lie "unconscious and bleeding from severe wounds" at the end of one chapter and find himself, at the beginning of the next, being "carefully nursed and on the way to recovery." Despite the dangers depicted in such stories, one reads them with a sense of security. The plots are of what we wish for, to triumph and to be tenderly cared for. In raw form such phantasies in adulthood would be too infantile to be admitted to others or to ourselves. Fictional stories are their transmutation into something acceptable.[4]

So far as I know, Freud was the first to connect fiction to childhood play and to dreams. He said that play in childhood is a source of intense pleasure. We don't generally give up our pleasures, Freud asserted, we exchange their sources. Although play declines towards the end of childhood, it's exchanged for equally pleasurable activities that derive from it, such as fiction and sports. In them we can identify with a protagonist, or with a team, or with a particular athlete, and take pleasure in their successes.

In the scenes with which I began this chapter – the two boys playing at pirates and the four girls watching a film – we see the childhood origins of fiction. These scenes of imagination are early stages in a sequence that leads to Dante, William Shakespeare, and Virginia Woolf.

Evolutionary bases
Some people say that we take pleasure in reading fiction and at the movies. What does this mean? Psychologists now think of pleasure as our genes' way of getting us to do this or that. Eating sweet things is pleasurable because we are genetically predisposed towards sweet tastes which, during evolutionary time, have prompted us human beings towards foods such as fruits that are nutritious. In the same kind of way sex is pleasurable. Our ancestors were those who survived and reproduced, in part because they were prompted towards the pleasures of nutritious foods and sex. Those who did not like sweet things and sex were not our ancestors. Their lines became extinct.[5]

For the experience of reading, hearing, or watching, fiction, I shall use the idea of enjoyment – being fully engaged in what we are doing – rather than pleasure. I agree that we do enjoy stories because our species is genetically predisposed to do so, but I think we should distinguish this from the pleasure of eating sweet foods, if only because fiction is a process whereas to eat a sweet food is a conclusion.

known cave paintings were made 31000 years ago. At around the same time, people started burying their dead. Manifestations of this kind show, says Mithen, the occurrence of human-made things that were metaphorical in the sense of being both themselves and something else. As shell was also a bead. A piece of wood was also a musical instrument. Charcoal and ochre marks on a cave wall were also a rhinoceros. In a story told at a burial, someone dead was alive still on another plane.

One of the intrinsic functions of the modern human mind, then, is art: both itself and something else. Art is based in our mind's ability to invent and comprehend metaphors. Mithen's theory about how this came about is that mental domains of knowledge were once extensive but separate. We can still see evidence of such separateness. Skills of riding a bicycle do not transfer to skills of doing algebra. But, says Mithen, less than 100000 years ago, some of the domains started to lose their separation. For instance, ancient people would know a lot about sources of food in their environment, and would also know a lot about social relationships within the social group in which they lived. Then these separate domains began to interpenetrate, a particular herb could be a friend. Metaphor was born. With metaphor came the possibility of models.

For a long time, metaphor was generally taken as something that occurred only in works of literature. If we follow Mithen's argument, it is far more significant: metaphor is fundamental to how we think. It's both useful and enjoyable.

Make-believe and what-if

Lest one might think that imagination is only necessary to more-or-less frivolous matters such as fiction, Harris shows that the imagination based in children's play is necessary for abstract thinking.[11]

A revealing psychological study of the development of abstract thinking was performed by Aleksandr Luria. In 1931 and 1932, he travelled to Uzbekistan to study effects of the USSR's newly introduced literacy programs.[12] Luria compared people who had attended these programs with people who had not. Among his cognitive tests he asked: "In the Far North, where there is snow, all bears are white. Novaya Zemlya is in the Far North. What color are the bears there?" The form is that of a syllogism. Luria reported a test of 15 people who had remained illiterate. Of these, only four were able to answer this question. The people who could not answer it replied, for instance, that they could not say because they had never been to Novaya Zemlya. By contrast, all 15 of those who had attended a literacy program could answer the question correctly. They were able to escape the literal and immediate, to think in verbal abstractions.

Luria's result did not occur because the educational programs made people widely knowledgeable. The programs were very elementary. Harris argues that the effects occurred because the programs enabled people to use their imagination to ask "what if," and to conceive states they had not directly experienced.[13] When shown how to do this, they could accomplish thoughts with mere symbols (words). This is a central idea in education. People who attain literacy have all been able to play as children, and in that play to pretend. When we take on education, we become able to use our child-derived imagination to abstract ourselves from the immediate, and to guide our thoughts by something else, for instance by words. The adults who had remained illiterate were lodged in the literal and the immediate.

Imagination gives us entry to abstraction, including mathematics.[14] We gain the ability to conceive alternatives and hence to evaluate. We gain the ability to think of futures and outcomes, skills of planning. The ability to think ethically also becomes a possibility.

In the branch of imagination called fiction, we can enter in imagination many more situations than a lifetime could contain.[15] In doing so we undertake mental enactments. We become for a while people who we are not, and have feelings for people we would not otherwise know.

Metaphor and metonymy

Among indications that metaphor is about the very nature of mind was an idea of the famous linguist, Roman Jakobson. In 1956 he proposed that all language is based on two operations: selection, as when I select the word I want to use next in this sentence, and combination, how I order words in the sentence.[16] When pressed, the selection function leads to metaphor and the combination function to metonymy.

In the selection function, metaphor is the selection of a word or phase that is apparently different from what one is talking about, but which has some similarity. There is a mapping between domains. So, in *Hamlet*, Rosencrantz and Guildenstern, Hamlet's friends from university in Germany, arrive unexpectedly at court, in Denmark. He asks them why they have come.

Hamlet:	What have you, my good friends, deserved at the hands of Fortune that she sends you to prison hither?
Guildenstern:	Prison, my lord?
Hamlet:	Denmark's a prison.

The mother of Gilgamesh, clever and wise, then interprets the dream:

You lifted it up, set it down by my feet,
    and I, Ninsun, I made it your equal,
Like a wife you loved it, caressed and embraced it:
    a mighty comrade will come to you, be his friend's saviour
    (Tablet I)[27]

Here is a series of metaphors: something falling from the sky is an important event, a boulder is a friend, a dream is something that will come to pass. In the story, Gilgamesh does indeed acquire a friend, Enkidu. We see a movement of metaphor applied not just to an idea or an event – the arrival of a star to earth as the arrival of a friend – but in the whole story, in a metaphor-in-the-large, or fable, or allegorical meaning in which we understand that humankind is separate from the all-powerful gods, and that much as we might rebel against these gods, the human condition is susceptible to loss of meaning with the loss of a close friend. We confront the human need to find meaning in other people.

Metaphor contributes to the enjoyment of fiction because we like to be discoverers. We are genetically predisposed to enjoy the new thoughts that can occur when a this becomes a that. Such discoveries are continuations of those made in pretend play, in which we can discover that a table can become a house.

A very social nature

Play includes discovery, but we have yet to come to an essential aspect: most play is social. It enables us to discover ourselves and others in the hyper-social world of humanity. Scenes such as the boys' pirate game that I presented at the start of this chapter involved not only invention, but sharing, and knowing another mind. Judy Dunn, from whose book the scene of pirate play was taken, wrote of it as the beginning of intimacy.

By the age of about four, children spend a good deal of time in imaginative play that involves roles. The assignment of roles by the four girls, which I also presented at the beginning of the chapter, was one example. Another example is hide-and-seek, which becomes interesting to children at about the age of four. To have a good time as hider in hide-and-seek you might sit in a cupboard under the stairs. Only if you also know the role of seeker can you imagine the seekers approaching, and looking there, and there, and at last here.

If you are a child who takes part in a game of wrestling with a sibling, or of Scrabble with a parent, or of pirates with a friend, you know play is both not real and real. Childhood wrestling, for instance, is not real fighting. But it is completely real in that you are taking part in a relationship with the other in which you compete (as you do in a real relationship) and in which you take care not to hurt the other (as you do in a real relationship).

Bears and teddy-bears

Here's an example that puts pretend play discussed in the first part of the chapter together with this all-important social idea. If you visit Canada and go for a walk in the countryside, you will be told about bears. The real Canada has a population of 34 million, and each year one may read in the papers that a person in Canada has been killed by a bear. The low likelihood is nevertheless sufficient to ensure that bears are a matter of shared attention. If you go for a walk in the countryside, Canadians are liable to give you earnest advice. They may tell you to make a noise, which will alert the bears who, they may say, are shy creatures and will therefore keep away from you. Or they may tell you the opposite: don't attract attention by making noise, and if you see a bear, avoid looking it in the eye . . . and so on. Then, because it is rare to encounter a bear and because the idea of doing so is quite exciting, they may say that if you really want to see one you should go, at dusk, to a municipal garbage dump, where bears go to pick through human rubbish. This is the ordinary world of bears.

Then there is the world of pretend-play bears, teddy bears, which draw us towards some further realizations about why models are so important in the way we think, and why they are important to fiction. There are certain correspondences between the ordinary kind of bear and the model kind of teddy bear: four limbs, two ears, soft fur, and so on. But some potential correspondences between model bears and real bears do not occur, for instance, if you have a teddy bear, you are not frightened, and you don't need to visit special sites. In the teddy-bear-world it is not correspondence that is at issue, but model-ness. If you are of the right age, and in the right mood, the model bear provides something entirely different. It affords a relational experience of what developmental psychologists call attachment, which includes the experience of cuddling and feeling close to a loved one.

As an adult, you may reflect on attachment and its meaning for us human beings. It is something we share with other mammals, including bears. It is the basis of trust in others, the basis of comfort in the presence of a loved one. Donald Winnicott invented the term "transitional object" for that special blanket or that special teddy bear beloved of the two-year-old child, which must never be lost or even washed. Winnicott explained how such objects are not so much invented as discovered in what he called a "potential space between the individual and the environment," originally a space in between an infant and its mother or other caregiver. Transitional objects stand in, as it were, for the attachment relationship and, like that relationship, they can become irreplaceable. They are transitional between the world of nature – of attachment to the mother or other caregiver – and the world of culture, which includes relationships, games, and fiction.[28] Such objects are, indeed, the beginnings of human culture. The arts, science, technology, indeed all aspects of human culture, grow from the space-in-between, and it is significant that however rarefied it might become, human culture never quite loses its relationship to other people.

The correspondence between the ordinary-world eye of a real Canadian bear and the glass eye of a teddy bear is not exact. What is being modeled in teddy bears is different. It is something to do with an imagined world of attachment, something relational, something abstract, and something intimate.

Fiction is both real and not-real in the same way. It is about real social worlds, but it's also imagined. In such play, and in such fiction, essential components are that we can discover aspects of others, for instance what kinds of people can be trusted, and find out about ourselves, for instance about whether we might use our ingenuity to prevail in this circumstance, or whether we can withstand the experience of being unable to prevail.

Ed Tan has argued that to understand the relation between play and fiction, we must separate immediate causes from evolutionarily adaptive causes. At the evolutionary level we can suppose there have been selective advantages to populations that have engaged in the pretend play of games of chase and the like, because they will have practiced social skills and know what it is to pursue and to be pursued. Children will have become able to enter the minds of those in the other role. Tan argues that once we have separated immediate and evolutionary causes we can see that what links them are social emotions, which are both immediate and the means by which genes pass on certain forms of motivation.

In terms of immediacy, to engage emotionally in play is enjoyable. Just as all mammals play, all have a repertoire of social emotions. Think, for instance, of the children's game of chase, a pretend version of pursuit. It can be seen in the playground of every primary school. It affords the emotional sense of urgency, the uncertainly of whether the pursuer will make the catch, whether the pursued will escape. So the immediate cause for play is to take part in emotional activities of this kind. Fiction extends this vicarious property, and the same game is played every time there is a car chase in an action movie, every time a police officer pursues a suspect in a detective story. Adults often provide props such as school playgrounds. For the adults themselves, the props include novels and movies. As Tan puts it: "The entertainment experience is an episode of emotions in response to an ongoing guided imagination." Just as our genes have made sweet things enjoyable because it is adaptive to be healthy, so it has made play – and its derivative, fiction – enjoyable because it is adaptive to acquire skills of interaction and of managing emotions.

Just as in a game of chase or hide-and-seek, one might be frightened of being caught, so too in fiction, fear – which in everyday life is to be avoided – becomes manageable, even enjoyable, in the larger context in which we can explore it and discover how it may be resolved.

Fun in games
The fullest exploration that I know of the psychology of games comes from Erving Goffman's[29] essay "Fun in games." "There seems to be," says Goffman, "no agent more effective than another person in bringing a world for oneself alive" (p. 41). Because we humans are such social beings a principal aspect of our enjoyment in life – our engagement in what we are doing – is in our interactions with each other.[30]

A game brings a world alive, but in a contained way. In most games, the human engagement in social interaction – that which makes the human way of life distinctively human – is maintained, but in a form that is safe and stripped-down to selected motivations (goals) such as competition, and selected events such as the turn of a card or the bounce of a ball.

So, for instance, chess is a miniature version of medieval warfare, with two equally matched armies. The goal is to protect the high aristocrats, the kings. Other aristocrats such as the queens, knights, and bishops, can dash about the field of battle in an exciting way, while the foot soldiers, humble peasants, can only plod forward one square at a time, and are liable to be killed with scarcely a thought. In some ancient games, for instance of gladiatorial contests, the proceedings were games for the spectators but not for the participants. Now games in which people are killed have largely disappeared. Only a few gestures remain: in cricket the hurling of a hard ball at the wicket instead of a spear at an opponent, in baseball the brandishing of a club.

One aspect of the constructed model world of a game is a set of rules. Another aspect is of roles that are afforded and actions that can be undertaken.[31] These rules, roles, and actions, are transformed versions of rules, roles, and actions, in ordinary life. For some aspects, the membrane between the real world and the world of the game is permeable. So, for instance, conflictual aspects of our relationships (us-versus-them) move easily between the day-to-day world and the worlds of competitive games.

As Goffman has shown, a game becomes a world in itself, a model world, whether it's an improvised game of childhood or a professional sport like cricket or baseball. It becomes a topic of conversation and commentary. A history is constructed, from which events are told and retold. The worlds of such games become peopled by beings who exist on a border between play and everyday life. Sports stars become fictional characters.

A novel or a film is not usually more effective than another person in "bringing a world for oneself alive," but it can be as effective because, in its world-making properties, the element of relationship with another person is maintained, along with the possibilities of a new kind of creativity: the world-making is not just something the author does, readers and audience do it too.

Friendship and theory-of-mind

Most mammals are social. But we humans are the most social of the mammals. Our ecological niche is the social world. Beavers make dams; humans make friends.

Interaction with others with whom we humans are friendly, then, is the source of much of our enjoyment in life: cuddling with loved ones, conversation with friends, shared activities of families and other social groups. Fiction extends this kind of enjoyment. It is symbolic, but it has the same basis of relationship: with fictional narrators and fictional characters. Also, it's based on the same set of emotions as occur in the ordinary social world, though without the damaging possibilities from which certain of these emotions sometimes derive in real life.

One of the best ways to think of our relationship to books, to their authors, and to their characters, is as friends.[32] Indeed, fiction introduces us to a mode of remarkable intimacy, which enables our mind to join with another or, rather, for that other mind to enter our own. So, says Marcel Proust in his essay "On reading":

> In reading, friendship is restored immediately to its original purity. With books there is no forced sociability. If we pass the evening with those friends – books – it's because we really want to. When we leave them, we do so with regret and, when we have left them, there are none of those thoughts that spoil friendship: "What did they think of us?" – "Did we make a mistake and say something tactless?" – "Did they like us?" – nor is there the anxiety of being forgotten because of displacement by someone else. All such agitating thoughts expire as we enter the pure and calm friendship of reading (p. 40, my translation).

In her book from which the scene of two boys playing pirates at the start of this chapter was taken, Judy Dunn shows the beginnings of friendship. Proust's idea about books as friends suggests how the shared worlds of play become bases of fiction, and how books of fiction, too, can offer a sense of intimacy: knowing the mind of another.

Theory-of-mind

How do we know other minds? One of the main rubrics under which this question is discussed in developmental psychology is theory-of-mind, which is also called perspective-taking, and mentalizing. Here, once again, is the metaphorical and the making of models: our own mind imagines – becomes an aspect of – someone else's mind. How, and at what point in development, do children start to be able to accomplish this?

Before the age of about four, children seem unable to think that what another person knows is any different from what they themselves know. They maintain only their own perspective. In this sense they can't really be said to have a theory of other minds. In 1983, an experiment by Heinz Wimmer and Josef Perner showed the change from this pre-four-year-old conception. Wimmer and Perner told children a story in which a little boy, Maxi, had some chocolate. He put the chocolate into a blue cupboard, and went out to play. While he was out, his mother took the chocolate from the blue cupboard, and used some of it to make a cake. Then she put the rest of the chocolate in a different place, in a green cupboard. In the experiment, the children were asked: "When Maxi comes back from the playground, he would like some of his chocolate. Where will he look for it?" Children who were under about four usually said: "In the green cupboard." They knew that was where the chocolate was, so they thought Maxi would look there. But children who were four and over tended to say, "In the blue cupboard." They could hold in their mind the perspective that this is where Maxi knew he had left his chocolate. They knew that Maxi knew something different from what they knew.

Much the same applies to children's own selves. Only after they are about four, do children realize that what they think and feel now can be different from what they thought and felt in the past. Alison Gopnik and Janet Astington looked into this question. In one experiment children aged three to five were shown a Smarties box (Smarties are small sweets) and asked what they thought was in it. "Smarties," the children replied. The experimenter then opened the box, and showed that it contained crayons. Then the children were asked what they had thought before the box was opened. The younger children said they thought the box had crayons in it, but the five-year-olds knew that previously they had thought it contained Smarties. As with being able to think about others as knowing things different from oneself, this change to being able to think of previous conceptions of oneself occurs at about the age of four.

Figure 2.3 A Smarties box with crayons, similar to that used by Gopnik and Astington. Photo Keith Oatley.

I don't remember Gopnik and Astington – who I have heard discuss this experiment on several occasions – relating it to Augustine's *Confessions* in which he writes that only by recognizing, and owning, the mistakes of one's earlier life can one hope to change. What Augustine did not know, which is implied by recent results on theory-of-mind, is that the soul enters the body not at conception, but at the age of four.

Acquisition of theory-of-mind seems to be a mental change that most of us acquire. An exception is people with autism, who remain largely unaware into adulthood of what others might be thinking and feeling.[33]

Social intelligence

An earlier step in our entry into the world of other people is that by the age of two children experience both themselves and others as agents, able to do things in the world. This is essential to the intensely social lives we lead, and it separates us from our nearest primate cousins, the chimpanzees.

When young chimpanzees are compared with human children, they are about the same in their understanding of how things work in the physical world. But, by the age of two, human children are more intelligent in how they think about the social world.[34] Young chimpanzees do not understand that they themselves are agents. They can act in the world, but they do not know that they and other chimpanzees are agents capable of action. By the age of two, human children do think of themselves in this way. John Donne seems to have had a sense of this when he said in a sermon: "The beast does but know, but the man knows that he knows" (p. 225)

Moreover, when children begin to speak in more than single words, which occurs is usually in the second half of their second year, the structure of their language is around actions – verbs like going, eating, putting – with slots that include who did these actions and other features of the action. For instance, in his account of the development of his daughter, Athena, the psychologist and novelist Charles Fernyhough recorded that at about eighteen months she asked him (interactively): "What we doing today?" (p. 116). In this sentence the verb Athena chose (using Jakobson's selection function) was "do:" an action of an agent. Then (using Jakobson's combination function) she arranged words around the action word: "what" to ask about the type of action, "we" to indicate the agents, and "today" to indicate the time of the action. At this period in her life, Athena's language started to organize her thoughts and plans. As Fernyhough put it: "Whatever thinking Athena was doing before language, it was disconnected, biological thinking. Language put it all together. When the faders went up on her consciousness, the story finally began to cohere" (p. 111).

Theory-of-mind and narrative

Several factors are thought to contribute to theory-of-mind. One is the ability of babies and caregivers to share attention to something they see, for instance by pointing. This is something babies start doing spontaneously at less than a year of age, and apes in the wild never do. Shared attention becomes an important aspect of communication, and of art.

Another contributor to theory-of-mind is language. In a longitudinal study, Janet Astington and Jennifer Jenkins tested three-year-olds. They found that earlier language abilities predicted better performance at theory-of-mind tasks (though earlier theory-of-mind did not predict future language performance).

In another study, Jenkins and Astington tested what effects theory-of-mind might have on children's playing of games that involved roles. They tested children who were three and four years of age, and assessed them three times over seven months. At each assessment point, children's theory-of-mind was measured, and the children were videotaped during play with a friend. Jenkins and Astington made measures of pretend play, and of how children made plans with each other. Theory-of-mind understanding was found to predict measures of making plans together during play, but none of the assessments of play predicted theory-of-mind.

Julie Comay worked with children aged between four and seven. Each child was asked to retell the stories of two fables and to dictate two stories he or she made up. Comay recorded the stories, and also took measures of the children's vocabulary, working memory, and two theory-of-mind tasks. She found significant development with age. The stories of the four-year-olds tended to be of simple action sequences, while those of the six- and seven-year-olds integrated both character and audience perspectives, and started to show complex plots. In terms of individual differences, each child's ability to represent perspective was consistent across the four stories. Children's ability to accommodate to an audience was significantly related to the tendency to portray inner worlds of characters.

To measure narrative skills in the stories that the children told, Comay assessed representation of the perspective of characters within the story, representation of the communicative needs of an audience, and representation of the narrative text as a self-contained story. She found that, after controlling for[35] age, language skills, and working memory, theory-of-mind made a significant and independent contribution to all three aspects of narrative skills. The more children were tuned in to others, the better were their stories in representing characters' perspectives, in considering the audience, and at working in their own terms as stories.[36]

With theory-of-mind we make mental models of ourselves and others, of what we and others know in the moment, and of our own and others' characteristics over longer periods. But this can go further. We can make models of other people's models, and this kind of embedded structure of what people think, feel, and believe often occurs in literature so that part of the interest in a story can be to work out who knows what, and what each one is up to. So, for instance, in *The human story,* Robin Dunbar pointed out that in *Othello,* Shakespeare needed five such layers (indicated by numbers in square brackets). Shakespeare:

> *intended* [1] that his audience *realize* [2] that the eponymous moor *believed* [3] that his servant Iago was being honest when he claimed to *know* [4] that his beloved Desdemona *loved* [5] Cassio (p. 162).[37]

To understand *Othello,* the audience needs to maintain four layers of mental states in their model, but the author needed five. If we follow Dunbar's style of numbering we can say that theory-of-mind is *guessing* [1] what another person might be *thinking* and *feeling* [2]. This reaches just the second of these layers. Ability to maintain a third layer may have been achieved in our hominid ancestors at about the same time that conversational language emerged. For us modern humans this third layer is easy. So in conversation we might *think* [1] and say: "You wouldn't tell him anything you didn't *want* [2] everyone else to *know* [3]." Chimpanzees can manage about one-and-a-half layers.

In the social world, we may know what someone is thinking because he or she has just told us, or we may know what the person is feeling because we have just seen him or her act in a demonstrative way. But to get a proper sense, even of something being said directly in a conversation, we have to put it together with a lot of other knowledge of the person, and of the situation. The method is not always accurate, but for most purposes it works well enough, both in the immediacy of an interaction, or for building a mental model of a person over time. We can imagine ourselves into the mind of a friend, or of a character in fiction.

Usually we build our model of another person by starting with our self. In "The Musgrave ritual" Arthur Conan-Doyle has Sherlock Holmes state this idea rather well: "I put myself in the man's place and, having first gauged his intelligence, I try to imagine how I should myself have proceeded under the same circumstances" (p. 394). G.K. Chesterton's detective, Father Brown, put the matter even more starkly: "When I tried to imagine the state of mind in which such a thing [the crime] would be done, I always realized that I might have done it myself under certain mental conditions, but not under others" (p. 170). We project some aspect of what we know about ourselves onto the other and we make adjustments for what we know of that person and the situation.[38] But often we project too much and adjust too little. There is always more to know about others, and about ourselves.

It is now well established that children about the age of four do start to understand what others think and feel, and that as adults we need to continue to develop our understanding of what others may be thinking and feeling. It is an essential human skill. And we do impute thoughts and feelings to others, based on what we know of ourselves. At the same time, we believe that people act for reasons. The very practice of explaining things by narrative depends on this idea.[39]

In *Why we read fiction*, Lisa Zunshine has proposed that fiction is all about – or nearly all about – theory-of-mind, or perspective-taking, and finding out why people act as they do. Her proposal for why we enjoy fiction is that we are good at working out what people are up to. Because we enjoy what we are good at, we enjoy fiction. In fiction, the author gives us information to enter into our theory-of-mind processes. Usually the characters of fiction are introduced so that we know something about them, but other aspects (as with people we know) are not so easy to discern. Perhaps they present themselves in one way, but beneath the surface other things are going on, sometimes from insecurity, sometimes from bitterness or envy, or sometimes from sadness. Some kinds of fiction such as the detective story (mystery) have, almost as their sole content, working out what someone is thinking and feeling when he or she is trying as hard as possible to conceal it, and one way of thinking of these is to do as Sherlock Holmes and Father Brown recommended, to put ourselves into the mind of the other.

Shakespeare's idea of enabling us to see beneath the shadow-surface of behavior is to prompt us to imagine why people act as they do. Our abilities to imagine such states are based on the social play of childhood, as we edge towards intimacy with others, where intimacy means being able to enter their minds.

A playful novel

I am pleased to announce the results of the competition for best first sentence of a novel, novella, or short story:

Third prize goes to Franz Kafka: "As Gregor Samsa awoke one morning from uneasy dreams he found himself transformed in his bed into a gigantic insect."

Second prize goes to Leo Tolstoy: "All happy families are alike; each unhappy family is unhappy in its own way."

First prize goes to Jane Austen: "It is a truth universally acknowledged, that a single man in possession of a good fortune, must be in want of a wife."

Among the reasons for awarding first prize to Austen (despite what to modern eyes seems a peculiarity in the domain of the comma) is that this sentence is both thought provoking and marvelously witty.

Jane Austen's irony has been widely remarked.[40] Irony is thought to be especially important in fiction because it enables a reader to think, playfully, about some possibility and then, at the same time to wonder about its opposite. The opening sentence of *Pride and prejudice* might mean what it says, but it might also mean what it doesn't say. Again, the function is of something which is both itself and something else. Irony, like play, has the quality of the provisional[41] and this, in turn, is important to fiction, in which we are not told what to think and feel, but are offered something about which we can think and feel. The opening sentence of *Pride and prejudice* is the very emblem of irony. Think about it like this. In America, one knows that life is serious but there is hope. In England, one knows that life is hopeless but it's not serious.

I am now – perilously – going to argue that *Pride and prejudice* is a playful novel, and indeed that irony and playfulness are often important in English fiction. I say "perilously" because I find myself in the position of having to explain a joke, than which few things can be more baleful. Jane Austen's novel is, I think, playful because middle-class women of the period in which she wrote (including Jane Austen herself) did not have gainful employment, but at the same time questions of love, friendship, and marriage, could not be disentangled from money. The matter could scarcely be more serious. Jane Austen never married, so when her father died, she with her mother and sister had to live in a cottage on the estate of one of Jane's brothers who had been given for adoption as a child to a rich relative who needed a male heir. How should one treat such subject matter? Earnestly, perhaps? Austen decides not. Her tone is playful. It is a delicate effect.

Austen's family was a literary one, and Brian Southam writes: "There was 'the flow of native wit, with all the fun and nonsense of a large and clever family,' conversation 'rich in shrewd remarks, bright with playfulness and humour'" (p. 4). Starting at an early age, and throughout her life Austen would read extracts of what she had written to members of her family. Here, is a piece from "Jack and Alice," written when she was about 14.

On enquiring for his House I was directed thro' this Wood, to the one you there see. With a heart elated by the expected happiness of beholding him I entered it and had proceeded thus far in my progress thro' it when

I found myself suddenly seized by the leg and on examining the cause of it found that I was caught in one of the steel traps so common in gentlemen's grounds.

"Ah," cried Lady Williams, "how fortunate we are to meet with you, since we might otherwise perhaps have shared the like misfortune" (Austen, 1993, p. 20).

The young Jane Austen was making fun of romantic novels of the period. You can almost hear the family's laughter. By the time her first novels were published, when she was in her early 30s, she had replaced satire with ironic understatement.

Here is the beginning of the first chapter of *Pride and prejudice*.[42]

It is a truth universally acknowledged, that a single man in possession of a good fortune, must be in want of a wife.

However little known the feelings or views of such a man may be on his first entering a neighbourhood, this truth is so well fixed in the minds of the surrounding families, that he is considered the rightful property of some one or other of their daughters.

"My dear Mr. Bennet," said his lady to him one day, "have you heard that Netherfield Park is let at last?"

Mr. Bennet replied that he had not.

"But it is," returned she; "for Mrs. Long has just been here, and she told me all about it."

Mr. Bennet made no answer.

"Do you not want to know who has taken it?" cried his wife impatiently.

"*You* want to tell me, and I have no objection to hearing it."

This was invitation enough.

"Why, my dear, you must know, Mrs. Long says that Netherfield is taken by a young man of large fortune from the north of England; that he came down on Monday in a chaise and four to see the place, and was so much delighted with it, that he agreed with Mr. Morris immediately; that he is to take possession before Michaelmas, and some of his servants are to be in the house by the end of next week."

"What is his name?"

"Bingley."

"Is he married or single?"

"Oh! Single, my dear, to be sure! A single man of large fortune; four or five thousand a year. What a fine thing for our girls!"

"How so? How can it affect them?"

"My dear Mr. Bennet," replied his wife, "how can you be so tiresome! You must know that I am thinking of his marrying one of them."

"Is that his design in settling here?"

"Design! Nonsense, how can you talk so! But it is very likely that he *may* fall in love with one of them, and therefore you must visit him as soon as he comes."

"I see no occasion for that. You and the girls may go, or you may send them by themselves, which perhaps will be still better, for as you are as handsome as any of them, Mr. Bingley may like you the best of the party."

At the beginning of the following chapter, we read that Mr Bennet was among the earliest callers on Mr Bingley, and that he had always intended to go.

Irony, then, like metaphor, is a mode of play in which something is both itself and something else. The first chapter of *Pride and prejudice* has a delicious but also bitter quality because it is not only ironical in itself but because it makes ironical fun of the in-itself-ironical activity of teasing.

Mr Bennet teases Mrs Bennet, and this is funny. But it's funny in an ironical way because the serious subject of how young women need to get married in order to live is approached via a playful portrait, depicted in their conversation, of the disastrous marriage of Mr and Mrs Bennet. We the readers are caught up in the same issues: how, in a world where disappointment is frequent, are we to understand our own involvement in these matters of love, and how even, in our own lives, might we find love?

The last paragraph of Chapter 1 of *Pride and prejudice* is as follows.

Mr. Bennet was so odd a mixture of quick parts, sarcastic humour, reserve, and caprice, that the experience of three-and-twenty years had been insufficient to make his wife understand his character. *Her* mind was less difficult to develop. She was a woman of mean understanding, little information, and uncertain temper. When she was discontented, she fancied herself nervous. The business of her life was to get her daughters married; its solace was visiting and news.

D.W. Harding refers to this final paragraph of the first chapter of *Pride and prejudice* as an example of what he calls Austen's "regulated hatred" of the situation in which love and money were tangled together for women of her time.

As the narrator of *Pride and prejudice* says, Mrs Bennet's main motive is straightforward: to get her daughters married. But like all of us, she has other motives. She wants what is proper and, with a real affection for them, she wants, too, what will make her daughters happy. Going on beneath the surface for Mr Bennet, in a way that grows more evident in the first part of the book, is that his motives are more mixed. Much goes on beneath the surface. He married because he needed a male heir to whom he could bequeath his property. Mrs Bennet had failed him in this; he didn't want all these daughters. Except for Elizabeth, whom he likes, he frequently calls them silly. He married Mrs Bennet because when young she was beautiful, but middle age has had its effect. She failed him, too, in being the lifelong friend and companion that is the ideal of marriage towards which *Pride and prejudice* strives. She's not very intelligent, and she's sometimes embarrassing. His sarcastic humor is a compromise to express his bitterness and disappointment, but at the same time to keep up a front for his family. It is by walking through the ashes of her parents dead marriage that Elizabeth Bennet has to take her first steps towards her own marital happiness. Is that ironical, or what?

3

Creativity

Figure 3.1 Sketch of an original drawing (in the top left corner) and a sequences of copies made by the method of serial reproduction in an experiment by Frederic Bartlett (1932). Bartlett, F.C. (1932). *Remembering: A study in experimental and social psychology.* Cambridge: Cambridge University Press. Reproduced with permission from Cambridge University Press.

Creativity: Imagined Worlds

The spring of creativity

In Xanadu did Kubla Khan
A stately pleasure dome decree:
Where Alph, the sacred river, ran
Through caverns measureless to man
Down to a sunless sea.

Thus begins the famous poem "Kubla Khan," by Samuel Taylor Coleridge, which he also calls "A vision in a dream, a fragment." It was published in 1816. As with Shakespeare's verse, the meter is iambic: "In **Xan**-a-**du** did **Kub**-la **Khan**." It is a poem based on the metaphor of art as the sacred river Alph, which rises from an enchanted spring ("As if the earth in fast thick pants were breathing"), runs through society, makes it fertile, and disturbs it.

Coleridge accompanied his poem with an account of how he created it:

In the summer of the year 1797, the Author then in ill health, had retired to a lonely farmhouse between Porlock and Linton . . . In consequence of a slight indisposition, an anodyne had been prescribed, from the effects of which he fell asleep . . . The Author continued for about three hours in a profound sleep, at least of the external senses, during which time he has the most vivid confidence, that he could not have composed less than two to three hundred lines; if that indeed can be called com-position in which all the images rose up before him as things, with a parallel production of the corresponding expressions, without any sen-sation or consciousness of effort. On awakening he appeared to himself to have a distinct recollection of the whole, and taking his pen, ink, and paper, instantly and eagerly wrote down the [54] lines that are here preserved. At this moment he was unfortunately called out by a person on business from Porlock, and detained by him above an hour, and on return to his room, found, to his no small surprise and mortification, that though he still retained some vague and dim recollection of the general purport of the vision, yet, with the exception of some eight or ten scattered lines and images, all the rest had passed away . . .

Here, at the beginning of the Romantic era, the theory of artistic creativity is stated forcefully.[1] An artist – a special person set apart from society and in touch with sources of inspiration – is an unconscious oracle for a special kind of utterance.[2] One might think that the Romantic poets were rather full of themselves. Another of them, Percy Bysshe Shelley, offers this as the concluding sentence of his essay "A defence of poetry:" "Poets are the unacknowledged legislators of the world."

Coleridge's account is not misleading in every respect. The sense of being apart from society does occur to many artists, and the experience of writing in which one can be taken up totally in what one is doing, and of having words come as if from some source apart from oneself, is described by some writers.[3] The account is only misleading in respect of two main issues.

The first misleading idea is that creativity is open only to a few: geniuses in touch with the muses. This is not true. Creativity is open to us all. It is open in many ways, one of which – the subject of this chapter – is what we do when we engage with fiction, as readers, watchers, or writers. The second misleading implication derives from Coleridge's failure to mention the amount of time, thought, and effort he himself had had put in over many years of learning to write poetry, to practice writing, and to think about it. I say a bit more about the issue of putting in a lot of time in the next section, but I'll concentrate on it in Chapter 6.

In this chapter I concentrate on the creative – constructive – aspects of fiction. If play is the origin of fiction in evolution and childhood, then creative construction is the origin of fiction in how the mind works. Dreams show one aspect of human constructive activity; reading and remembering show this activity in other ways.

The extraordinary and the ordinary

Understanding of creativity has come on quite a bit since Coleridge's statement of how he wrote "Kubla Khan." At first this psychology was about those few celebrated people in the arts and sciences who had made contributions that were widely recognized. One famous psychological theory was that creativity had four stages: Preparation, Incubation, Illumination, and Verification.[4] A creative person could contribute voluntarily during the stage of preparation, in which, perhaps over weeks or years, he or she might work on a problem or a piece of art, or a set of such pieces. The final stage of Verification, implementing the idea to see how well it worked, could also be conscious and deliberate. But incubation of the problem occurred when the person deliberately did not think of the work in hand, and only when this had occurred did the unwilled moment of Illumination come.

For every act of human creation, events do indeed occur in the brain and mind for which no-one can give an account. We may, ourselves, have had experiences of solutions to problems coming when we've not been thinking about them. Recent research has, however, both offered explanations, and brought some of the processes of creativity close to the experience of ordinary people. A good deal is now understood, for instance, about how Charles Darwin approached and then formulated his theory of evolution which, as one prominent commentator has put it, is "the single best idea anyone has ever had."[5] Each step by which he approached his solution is understandable to us. The steps are not very different from those that we have taken when we have applied ourselves in a determined way to a difficult problem.

Darwin's idea was reached after a five-and-a-half-year voyage of exploration on the ship *Beagle,* to which he had been appointed ship's naturalist, followed by an additional year-and-a-half of note-making, reading, and thinking, before he was able to write a complete version of his theory, and then, after a pause of many more years, his famous book *On the origin of species.* Darwin approached his theory by steps that were each small and comprehensible.[6] Each depended on the steps he'd made before.

Darwin started by wanting to answer specific questions, about whether the earth and its creatures have changed since the world began. A starting point, as he set off on his voyage on the *Beagle,* was to question the idea that most people held: that the world was created at a particular time, and that each species was created at the same time to fit perfectly in its place in that world. Before he went on his voyage, Darwin knew, from one of his mentors, of evidence that the earth had changed since its first creation. Part of his purpose was to see if he could find new and more convincing evidence of such change. He did indeed find it. He discovered, for instance that coral reefs, which make up huge areas of tropical and sub-tropical seas, are composed from accumulations of the skeletons of untold numbers of small coral organisms. These organisms made the reefs which, therefore, weren't there at the earth's creation. That was one step. Next – he inferred – species that are fitted to live in the distinctive environment of the reefs cannot have been fitted in this way since the earth's creation. That was another step.

Perhaps Darwin's largest breakthrough – a point at which he might have shouted "Eureka" – came from reading. After his return from his voyage he read a book by Thomas Malthus, on how human populations tend to expand beyond the resources that can support them. With this he realized that each species produces more offspring than can survive. He called this principle "superabundance." He then went on, by means of further steps, to think that therefore only the fittest among the superabundant progeny of a species would survive, and that the lines of the less fit would die out. From this he formulated his most famous principle, natural selection, which operated to enable the fittest of each species to survive in a particular kind of environment and pass on to the next generation the characteristics that had enabled them to do so.

Darwin's creativity – extraordinary and influential – occurred by application of psychological processes that are, in themselves, ordinary: step-by-step asking of questions and going out to find answers. In Chapter 6, I offer more discussion of individuals – writers – whose work has been widely recognized.

The space-in-between

It's not only celebrated people like Darwin who are creative. In the previous chapter I suggested that fiction – indeed art generally – arises from play, a creative activity that we all do. In his book *Playing and reality*, Donald Winnicott proposed that play is the beginning of creativity, and that without at least some creativity in our lives, not just in childhood, we experience ourselves almost as dead.[7] It is creativity, says Winnicott:

> more than anything else that makes the individual feel that life is worth living . . . In a tantalizing way many individuals have experienced just enough of creative living to recognize that for most of their time they are living uncreatively, as if caught up in the creativity of someone else, or of a machine (p. 65).

The opposite of creativity is compliance to external imposition, having for one reason or another to bend to the will of another. Fiction is a continuation of the creative play of childhood, not just for authors but for readers. It takes place, as I mentioned in the previous chapter, in what Winnicott called the space-in-between: originally the space between the infant and mother or other caregiver, but expanding to become the space of self with others. It's the space within which culture grows. It is here that the reader's imagination can expand without coercion. It is in this space that the reader can take up and turn over the words of the writer. The experience of the book can become the reader's own. Games, conversation, and art, are the creative continuations of childhood play.

Experience sampling and flow

A strong sense of being creatively engaged – as happens in a close conversation and when reading or watching a fiction – is of becoming one with what we are doing, or reading, or watching. An important researcher on this sense of engagement, which he identifies with creativity, is Mihaly Csikszentmihalyi who has written: "Creativity is a central source of meaning in our lives [because] when we are involved in it, we feel that we are living more fully than during the rest of life" (pp. 1–2). With a colleague, Csikszentmihalyi used a method in which he gave adolescents signals at random moments during the day, and asked them to say what they were doing and what their emotions were at that moment. Among the findings was that although adolescents spend a good deal of time watching television, they do it more or less to pass the time, and it's generally experienced as not particularly enjoyable.[8] Enjoyment is based on experiences that Csikszentmihalyi calls "flow," in occupations that are active, in which the person is contributing, and is fully engaged.

Csikszentmihalyi also interviewed participants in his studies. One was 62 years old and lived in the Italian Alps. She found that tending her cows and her orchard had the quality of flow. "I find a special satisfaction in caring for the plants," she said. "I like to see them grow each day." Another interviewee was a dancer who described what it was like for a performance to go well: "Your concentration is very complete. Your mind isn't wandering, you are not thinking of something else; you are totally involved in what you are doing." A young woman with a small daughter said: "She reads to me, and I read to her, and that's a time when I sort of lose touch with the rest of the world. I'm totally absorbed in what I'm doing."

The essential aspect of flow – that is to say of creative living – is of being fully engaged in what one is doing. Self and activity become one, and that, of course, is what occurs when we read a novel, or go to a play or film that we enjoy. It is not a matter of waiting for the world to bring one pleasures. Enjoyment is that state in which we choose to do what we are doing.

The individual relationship with literature

What evidence is there that ordinary people do engage creatively with works of fiction as they read? An early piece of evidence comes from I. A. Richards's book *Practical criticism:* about what people make of literature. Richards did the study when he was teaching English literature. Each week he gave his undergraduate students a short poem, asked them to read it and to comment freely in writing on what they made of it. He did not tell his students who the authors were, and he took care not to influence them about the poems before they wrote about them. After he had collected the students' comments he would lecture each following week on the poem and the comments.

He repeated this procedure with 13 poems. He writes that the undergraduates whom he was teaching, highly selected students of English at Cambridge and some other universities, revealed an "astonishing variety of human responses." Most of them seemed not to understand the meanings of the poems he gave them.

What Richards might have concluded from his study was that poems (and other works of literature) have different meanings for different people, and that unlike scientific writing, which strives towards a single agreed meaning,[9] a work of fiction is essentially suggestive. It has a different significance for each person who hears or reads it. It even has different meanings for one person reading it on different occasions.

Richards's third poem in his series, was John Donne's "Holy sonnet VII," which starts as follows:

At the round earth's imagined corners blow
Your trumpets, angels, and arise, arise.

Comments from different readers of the poem included the following: "No appeal whatsoever" . . . "Somehow the poem does not raise as much emotion as one feels it ought to have raised" . . . "Vigorous but obscure" . . . "After repeated reading, I can find no reaction except disgust" . . . "It is impressive but leaves no very clear impression, there are no pictures in it" . . . "In the sestet the voice is lowered, the poet's desire for a revelation changes to a sense of humility" (pp. 43–48).

Richards regarded most of the comments on this poem as attempts to ward it off, as derived from insufficient poetic experience, as technical objections made in order to justify negative judgments, and so on. Richards regarded only three of the 22 sets of comments on this sonnet (including the last one quoted above) as having come from "readers who seem to have understood the poem" (p. 47).

Richards's book launched the movement that became known as New Criticism, in which students were taught close readings of works of literature, and the idea that for any work of literature there was a correct understanding – or understandings if the work was ambiguous – to which the reader should progress.

One knows what Richards meant with his idea that poetry often needs to be explained. Some literature is difficult, and instruction by a thoughtful teacher can enable us to see a poem or novel in ways that we would not have seen ourselves, at least to start with.[10] At the same time, something else was going on in Richards's study. The comments he collected were also indications of whether his students took to a poem, of whether they wanted a relationship with it. The readers used their ingenuity, and the knowledge they had, to try and make sense of works that are less straightforward than newspaper articles. We can therefore see the comments as indications of readers' creative engagement with problems of what relationship they want with a poem. Only some works resonate, and whether or not they do, readers take them up in individual ways.

A movement to think about literature in this manner has occurred. It is called reader response theory, and it does indeed focus on how different people respond to works in different ways, but this movement did not gather momentum until the influence of the New Critics began to decline. The reader-response movement is now one of the dominant approaches to teaching literature in high school and university.[11]

If Richards's study of reading poems and the reader-response movement indicate readers' creativity by means of the variety of ways in which they engage with a work of literature, how can we understand the psychological processes by which any particular engagement takes place?

Making a story one's own

In 1932, Frederic Bartlett published an experiment that became famous, and that can be regarded as the beginning of cognitive psychology, on which this book is based.[12] "Cognitive" means: about knowledge (conscious and unconscious) and how it is organized and used in the mind, in perception, thinking, reading, writing, and so on. Bartlett's study shows the creative involvement of the individual in reading and remembering a story.

Bartlett asked people to read a story from a culture that was different from their own. One story he chose had been collected by an ethnologist at the end of the nineteenth century from an indigenous group in Oregon. The story is called "The war of the ghosts." Bartlett did not tell his participants anything about the story, but just asked them to read it through twice at their normal reading speed and then, 15 minutes later, to reproduce it as accurately as they could. Then they were asked to return to the laboratory from time to time, to make further reproductions. (He called this method "repeated reproduction.")

Here is how "The war of the ghosts" begins:

One night two young men from Egulac went down to the river to hunt seals, and while there were there it became foggy and calm. Then they heard war cries, and they thought "Maybe this is a war-party." They escaped to the shore and hid behind a log (p. 65).

The story then tells that a canoe came up, and the men in the canoe invited the two young men to go with them to make war on some people up the river. One of the young men did not want to go and said, first, that he had no arrows, and then that his relatives would not know where he had gone. But the other young man went with the men in the canoe. In the fight that took place, the young man was shot but did not feel sick, and he thought, "Oh, they are ghosts." After the fight, he went back home, and the story ends like this.

He told it all, and then he became quiet. When the sun rose he fell down. Something black came out of his mouth. The people jumped up and cried.

He was dead.

The English readers did not reproduce the story accurately. They omitted some parts. But they did not just forget, they actively changed the story. It became more English. For instance, after an interval of 20 hours, Subject H wrote: "Two men from Edulac went fishing. While thus occupied by the river they heard a noise in the distance." "Hunting seals" has become "fishing," and the eerie motif at the start of the story "foggy and calm" has been replaced by something like a newspaper report.

Almost all the participants in the experiment remembered certain salient details, for instance that "something black" came out of the young man's mouth. But whereas, in the original story, the young man died when the sun rose, for some readers he died when the sun set, for the English a more appropriate time to die.

For certain purposes, for instance if we have to give evidence in a court case, it is important to be accurate but, in this and similar experiments,

Bartlett found that we seldom achieve accuracy. When we remember a story or a picture, or anything else, our remembering is based on construction from a schematic outline, a general sense of the whole, and certain salient details. From these and from what we know about how the world works, we create our own version.

Although some people have vivid mental images, anything that might be called photographic memory is vanishingly rare.[13] Memory is not fixed and lifeless as the idea of photographic memory suggests. Bartlett also performed experiments on visual images. He gave, for instance (in a method he called "serial reproduction") a visual image from another culture, then asked an English person to copy it, then for another to copy the copy, and so on. After not very many copies the image ceased to look like anything from another culture. It had become something schematic, recognizably from English culture (you can see some of the images from such a series in the figure at the head of this chapter).

Bartlett dispelled the idea that most people's memory is anything like a photograph. He concluded from his experiments that remembering:

> . . . is an imaginative reconstruction, built out of the relation of our attitude towards a whole active mass of organized past reactions and experience, and to a little outstanding detail . . . It is thus hardly ever really exact . . . and it is not at all important that it should be (p. 213).

Although he did not publish *Remembering* until 1932, Bartlett ran his experiment on "The war of the ghosts" towards the end of World War I. Most of his male participants had been in the war or faced the prospect of going, so the subject matter of being asked to go to fight was relevant to them. For the female participants, too, the issue of losing relatives and friends was salient. Bartlett says that in one of his groups of 20 participants, only ten remembered, in their early reproductions, the excuse of the young man saying he had no arrows, but all except one male and one female remembered the excuse that the man's relatives would not know where he had gone. Bartlett wrote that anxieties about separation were salient at this time. Participants were concerned with separation, and so this, perhaps, was why the idea could easily enter their minds, and why they remembered it.

Schema and variation
The process of construction that Bartlett described is not just about memory. It is about what happens in the experience of reading a story, or indeed in the experience of perceiving the world around us. What we read

or what we see is assimilated by means of what we can understand. We understand in terms of what we bring to a story or a scene. Bartlett used the term "schema" for the structure of what we know. The term is based on the idea of a schematic drawing, for instance from an instruction manual for a device, showing how it works. In the cognitive psychology that Bartlett initiated, our schemas develop continually, and are internally coherent: working models of what we know about how the world works. When events occur, or things are said, in a story or in a life, we assimilate them to our own schemas. Events that happen and words that are said are not just absorbed in an unprocessed fashion. We are not video cameras. What we see and what we read are taken in insofar as they achieve significance for us, by becoming parts of our schematic models, our implicit theories of what we know about the world.

In the best book (that I know) on the psychology of visual art, *Art and illusion*, Ernst Gombrich uses this same idea (adopted from Bartlett) to show how the depiction of a scene by a painter involves first a schema, from which the painting will be generated, and then some variations on the schema to indicate the particularity of what is being depicted and to make the work of art new and striking. Understanding the painting also involves a schema and the recognition of variations on it.

Fiction (as well as other art) therefore works not by us simply receiving it. We each construct our own understandings of a piece of literary, visual, or musical, art that we read, see, or hear, based on our own schemas. We take in the material by creatively transforming it to make it comprehensible to us personally. Bartlett's PhD student, Kenneth Craik would later elaborate Bartlett's idea of schemas into a theory of thinking by means of mental models that I discussed in Chapter 2. This same idea is central to this book. When we encounter an aspect of the world or a piece of literary art, we base our understanding of it on our dreams, models, and simulations, and make it our own, with our own variations.

When people read, they are active. If you have been in a reading group, you will know vividly that the same story is somewhat different for everyone. (Reading groups are, I think, a significant phenomenon in the psychology of fiction and I discuss them in Chapter 8.)

Readerly and writerly reading
We can think of the demonstrations of Richards and Bartlett as indicating that fiction has different meanings for different people. This can be put more strongly: fiction should have many meanings.[14]

The medieval formulation, discussed in Chapter 1, of texts as consisting of the literal, the allegorical, the moral, and the anagogical, is a version of this idea of the multiple quality of literary works. Roland Barthes has written a commentary on Balzac's *Sarrasine*, which follows the same kind of idea. He proposes that five different codes are carried in its text. He describes these codes as

(i)   the hermeneutic, the means by which a reader solves mysteries of the text,
(ii)   the semic, a code by which material objects suggest abstract entities,
(iii)   the proairetic, a code of actions and the sequences of what follows what,
(iv)   the symbolic, a code by which ambiguities are read into a text,
(v)   the cultural, the code by which a text refers to shared meanings within a culture.

A reader might take up, for instance the first code, to follow the mysteries of the text. Some texts – detective stories – invite us to do just that. Or a reader may follow the third code, to follow actions and their effects, attending to the plot to find out what will happen next. Some readers may follow now one of these codes, now another, now two in combination, and so on. And the next time a reader reads the same text, the codes may be taken up in different orders and in different ways.

Barthes suggests that, as well as what he calls readerly readings (receiving texts somewhat passively), there are writerly readings in which the reader writes (or rewrites) what he or she reads. I want to make a stronger proposal: even in the most passive readings, we write our own versions of what we read.

Some genres tend to constrain readers to a narrow set of interpretations and experiences. I like to think of these genres as roller coasters at Disneyland. The Disney engineers have specified a particular set of experiences, in your body as it is swung round corners and is rushed down steep slopes, as well as in your perception of sights and sounds. This is also what certain kinds of genre fiction do. They take you on a carefully-specified ride. In the thriller, the formula is first to be introduced to someone likable, the protagonist. Then this person – indeed perhaps the whole world – is subjected to a seemingly inescapable danger. You turn the pages anxiously until, at last, the protagonist, the world, and you, attain the relief of safety. In Bartlett's terms, such a formulaic work elicits a particular schema (for which I have just told you the outline). What is offered is pretty much what you would expect from it, and it can be enjoyable. Just as when you get off a roller coaster, although you may remember the ride and remember a certain cardiac perturbation, your schemas and your selfhood remain unchanged. With more complex fiction not everything is as expected. In our more writerly readings, our schemas can change. As the cognitive psychologist, Jerome Bruner, has put it in *Actual minds, possible worlds:* "I believe that the *great* writer's gift to a reader is to make him a *better* writer" (p. 37).

The reader's contribution

I am going to introduce Kate Chopin's two-page story of 1894, "The dream of an hour."[15] I am also going to suggest a method of recording some of

Figure 3.2 Kate Chopin in 1894, the year in which she wrote "The dream of an hour." Source: Missouri History Museum Photographs and Prints Collections. Portraits. N1 1979.

your contributions to the story. As you read its first half (below) please pencil an M in the margin when a memory from your own life comes to mind, an E when you experience an emotion while reading, and a T when you have a thought of your own that doesn't just repeat what you have just read. When you have finished reading this part of the story, please go back over your Ms (memories) and find the one that was most significant to you. If you would like to, please write a few lines to describe the memory, and include any emotions that occurred in the memory. Please now go back over the Es (emotions) you have marked. Write alongside each E the name of the emotion (sadness, relief, etc.) along with a number to indicate how intense each was on a scale in which 0 means no emotion at all, and 10 means the most intense emotion I have experienced in my life. Next go back over your thoughts – marked with Ts – select the one that was the most interesting to you, and write, briefly, what the content of this thought was.[16] If you don't want to mark Ms, Es, and Ts, don't worry. Just read on, and I'll later give you some examples from other people.

The dream of an hour

by Kate Chopin

Knowing that Mrs Mallard was afflicted with a heart trouble, great care was taken to break to her as gently as possible the news of her husband's death.

It was her sister Josephine who told her, in broken sentences; veiled hints that revealed in half concealing. Her husband's friend Richards was there, too, near her. It was he who had been in the newspaper office when intelligence of the railroad disaster was received, with Brently Mallard's name leading the list of "killed." He had only taken the time to assure himself of its truth by a second telegram, and had hastened to forestall any less careful, less tender friend in bearing the sad message.

She did not hear the story as many women have heard the same, with a paralyzed inability to accept its significance. She wept at once, with sudden, wild abandonment, in her sister's arms. When the storm of grief had spent itself she went away to her room alone. She would have no one follow her.

(Continued)

There stood, facing the open window, a comfortable, roomy, arm-chair. Into this she sank, pressed down by a physical exhaustion that haunted her body and seemed to reach into her soul.

She could see in the open square before her house the tops of trees that were all aquiver with the new spring life. The delicious breath of rain was in the air. In the street below a peddler was crying his wares. The notes of a distant song which someone was singing reached her faintly, and countless sparrows were twittering in the eaves.

There were patches of blue sky showing here and there through the clouds that had met and piled one above the other in the west facing her window.

She saw with her head thrown back upon the cushion of the chair, quite motionless, except when a sob came up into her throat and shook her, as a child who has cried itself to sleep continues to sob in its dreams.

She was young, with a fair, calm face, whose lines bespoke repression and even a certain strength. But now there was a dull stare in her eyes, whose gaze was fixed away off yonder on one of those patches of blue sky. It was not a glance of reflection, but rather indicated a suspension of intelligent thought.

There was something coming to her and she was waiting for it, fearfully. What was it? She did not know; it was too subtle and elusive to name. But she felt it, creeping out of the sky, reaching toward her through the sounds, the scents, the color that filled the air.

Now her bosom rose and fell tumultuously. She was beginning to recognize this thing that was approaching to possess her, and she was striving to beat it back with her will – as powerless as her two white slender hands would have been.

When she abandoned herself, a little whispered word escaped her slightly parted lips. She said it over and over under her breath: "free, free, free!"

First, let's compare different takes on the story: yours and mine. My take is that this is a story written during the early years of the feminist movement in the United States in which the writer invites readers into alternative ways of thinking about marital relationships. I imagine that Kate Chopin quite likes shocking her readers. I much appreciate her depiction of an emotion growing from something noticeable but inarticulate to something strong and distinct, along with its implicit allegory for how the women's movement might grow.

What do you think?

I have used this story in research. Here is a memory (M) set off in one person who was in a group of readers to whom I gave the story in much the same way as I have given it to you. Reader 25 wrote as her most significant memory, one that was set off by the sentence about seeing "the tops of the trees that were all aquiver."

> This memory is from my childhood and I was not yet tall enough to see outside my window when standing . . . I could see the trees ruffling in the breeze outside my bedroom. I called for my mother to come and get me out of bed like I did every morning. I was four and an only child. This time, however, my grandmother appeared and told me I had a new baby sister.

In this group of participants, emotions (Es) elicited at different moments of the story ranged from grief and sadness, to shock, dread and frustration, to surprise and happiness. The intensities readers experience ranged from 1 to 8 on the 0–10 scale we asked people to use.

From the same group of participants, here is a Thought (T) set off for Reader 20 by the word "free:"

> I had a thought that I wanted a situation such as this, only without death, to occur to X. I wished that she would be free and happy without her boyfriend.

The Ms, E's and Ts – memories, emotions, thoughts – that can be marked in the margin as we read, indicate that even when we seem just to be taking in what is written in a story, we are creatively adding to it.

In an experiment, Elise Axelrad and I[17] combined Bartlett's idea of asking people to reproduce a story they had read with the idea of asking people what memories came to mind as they were reading. Participants first read James Joyce's short story "Clay" and marked Ms wherever memories occurred. We then asked them to write brief descriptions of all the memories. Later, we asked participants to reproduce the story. We found that pieces of some of the readers' memories found their way into their reproductions of the story.

In another experiment Seema Nundy and I found that emotions that people experienced when they read a story affected how they understood it. We asked participants to read Russell Banks's short story, "Sarah Cole: A type of love story." It begins with a first-person narrator who says that at the time of the story's events: "I was extremely handsome," and that Sarah was "the homliest woman I have ever known." He says he is telling the story ten years after its events, and that he will tell it objectively, so as not to be biased. He then continues in the third person, calling himself "the man." The man starts an affair with Sarah. After the affair has continued for some months, he ends it cruelly, saying, "Leave me now, you disgusting, ugly bitch."

Nundy and I did not ask readers to indicate emotions by E's in the margin. Instead we asked them to rate the intensity (from 0 to 10) of a set of emotions they were feeling before reading the story, and again just after they had read it. The emotions were indicated by a list of emotion words: happiness, sadness, anger, anxiety, and so forth. We classified people's overall emotional response to the story according to the largest change in any emotion that the readers indicated from before to after reading. The story gave rise to different emotions in different readers: some people became mainly angry, some became mainly sad, and some were disgusted.

Also, after reading the story, we asked the readers three interpretive questions about the story's ambiguous ending. We found that those made sad by reading the story tended to reason in a way that cognitive psychologists call backward chaining. They started with a conclusion, and then stated reasons for holding it. Here is an example of this kind of response to our first question, which was: "From the narrator's point of view, why do you think the story says, 'She's transformed into the most beautiful woman he had ever seen?'"

> He no longer sees Sarah as belonging to him. She breaks away from him probably more strongly than he tries to separate from her. He is also not truly capable of a true respectful love . . . and maybe feels guilty and envious that she was giving in the relationship he was never honestly in.

By contrast, those who were made angry by the story, tended to reason by forward chaining. They started with premises, and then drew a conclusion. Here is an example of a forward chaining response to our second question, which was: "From the narrator's point of view, why do you think the story says, 'It's not as if she has died; it's as if he has killed her?'"

He knew she knew and everyone else that she was "homely." Perhaps it was perverse or pity that he engaged in a relationship with her. But despite her physical appearance which she struggled with, she had feelings . . . So out of guilt he might as well have killed emotionally – cut deep into the soul at any rate.

The way people thought about this story was affected by the emotions they experienced.[18] The emotions were the readers' own. And the ways in which the readers thought about the story, affected by their emotions, were also their own.

We were struck by the close correspondence of predominant emotions that readers experienced with the kinds of thinking that typically occur with particular emotions. In sadness, one searches backwards for reasons to explain the loss that has caused the sadness; among readers who became sad at the story the mode of reasoning was predominantly (and significantly) of backward chaining. In anger one looks forward in plans of asserting oneself against the person who has made one angry; among readers who became angry at the story, the mode of reasoning was predominantly (and significantly) of forward chaining.

Components of construction

To move further with the question of creativity in engagement with literature, I think we need to look at some of the components of stories, to see what kind of creativity is required of writers and readers with each of them.

A division of fiction into two components was introduced by the Russian Formalists in the second decade of the twentieth century. These components are: *fabula*; the set of events of a story, and *syuzhet*; how these events are presented by the writer.[19]

The Formalists included Roman Jakobson and Viktor Shklovsky,[20] who introduced the approach I am following here: scientific as well as literary. The guiding principles of the Formalist movement were to study literature as such, and to give priority to literary facts, as compared with political or moral positions of the kind that are sometimes taken up in literary criticism.

Fabula and syuzhet
Fabula and *syuzhet* are usually translated in English as "story" and "plot," but this is a bit misleading. A story is something that can come alive in the

mind of a reader or listener, and plot is best thought of in the way that Aristotle said, of a working-out of the implications of human action. The Formalists were driving at something different. Better translations are that *fabula* is "event structure" and *syuzhet* is "discourse structure."[21] The event structure is the chronological sequence of events in a story: this happened, then this, then this. It's not, as such, a story. If you want to demonstrate this to yourself, ask a thirteen-year-old to tell you what happened in a film he or she just saw. The teenager will tell you that this occurred, then this, then this. You quickly wish he or she would stop because thirteen-year-olds have good memories, and they are just telling you what you asked, not telling you a story.

Here, told in the same kind of way are the events of *Hamlet* in chronological sequence. Claudius has murdered the king, his brother. He becomes king and marries Gertrude, the late king's wife and Prince Hamlet's mother. The late king's ghost appears to sentinels of the watch and to Horatio, friend of Hamlet, who tells him of the appearance. Next night, the ghost of his father appears to Hamlet, and demands vengeance for his murder. A travelling theater company arrives at court, and Hamlet asks them to perform a particular play, into which he says he will insert some lines.

The event structure of a story is, in a way, the least creative of its aspects. Shakespeare, for instance, in *Hamlet* and generally, wrote plays around event sequences from history books or from previously published stories.[22] The same practice continues in adaptations of novels into movies. No mere set of events, one after the other, constitutes a story. A story requires both the events and a set of instructions or cues as to what to do with them: how to turn the events into a story. It was this set of instructions that the Formalists called the *syuzhet,* and that William Brewer and Ed Lichtenstein call the discourse structure.

In one sense the *syuzhet,* or discourse structure, is the text of the piece of fiction on the page, or the performance that an audience sees. Really it is a set of indications as to what the events are (in the event structure) plus the cues or instructions as to what to do with them, which prompt each reader or audience member into an imagined construction that brings the events to life.

In his play *King Henry V.,* Shakespeare tells the audience about the relation of events to the instructions that he and the actors will give and the audience's job, which is to create the story in their imagination. The play is about an event in English history, the Battle of Agincourt, "this great accompt." Here is what an actor tells the audience.

Chorus: And let us, ciphers to this great accompt,
  On your imaginary forces work . . .
  Think when we talk of horses that you see them
  Printing their proud hoofs i' the receiving earth:
  For 'tis your thoughts that now must deck our kings (1, 1, 18*).*

The actors – "ciphers" – enact the events (in the event structure), and at the same time implicitly give the audience instructions about what to do with them. It is the audience members who have to take what they see and hear, apply the instructions, and make the whole thing go.

Authors are not usually so explicit. If, for instance, you go to a performance of *Hamlet* that has not been set in modern times, you will most typically see two armour-wearing actors come onto the stage, perhaps together, perhaps one at a time. Here are the opening words of the play:

Barnardo: Who's there?
Francisco: Nay, answer me. Stand and unfold yourself.
Barnardo: Long live the King!
Francisco: Barnardo?
Barnardo: He.
Francisco: You come most carefully upon your hour.

The actors' movements and speech are not just events. They also constitute instructions to the audience to imagine an anxious scene on the battlements of a castle in a country prepared for war 400 years ago. In *Hamlet,* no actor says: "The sentinels we play are anxious, so will you in the audience please feel anxious too." But this is what they mean. If you read the play, you infer that Barnardo's first utterance is a challenge. The second utterance, by Francisco, is a reciprocal challenge: "Nay, answer me." The implicit instruction is that for both sentinels there is at first uncertainty as to who the other is. Is he friend or foe? If you see this exchange on the stage, the actors will play it in a way such that their edginess instructs you to feel edgy too.

To enjoy the play – really get into it – the construction you make should be anxious. If you were to write an E (for an Emotion that you experience) in the margin the opening battlement scene in *Hamlet,* you might label it "Anxiety." It's just the beginning of the play, and you may just have been riffling through your program, so the intensity tends to be mild, perhaps a 2 or a 3. Then Shakespeare turns up the intensity of anxiety with the appearance of a ghost.[23]

Or take the two opening sentences of *Pride and prejudice.* They are instructions to start imagining middle-class England 200 years ago, and to start thinking how love and property are related. The first event in the story is Mrs Bennet saying, "My dear Mr. Bennet, have you heard that Netherfield Park is let at last?" So the story-teller both lets us readers know about events such as this utterance by Mrs Bennet, and gives us instructions about what to do with it. How should we imagine the event of Mrs Bennet saying that Netherfield is let? We should imagine it in the way for which the first two paragraphs of the chapter have primed us: that any wealthy young man who comes into a neighborhood will be considered the rightful property of someone's daughter. Mrs Bennet goes on to say that Mr Bingley, the new tenant of Netherfield, is a young man of large fortune. Mrs Bennet is thinking that this fortune, along with its owner, might become the property of one of her daughters.

The instructions of *Pride and prejudice* are to be playful. The novel's first sentence is ironical, and this perhaps might instruct us to take the scene somewhat lightly. In doing so we might wonder whether Mrs Bennet is too naïve to realize her husband is teasing her. Or we might wonder whether, despite the unkind teasing by her husband, Mrs Bennet's ambitions for her daughters are to be taken very seriously indeed.

It is the audience member or reader who takes the instructions and events, and puts them together in his or her own way. And, as you may see, the ways in which we can take these events and these instructions are various.

It is the audience members and readers who must animate the characters. Without this creativity, the words of fiction are dead. In reading fiction we engage with the *syuzhet* so that it comes alive; by means of it we construct, for ourselves, the *fabula*, the event structure, in a way that – instead of being just a sequence – it has meaning.

Dhvani

The discourse structure (*syuzhet*) contains a set of general instructions about how to start up and sustain the simulation. As William Benzon has shown, each piece is marked by a specific form that is the same for all readers. But there is another component that requires even more of the reader's creativity. It's about what a story means to you. The Memories, Emotions, and Thoughts, we experience are indications of this third component, not general, but personal. This component is the prompting towards your own contributions to the story. It's a component that has not been much elaborated in Western literary theory, but it has been discussed in Eastern literary-psychological theory, which started in India with Bharata Muni, who is thought to have lived one or two hundred years after Aristotle.

In this tradition, the heart of poetry and of literary stories is suggestion, which in Sanskrit is called *dhvani*. This is a third component of stories.

Among the most interesting of the Indian literary theorists was Abhinavagupta, a literary theorist, dramatist, and philosopher (famous in his time and since) who lived and wrote about 1000 years ago in the area that is now Kashmir. He gives the following example of *dhvani*. In a play, a traveler arrives at a house in which he meets a young woman and her mother-in-law. The young woman's husband is away. An intuition of love passes between the young woman and the traveler, and she speaks this verse:

> Mother-in-law sleeps here, I there:
> Look, traveler, while it is light.
> For at night when you cannot see
> You must not fall into my bed.[24]

The verse seems rather literal. It works by suggestion or – we might even say – by suggestiveness. Abhinavagupta proposes that, in this little verse, the young woman speaks openly in the presence of her mother-in-law, and at the same time, by means of a prohibition she makes the traveller an invitation. In a piece of good fiction, one often finds that suggestions are made by something being said that does not mean what it says. If the mother-in-law doesn't understand what the young woman says, that's what was intended. If the traveler doesn't understand it, too bad. If you, the reader, don't understand it, you miss the point but can have it explained to you, and then you see it.

As well as the event structure (*fabula*) the discourse structure (*syuzhet*), we have therefore, in addition, the suggestion structure (*dhvani*). Whereas the discourse structure contains instructions of a general kind about how to run the simulation, the suggestion structure is a set of hints to be taken up in a personal way, so they depend on what the particular reader or audience member brings. We can recognize this understanding in Bartlett's finding of a culturally influenced, personal set of schemas to which we assimilate a work of fiction, and in the personal memories, emotions, and thoughts (Ms, Es and Ts) prompted by reading as discussed above.

With these three components – event structure, discourse structure, and suggestion structure – each reader or audience member creates something new. In *The implied reader*, Wolfgang Iser has proposed that to do this, the reader "Must actively participate in bringing out the meaning and this participation is an essential precondition for communication between the author and the reader" (p. 30). Iser also talks of the "fulfillment" and the "actualization" of a fictional text. We can call this actualization of a text the realization structure: the inner performance, or the inner enactment.[25]

People's realizations of the same story will contain common elements. For instance unless there are deliberate ambiguities, created by the writer, people generally agree on the events of the story. The personal meanings for each person will, however, be somewhat different. Even if the story is in the form of a film which seems to take short cuts to imagining characters and settings, the viewer must still do his or her part, putting together the film shots in the story that he or she creates in his or her distinctive realization, a story that prompts his or her own memories and emotions, and suggests his or her own thoughts.

There is a difference, of course, between reading a novel and seeing a screen adaptation of it. Even in a screen version of *Pride and prejudice*, you the viewer have to imagine your version of Mr and Mrs Bennet, somewhat as when you read the book. You have to decide whether Mr Bennet's teasing of his wife is cruel or merely playful. You have to see him as resigned in his marriage to a woman who was once beautiful, or as irritated at everything she does. You, the viewer of an adaptation, like you the reader of the novel, have to decide whether Mrs Bennet really is simple minded. You have to decide what the dynamic might be between Mrs Bennet and her daughter Elizabeth who is intelligent and perceptive but caught, like other middle class young women of her era, in the prospect of having to auction herself off to possible marriage partners.

In the next chapter we move further into these matters of characters in fiction, and of how to think about incidents that arise from their actions, but first something about how language invites our creativity.

Creative language

At the beginning of the previous main section, I introduced the Russian Formalists, with their idea that stories consist of *fabula*, (the sequence of events in a story), and *syuzhet* or discourse structure (which includes the cues or instructions from which readers construct an inner enactment of the story). But creativity depends, too, on a writer drawing attention to certain aspects of a text, and on a reader doing something with the object of shared attention. One of the Formalists' ideas was that a writer draws attention to that which has become so familiar that it is not noticed. The writer does this by means of careful juxtaposition of words or ideas.

Attention is drawn, and the reader makes some aspect of the juxtaposition his or her own.

Defamiliarization

The term usually used for drawing attention, as discussed by the Russian Formalists, is "defamiliarization." In a 1917 paper called "Art as technique," Viktor Shklovsky, quotes an entry in Tolstoy's diary of 29 February 1897 (the date is transcribed incorrectly, and it should read 1 March 1897):

> I was cleaning a room and, meandering about, approached the divan and couldn't remember whether or not I had dusted it. Since these movements are habitual and unconscious, I could not remember and felt it was impossible to remember . . . if the whole complex lives of many people go on unconsciously, such lives are as if they have never been.

So, argues Shklovsky, a principal function of literature is to make the familiar strange, so that one's attention is drawn to it, so that one notices it.[26] He quotes a passage from Tolstoy's short story "Kholstomer" (Strider) which is narrated by a horse:

> I understood full well what he said about flogging . . . But then I found it impossible how and why I could be called man's property. The words my horse referring to me, a living creature, struck me as strange, just as if someone had said my earth, my air, my water (Tolstoy, p. 86).

Anticipating the Formalists' statement of defamiliarization, Thomas Hardy put it like this:

> Art is a disproportioning – (i.e. distorting, throwing out of proportion) – of realities, to show more clearly the features that matter in those realities, which, if merely copied or reported inventorially, might possibly be observed, but would more probably be overlooked. Hence, "realism" is not Art (p. 239).

In one of the earliest pieces of research on the psychological effects of literature, Willie van Peer investigated the effects of linguistic defamiliarization. He called the process "foregrounding,"[27] and argued that it is accomplished by offering something unusual: creating variations from ordinary usage. He asked people to read six short poems, the linguistic content of which he had analyzed to determine what phrases were foregrounded. He found that

Figure 3.3 Viktor Shklovsky, a prominent member of the Russian Formalists, a group who advocated an approach to understanding literature that I have followed in this book. Source: Igor Palmin/Writer Pictures.

phrases which (on linguistic grounds) were foregrounded were experienced by readers as more attention-drawing, more striking, more important, and more worthy of discussion, than other phrases.[28]

The artist offers something that attracts interest, and enables the imagination of the reader or viewer to expand creatively within its context, and within the structure of the attention that the artist shares with us.[29]

In *Literature and the brain*, Norman Holland puts the matter like this:

When we read, then, two systems are at work. The form of the literary work provides the first. It establishes what we are likely to pay attention to and what we will perceive when we do pay attention. The second comes from within us, our own defenses. We perceive the work in such a way as to use our own defenses to guarantee our pleasure (p. 159).

"Form" in Holland's sense depends on such devices as defamiliarization. In using the word "defenses," Holland offers a psychoanalytic concept based on the idea of schema. A defense is a schema with the added implication of being tuned to admit what is emotionally acceptable to us, and fend off what is not. Holland goes on to say this:

> Language only becomes "literary" when it enables us to do certain things with it, namely, to make it a satisfying part of our patterns of expectation, unpleasure-avoiding, goal-imagining, and goal-achieving. Having found it "surprising," we make it "right." That is when it becomes "literary" (p. 246).

So, although the techniques of defamiliarization depend on the creativity of the writer, they depend, too, on the creativity of the reader. It's the reader whose attention is drawn by unusual juxtapositions of words, or unusual ways of seeing, who then brings the idea alive, in him- or her-self. The issue can, think, be illuminated by the following idea about the relation of verbal expressions to their meanings.

The hybrid mind

An idea due to Andy Clark is that the human mind is a hybrid. It can be thought of as two mental processors that have entirely different characteristics. The older processor works in a similar way to the mental processor of our cousins the great apes. We can think of it as intuitive. It enables us to know other individuals and to associate our idea of them with ideas of whether we like them and whether we trust them.[30] It enables us to make mental models of them, to interact with them, prompted by social goals of assertion, attachment and affiliation and the emotions that arise in relation to them. It has almost limitless memory. It can process and represent sequence, but it works largely by associations, and simple heuristics.[31]

According to Clark, a newer processor was installed perhaps half a million years ago, when our ancestors acquired language. He thinks of it as a linguistic processor. It has the limited capacity of short-term working memory, and it works in a different way from the associative-intuitive processing of the non-verbal mind.[32] The problem for the writer, then, is to create pathways from the associative processor to the linguistic processor: to produce translations into words. The problem for the reader is to take in a language-based story and to create pathways to the layer of associations, to translate it into terms of intuitions and experience, in an inner mental enactment.

Words and imaginings

Elaine Scarry describes the depiction of physical settings as the writer having to give the reader instructions for how to construct a scene. She offers a set of principles, and examples from writers who are particularly good at this, such as Thomas Hardy and Marcel Proust. Among the principles are for the writer to depict reflections, shadows and lights shining onto walls and furniture. These plays of insubstantial darkness and light on surfaces prompt the reader into constructing a mental scene of three dimensions with objects arrayed in a spatial layout. Scarry recommends, too, that the author should depict actions of a protagonist through space, and actions on objects. This fits in with the finding that Scarry did not know about, of specific parts of the brain being activated by particular kinds of actions.

Following the advice from Scarry, and taking note of the evidence that brain activation occurs in a way that mirrors imagined actions when one reads about them, here is a scene I have written at the beginning of Chapter 7 of my recent novel, *Therefore choose*:

Two stairs at a time, George ran up the big circular staircase towards the flat. In one hand he held a bag of groceries and, as part of each upward movement, he pulled with his other hand on the polished mahogany banister. As he reached the first landing, still moving quickly, he looked up into the octagonal skylight. In the morning the sun shone on the wall that was behind him. At midday, it reached far down the stairwell. At this time, in the afternoon, it cast bright illumination on the embossed beige wallpaper of the upper wall in front of him. The stairwell was not quite exotic, but it was hard to think of as familiar. When he reached the top, George took the key from his pocket, let himself into the flat, and peered down the corridor of carpets and bookshelves. The feeling of foreignness intensified.[33]

An appealing thought is that when we understand something we process it both as verbal phrases and as intuitions. When we do this in the passage above, our reading of the phrases prompts an imagination of a stairwell with a skylight, and activates in our brains regions concerned with running up stairs, grasping a bannister, opening a door.

Almost a remembrance

One of the profound experiences of poetry and prose fiction is to give one's assent as a reader to the words offered by the writer, while at the same time accomplishing a recognition in experience within the associative-intuitive processor. This is how John Keats put it in a letter to a friend. "Poetry ... should strike the Reader as a wording of his own highest thoughts, and appear almost a Remembrance" (p. 267). The "wording of ... thoughts" acquires such a rightness that its correspondence with experience seems "almost a Remembrance."

Thus after the author has offered something unusual, readers have to connect the words to their intuitions, and make the words their own. When readers are able to do this, they construct a path of the words in the language layer and at the same time create connections to the layer of associations and intuitions.

One might suppose that writers are special in being able to create such connections, but in *Le temps retrouvé,* the last book of *À la recherche du temps perdu,* Marcel Proust's narrator insists that it is not just the artist-writer who can do this.

> Real life, life that is finally discovered and made clear, the only life therefore that is lived completely, is literature. This life, in a sense exists all the time in everyone, just as much as in the artist. But most people don't realize it, because they are not trying to make it clear (p. 257, my translation).

Proust's narrator thought that the novel he was writing would enable us, as readers, to do something of what he had done, which was to make meaningful sense – in verbal forms – of aspects of the life he knew. He proposed that we readers could do something similar by making his words our own, to see how comparable verbal meanings could connect with the experience of our own lives. Thus the words we read can enable us to make connections within our intuitive selves, and to enable meaning and experience to come together. And so, says Proust's narrator:

. . . it would even be inexact to say that I thought of those who read it, as readers of my book. Because they were not, as I saw it, my readers. More exactly they were readers of themselves, my book being a sort of magnifying glass . . . by which I could give them the means to read within themselves (p. 424, my translation).

Having talked in this chapter about creativity, about language and about making verbal connections with our experience, in the next chapter I turn to some of the principal contents of fiction: characters, and the incidents that happen when characters act and interact.

4

Character, Action, Incident

Figure 4.1 Colin Firth as Darcy in a screen adaptation of *Pride and prejudice*.
Source: AF archive/Alamy.

Such Stuff as Dreams: The Psychology of Fiction, First Edition. K. Oatley.
© 2011 K. Oatley. Published 2011 by John Wiley & Sons, Ltd.

Character, Action, Incident: Mental Models of People and Their Doings

Depiction of character

On 18 May 1924, Virginia Woolf was invited to give a talk at Cambridge. She had been disappointed not to have gone to Cambridge as an undergraduate. She couldn't go because she was a woman. But now, at the time of her talk, she was beyond studenthood. She was a novelist.

> It seems to me possible [she said, archly] that I may be the only person in this room who has committed the folly of writing, trying to write, or failing to write, a novel (p. 69).[1]

Then she began to discuss the topic of character. Although, she said, "everyone in this room is a judge of character," and although, too, "it would be impossible to live for a year without disaster unless one practiced character-reading and had some skill in the art" (p. 70), the idea of character is a "will-o'-the-wisp." It is the novelist's obsession somehow to get hold of it.

Then said Woolf, even more archly: ". . . in or about December 1910 human character changed" (p. 70).[2]

Virginia Woolf went on, in her talk, to describe one of the games she liked to play. Perhaps it's not a game but an exercise in fiction, an exercise in world-making: to see a stranger and imagine that person as a literary character.

Woolf described how she had been late for a train from Richmond to Waterloo, and had jumped into the first carriage she came to. "As I sat down," she said, "I had the strange and uncomfortable feeling that I was interrupting a conversation between two people who were already sitting there." They sat opposite each other. One, whom she called Mr Smith, aged over forty "had been leaning over and talking emphatically to judge by his attitude and the flush on his face." Woolf called the woman to whom the man had been talking, Mrs Brown. "She was one of those clean, threadbare old ladies whose extreme tidiness – everything buttoned, fastened, tied together, mended and brushed up – suggests more extreme poverty than rags and dirt."

Although Mr Smith was evidently annoyed at being interrupted, Mrs Brown seemed rather relieved. Woolf surmised that Mr Smith was not a relative of Mrs Brown. He was, perhaps, a man of business, from the North.

"Obviously," said Woolf, "he had some unpleasant business to settle with Mrs Brown; a secret, perhaps sinister business, which they did not intend to discuss in my presence" (p. 72). To give the proper impression to a stranger, they talked instead of how caterpillars can eat the leaves off of oak trees. Meanwhile, Woolf had started to construct mentally a piece of fiction. She imagined that Mrs Brown might have a son who was beginning to go to the bad, imagined what might be going on between Mr Smith and Mrs Brown.

When the train approached Clapham Junction, Mr Smith said: "So about that matter we were discussing. It'll be all right? George will be there on Tuesday?" As the train pulled into the station, "he buttoned his coat, reached his bag down, and jumped out of the train before it had stopped" (pp. 73–74).

Virginia Woolf and Mrs Brown were alone together. "She sat in her corner opposite," wrote Woolf, "very clean, very small, rather queer, and suffering intensely. The impression she made was overwhelming. It came pouring out like a draught, like a smell of burning" (p. 74).

Woolf here offers a sketch of a character in the style of Shakespeare in his depictions of Cassius and Brutus in *Julius Caesar,* in the style of Jane Austen in her depiction of Mrs Bennet in *Pride and prejudice,* in the style of George Eliot in her depiction of Mr Casaubon in *Middlemarch.* In her character sketch, Woolf offers us Mrs Brown: tightly buttoned and suffering, being bullied on the train to Waterloo by a certain Mr Smith. In this idea of character we see a person somewhat from the outside, as he or she is seen by others, but with occasional glimpses of the person's inner life, of which we hope to understand more as a story unfolds.

In 1925 a year after Virginia Woolf gave her talk in Cambridge, and 15 years after the date when she said that human character changed, she herself depicted the new style of character in her novel, *Mrs Dalloway.* In this new style, emphasis falls more strongly on inwardness, its myriad impressions, its evanescent feelings, some of which contradict others, with only occasional glimpses of how the person is seen from the outside.

Here is the new type of character, Clarissa Dalloway, as she walks up Bond Street in London on a June morning, a year or two after the end of the First World War.

Bond Street fascinated her; Bond Street early in the morning in the season; its flags flying; its shops; no splash; no glitter; one roll of tweed in the shop where her father had bought his suits for fifty years; a few pearls; salmon on an iceblock.

"That is all," she said, looking at the fishmongers. "That is all," she repeated, pausing for a moment at the window of a glove shop where, before the War, you could buy almost perfect gloves. And her old Uncle William used to say a lady is known by her shoes and her gloves. He had turned on his bed one morning in the middle of the War. He had said, "I have had enough." Gloves and shoes; she had a passion for gloves, but her own daughter, Elizabeth, cared not a straw for either of them (pp. 11–12).

Woolf's dream here is accomplished in a paragraph about what Mrs Dalloway sees as determined by her character (with each perception separated from the previous one by a semi-colon), followed by a paragraph within her mind. In this second paragraph, thoughts at first prompted by her perceptions now prompt each other in a set of associations that gravitate towards one of her preoccupations: whether she is bringing up her daughter properly.

Woolf articulates how thoughts cue further thoughts in our minds. Perfect!

Character in prehistory

In this book I take character to be one of the three central issues of fiction, the other two being action (which I treat here along with character) and emotion (which I treat in the next chapter). Character is the issue for which Shakespeare wanted to look beneath the shadow-play of behavior, to see what is generally hidden. Why are some of our aspects hidden?

The idea of character is at the very core of being human. One human being is no human being. Look around: at the objects close to you, or at the book you are holding, all made by people in the distributed social networks in which we live, evidence of our intense and pervasive sociality. Our interconnections with each other in turn rest – as Virginia Woolf said – on our ability to judge character, and indeed to be characters.

Character is what we know about other people, whether we feel warmly towards them, or whether we dislike them, whether we understand what they say, and how far we can trust them. Character is also what we know of ourselves, whether we can depend on ourselves, and be reliable for others. In order to live in any human society, we make judgments of character, which we compile into mental models, one for each person we know well, one for our self. These models are critical to how we behave with those we know, and their models of us are critical to how they behave with us.

Leslie Aiello and Robin Dunbar[3] proposed that, between 500,000 and 200,000 years ago, language arose. Really, it was not so much that language arose. What arose was conversation. Its function is to maintain relationships. Dunbar argues that it happened like this.

Primates – an order that includes lemurs, monkeys, apes, and humans – live in social groups, the size of which has increased as primates have evolved. The maximum size of the social group for lemurs (a relatively primitive primate) is about 9, for cebus monkeys it is about 18, for chimpanzees about 50, and for humans about 150. This number for humans is of individuals with whom personal relationships are maintained. For instance, 150 is about the largest size in which villages thrive before pressures arise to split into two. For urban people it is not the set of those you recognize by sight, but those you know well, for instance, with whom you have had a meal. Dunbar found a close correlation between the maximum size of the social group for a species and the size of the cortex of the brain for that species: the larger the maximum size of social group, the larger the brain. For example in lemurs the cortex is 1.2 times the size of the rest of the brain, in cebus monkeys 2.4 times, in chimpanzees about 3.2 times, and in humans about 4.1 times. In other words, in us, the cortex is the by far the largest part of the brain. It is more than 80% of the whole.

Why this increase in brain size, as one goes from primates that emerged longer ago in evolution to those that emerged more recently? Dunbar's hypothesis is that it was because with larger groups of others among whom they lived, individuals needed more brain space to maintain more mental models, information about the character of everyone in the group, including everyone's history in relation to him or herself. And that, says Dunbar, is why the brains of chimpanzees, and even more so the brains of humans, have grown so large.

How do primates maintain their relationships? It's by grooming. To do grooming, one individual sits quietly and closely with another, and picks through the other's fur for insects and twigs. There is hugging and stroking too. Doing this maintains trust. One has to do it, in turn, with all the members of the group with whom one is close. In chimpanzees it occupies about 20% of each individual's time. Dunbar has proposed that as brain size and group size kept increasing in our forebears (species of hominids such as *homo erectus,* and *homo habilis*), an impasse was reached. As group size increased, the amount of grooming time needed to maintain an increasing number of relationships reached about 30%. This was a limit. For a primate to devote more than 30% of the time to grooming would

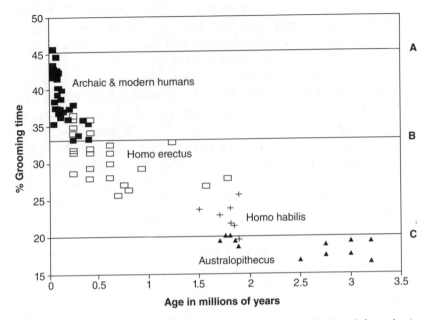

Figure 4.2 Group size of different hominid species (calculated from brain size) plotted against time before the present (BP). From the bottom right (about 3 million years ago) a more or less a straight line runs forward in time (leftwards on the graph) to 0.5 million years ago, at which point there is a change to a much steeper slope towards the present, as conversation enabled hominid species to live in larger groups, from Dunbar (2004).

not allow for obtaining food, for travel, for sleep, and for the other things that primates need to do. This point was reached about half a million years ago. That is when conversation arose: verbal grooming.

One can see in Dunbar's graph of hominid evolution that the straight line relating brain-cortex size and group size (on the x-axis) to group size (on the y-axis) became steeper about half a million years ago. In human ancestors, the problem of how to find enough time to groom with all those with whom one needed to remain close was solved by the replacement of grooming by conversation. So language arose not to talk about practical matters such as where to find food or how to make flint tools, but for social reasons, in order to converse. The primary function of conversation is to maintain relationships – a large number of relationships – and to maintain intimacy in relationships.

We humans have not lost the influence of touch, and cuddling. Conversational language emerged to augment these ways. By means of conversation, we humans can maintain three times more relationships than chimpanzees. We can converse in groups. We can converse when gathering or preparing food, when we are travelling, when we are working.

Dunbar's hypothesis is known as the social brain hypothesis. Although it has met with some skepticism among linguists and paleontologists, many now regard it as an important component in our understanding of how language began.

What did our ancestors talk about in conversation? What do we talk about now? Dunbar has found from recording conversations in a university refectory that some 70% of conversation is about our own plans, our emotions, and the doings of people we know. And when we talk in this way, we often include in the exchanges little verbal summaries of mental models we hold about others; character sketches, embedded in anecdotes, perhaps something like this:

"Paul always had a lot of women, quite nice women, but a lot of them.
    When he got together with Chloe, all that stopped."
"She said something?"
"Maybe he just realized."
"She must have put her foot down."
"Whatever it was, he's become quite devoted."

Here two people whom I have imagined talk about an event: and so skilled are we as readers that, given these minimal cues, we easily pick up what's going on between Paul and Chloe. For half-a-million years people will have talked about who has got together with whom and what the consequences were, or who has fought with whom and what happened as a result. With the above conversation we can start to form mental models of Paul and Chloe, to form judgments of their character.

Almost seamlessly, then, we can imagine that informal stories, of the kind we still exchange with each other when we converse, were elaborated into longer accounts, or into engaging anecdotes. Some people found they could do this well, and thereby enjoyed the attention of the group. You may have someone in your social group who is especially good at anecdotes. At the center of story is character. Character may be thought of, in a resonant phrase of Erving Goffman, as "the presentation of self in everyday life." Fiction is a set of carefully crafted versions of this kind. It is of interest to us because it is close to the very core of being human: understanding others, understanding them in relation to ourselves, understanding ourselves.

By reading from all round the world stories that originated before the age of European colonization, Patrick Hogan has found that three kinds of stories are so common as to be universal. They explore matters that are central to fiction: character, action, and emotion. The most common is the love story. Lovers long to be together but are impeded from being united, often by a male relative or by a rival. The engine of such stories is a set of questions. Who are these lovers? What might they do about their situation? What emotions occur as a result? *Romeo and Juliet,* which I discussed in Chapter 1, is a prototypical story of this kind. A second, only slightly less common, kind of story is the heroic. Once again, character, action, and emotion, are central. Hogan gives the example of the Indian epic, the *Rāmāyana.*[4] Rāmā's father, the king, is getting old. After a dispute, his brother becomes the ruler and sends Rama into exile where he encounters the wicked Rāvāna, who is a threat not just to the kingdom, but to the whole of society. Rāma defeats Rāvāna in a long and angry battle, then returns to the kingdom to take his place as king. The third kind of story is the sacrificial, in which an ill has befallen society so that people are in anguish. Someone identifies the nature of the problem, and sacrifices him- or her-self, so that society can be made whole. The Christian gospel is a version of this story.

What people are like, as characters, in how they act in their loving, anger, and anguish, are also frequent topics of human conversation. Like conversation, fiction is a way of exploring such concerns, as they affect ourselves and as they help us to understand others.

Among the depictions of mental models of character, in both conversation and fiction, condensed summaries appear. In the simplest cases they are behavioral dispositions, "Romeo is full of adoration." Psychologists call these dispositions personality traits, and tend to think that they remain constant over time,[5] that they tell us something useful about who these people are, which helps us understand them next time we see them, or have to rely on them.

The idea of such traits is rather basic. It starts in childhood: a child does something mean, and in the mental model constructed by other children, that child IS mean. Imputation of such a trait to others often persists independently of events that might be thought to change it. In everyday life, imputations of this kind form the basis for reputation, which tends to become fixed in the minds of others. At the same time, we humans are responsive to social contexts.[6] We might say, indeed, that the literary idea of character, at least from Shakespeare onwards, is an advance on the older idea of fixed personality traits, in that although there is continuity, character is also affected by events, especially events of emotional significance.

Character in history

One of the lovely things about written fiction is that it leaves evidence of its own history. The methods and preoccupations of fiction did not come into being all at once. They developed. Among the earliest written forms are epics, stories in poetry, probably derived from oral presentations. Such is the *Epic of Gilgamesh*, from Sumer. There were also dialogues such as the "Dialogue of a man with his soul," from Ancient Egypt. And there were stories of religious significance, such as those in the Bible.

Around 2700 years ago, pastoral and lyric poetry emerged in Greece, and a few hundred years later, drama emerged in Greece and India. Yarns, tales, folk stories, and fables, have probably abounded in the oral traditions of many peoples for thousands of years. With the invention of alphabetic writing in Greece, some of these stories were written down. Aesop's fables are an example. Subsequently, many more tales, stories, and yarns were committed to writing in collections such as the *Thousand-and-one nights* (the *Arabian nights*), Boccaccio's *Decameron*, and Chaucer's *Canterbury tales*.

Novels are different. They are longer and by definition they are conceived in written form. Margaret Doody has argued that the oldest novels emerged in the Greek world and persisted into Roman times. Perhaps the best known such novel, the only one to make it into a paperback that you can buy in an ordinary bookshop, is *The golden ass*, written in Latin by Apuleius towards the end of the second century of the Common Era.

Within the set of evolving genres, a development occurred, of the idea of character. The first literary characters have traits, very much like personality traits in psychology or reputations in the minds of others: more-or-less unchanging dispositions.[7]

In his essay on "The art of fiction" (discussed in Chapter 1), Henry James put the relation of action to character like this: "What is character but the determination of incident? What is incident but the illustration of character?" So, in the *Iliad* the traits of Achilles are that he is fierce, and he is proud. The incident related to at the beginning of the *Iliad* is that he gets into a rage with the commander-in-chief of the Greek army at Troy. He draws his sword and is on the verge of killing the commander. From traits of his character flow incidents of emotion-driven action. Because killing the commander is impermissible, Achilles goes into a sulk, and refuses to fight against the Trojans. In consequence there occurs a further set of incidents. Without their best fighter, the Greeks start losing the war.

Incident (in the sense meant by James) involves action which, as Aristotle said, typically gives the structure of a story's plot. It flows from character, which is at the center of fiction because it is at the center of being human.

In early literature, certain aspects of character that we find important in fiction remained relatively unexplored, for instance the developmental: what events, relationships, and experiences, are responsible for a character becoming who he or she is? A second, and related, aspect is of characters actively choosing who they will be. Fuller approaches to these aspects emerged towards the end of medieval times, with Renaissance individualism and humanism.[8]

Character as choice

According to Erich Auerbach, in his magisterial book *Mimesis,* the first writer to depict character in the modern sense was Dante.[9] In the *Divina Commedia* (Divine Comedy), especially in its first part, *Inferno,* Dante depicts people who have freely chosen how to live. Auerbach shows how the *Divine Comedy* presents the universe as determinate. Everything has been arranged by God, except for the choices that humans make in their lives, choices that affect who they are. Dante can be thought of as an early existentialist.

In Canto X of the *Inferno,* Dante meets the shade of Cavalcante, father of his best friend and mentor Guido Cavalcanti. The shade recognizes Dante, kneels up in his tomb, looks around and asks where his son is. Dante says he is not alone, but with Virgil, whom, perhaps, his son held in disdain. The shade picks up the past tense in Dante's reply about his son, and cries: "What did you say? He held? Is he not alive?" When Dante delayed his answer, the shade fell back into his tomb.

Cavalcante's son is more important to him than all the torments of Hell. He has made a choice: that Guido is the center of his life. Auerbach argues that this is an important moment in the literary idea of character. *The divine comedy* is a profoundly religious story but, for Dante, the real action takes place not in the universe as arranged immutably by God, but in what Auerbach calls "the secular world," the world in which we mortals live, the world of our relationships and choices.

Figure 4.3 Portrait of Dante, painted by Giotto before Dante's exile from Florence. Source: Museo Nazionale del Bargello, Florence, Italy/Alinari/The Bridgeman Art Library.

As Auerbach explains, Dante here makes an important move in European literature. He transfers action and truth from heaven, or from some ideal Platonic plane, to here on earth. The idea of character is not of people whose traits of personality remain unexplained, or of fate which cannot be apprehended. It's of people appraising events for their emotional implications and, as a result, acting on matters that are important to them here on earth. In an earlier work, *La vita nuova*, Dante depicts people (including the writer himself) making such emotional appraisals. For instance, people are awed when they see Dante's beloved, Beatrice, walking along an ordinary street.

So gentle and so honest appears
my lady when she greets others
that every tongue, trembling, becomes mute (p. 111).

It's here on earth that the critical events of life occur, and are appraised for
their importance.[10]

Character derived from experience

In English literature, the depiction of character was taken forward by
Geoffrey Chaucer. In *The Canterbury Tales,* his characters are on a pilgrimage. Most interesting of them is Alisoun, the Wife of Bath. Her traits, which
she describes in herself, are *jolitee* and a certain sexual energy. She explains
how on occasion she has duped people by lying to them but, through her
life, she has acquired a thoughtful understanding of the relations between
the sexes. It is this that makes her a character. It is she who asks and answers
the question that has resounded since: *What thyng is it that wommen moost
desiren?* (What do women really want?) Her understanding of this question
is not just an aspect of personality as a persisting trait. It developed – as
her story has it – from her experience of being married and widowed
five times.

Several generations later, Shakespeare made his first really successful leap
into character with the hump-backed Richard III, who – at the end of a
civil war – limps onto the stage and says:

Now is the winter of our discontent
Made glorious summer by this son of York (*Richard III,* 1, 1, 1)

Shakespeare's idea of character, here, is based on the relation between
shadow and substance that I introduced in Chapter 1. Richard has an outwardly deformed body which, he says, has made him unable to take part
in pursuits such as love. Therefore, he says, he will create himself, not as
others expect him to be, but to satisfy himself. The Richard who appears
in this play makes us shudder. We watch him as we might watch a cobra
about to strike. In the play he confides to us, the audience, about what he
is about to do before he does it, and this makes the effect of shadow and
substance more gripping.

For a Renaissance audience, a hump-back and a limp could be outward
and visible signs of inner and spiritual deformity, embodiments of evil.[11]

Shakespeare reverses the relation. Richard explains that circumstance of his outward disfigurement is the reason for his scheming. Notice how Shakespeare uses the words "looking glass" (mirror), and "shadow."

> . . . I, that am not shap'd for sportive tricks,
> Nor made to court an amorous looking glass . . .
> Why, I in this weak piping time of peace
> Have no delight to pass away the time,
> Unless to spy my shadow in the sun
> And descant on mine own deformity.
> And therefore, since I cannot prove a lover
> To entertain these fair well-spoken days,
> I am determinèd to prove a villain (*Richard III*, 1, 1, 15).

As I explained in Chapter 1, for Shakespeare, shadow is outer behavior. Character is shadow's counterpoint with inner substance.

Emotional goals and the unconscious

The first play to be performed at the new Globe Theatre was *Julius Caesar*, about the assassination of Caesar and its repercussions. In it, Shakespeare bases his characters on Plutarch's biographies of Caesar and Brutus. Plutarch offered verbal summaries of traits and emotional dispositions. For instance in the "Life of Caesar," Plutarch says: "What made Caesar most openly and mortally hated was his passion to be made King" (p. 299), and in his "Life of Brutus," Plutarch says: ". . . it was Cassius with his violent temper and his hatred of Caesar – which had its roots in personal animosity rather than in any disinterested aversion to tyranny – who inflamed Brutus's feelings" (pp. 229–230).

Shakespeare took traits ("violent temper") and amorphous descriptions of action ("Cassius .... inflamed Brutus's feelings") offered by Plutarch and imagined them into Cassius as an individual who feels and acts in distinct incidents,[12] a character of a modern kind.

How does Shakespeare do it? He depicts the substance of Cassius both as self-chosen (as conceived by Dante) and emotional. So, Shakespeare's Cassius tells Brutus that, once "upon a raw and gusty day," he and Caesar made a dare with each other to swim across the River Tiber. Before they reached the other side, Caesar cried "Help me Cassius, or I sink," and Cassius saved his life. Cassius continues:

> ... And this man
> Is now become a god, and Cassius is
> A wretched creature, and must bend his body
> If Caesar carelessly but nod on him (1, 2, 205).

Shakespeare imagined scenes that could have formative effects: events such as being humiliated, beneath the notice of Caesar: someone who once was a close friend but who is now become so important that "he doth bestride the narrow world/ Like a Colossus." Shakespeare's invention, here, was that the emotions that arise from character-shaping events in Cassius are shame and envy. A pressing outcome of shame is anger. The goal of envy is to destroy, and the principal action of the play (which gives the structure to its plot) is the assassination of Caesar. One sees more deeply into the substance of Cassius.[13]

Cassius recruits Brutus to the conspiracy to kill Caesar. He asks Brutus why he has not been as affectionate as usual. Brutus apologizes for neglecting his friend and says that he has been "with himself at war." Then follows this:

> *Cassius.* Then, Brutus, I have much mistook your passion . . .
>   Tell me, good Brutus, can you see your face?
> *Brutus.* No Cassius, for the eye sees not itself
>   But by reflection, by some other things.
> *Cassius.* 'Tis just;
>   And it is very much lamented, Brutus,
>   That you have no such mirrors as will turn
>   Your hidden worthiness into your eye,
>   That you might see your shadow (1, 2, 139).

Cassius says he will be a mirror for Brutus. He offers an interpretation of Brutus's inner conflict as dissatisfaction with Caesar's ambition. Without Cassius's interpretation he might be unwilling to acknowledge it. Cassius will help him:

> *Cassius.*   I, your glass,
>   Will modestly discover to yourself
>   That of yourself you yet know not of (1, 2, 156).

For Shakespeare a character can be at conflict with himself, as Brutus is. And, in his exploration of shadow and substance, Shakespeare depicts what we now call the unconscious.[14] Thus we reach the very pregnant idea of a character in fiction who can be impelled by goals that he or she does not know of, but which other characters, or we readers, might discern. One can't say that Shakespeare offered a hypothesis about character. A hypothesis would be in a different mode than the one in which he wrote. What he did, I think, was to introduce a way of thinking and talking about character that has become accepted, that enables us to understand others and ourselves more deeply.

Action, plot, and character

So, character derives from mental models we make of other people, and ourselves, and is a principal component of a literary simulation-dream. It is from character that flow goals, plans, and actions. In a typically structured narrative plot, actions generate incidents, which typically occur because of vicissitudes encountered in characters' plans. In well-constructed plots, these lead to outcomes that are somewhat unexpected, but that when we read the story, they seem to have a rightness about them, given the circumstances. The reason the idea of plot continues to be important in world literature is that not only do our human actions have effects we can't fully anticipate, but we don't always know what we want and we often act for reasons we don't fully understand. Plots are studies of such problems, and of how we negotiate them.

As I explained in Chapter 1, Aristotle called the unexpected change of circumstance in a narrative *peripeteia,* and argued that it is essential to a plot. Perhaps it is essential because emotions typically occur with the unexpected, and emotions are essential to fiction. We have then, as a schema of the structure of everyday life, and of the plots of narratives, something like this.

Goals $\rightarrow$ Actions $\rightarrow$ Incidents $\rightarrow$ Outcomes $\rightarrow$ Emotions
(of an emotional kind)

The literary idea of character's substance is of an ensemble of goals that derive from emotional aspects of relationships. From these goals, intentions are formed, which issue in characteristic actions. The idea that Shakespeare implemented, of character as formed by incidents of emotional significance, and of emotionally significant actions that flow from it, has diffused into society.[15] This idea was devised in the simulations of fiction. In turn, the simulations seem to have inserted the idea into everyday understandings.

The most famous, perhaps still the best, discussion of character in fiction is by E. M. Forster in *Aspects of the novel*. Forster makes the distinction between flat and round characters. A flat character is a cardboard cut-out, depicted as a single characteristic, or as driven to the actions about which we read by a single motivation (as villains are in many stories), or as employed to serve a particular function in a plot. Round characters feel and do things beyond a single characteristic, motivation, or plot function. They may have motivations that are at odds with each other, or be in inner turmoil. Such characters are interesting in themselves. They come alive beyond the page: alive – that is – in our minds, in something like the way of people we know. "They are," says Forster, "real not because they are like ourselves (though they might be) but because they are convincing" (p. 61).[16]

Theory-of-mind is important to fiction because characters (like ourselves and others we know) have not just one motive but many.[17] Some motives are not known by the characters themselves. Others, of insecurity and of desires that are inappropriate, may be known by characters but kept carefully hidden. The reader is set to wonder "what does she really want," or to think "he's concerned about doing the right thing, but is his real motive vindictiveness?" Fiction is a world in which we not only wonder about such matters but come, in the best instances, to understand them.

The emergence of character from relationship

Fiction has been good at exploring how character can determine incident, and how incident can illustrate character. But in novels and short stories character is typically depicted in adulthood. We know, however, that the most formative changes of character occur in childhood, usually with parents, sometimes without parents. In this, psychology is perhaps ahead of most fiction.

The important research in this area indicates that foundations of character are built in the first few years of life, in our relationship with our mother or other caregiver. This theory was proposed by John Bowlby, a psychoanalyst who, during World War II worked with children who had lost their parents because of the war. Such losses propelled children through stages of distress and protest, before finally they reached a despairing resignation. Something essential to their development – the relationship with the caregiver –had been damaged and this had a profound effect on their character. Bowlby was told by colleagues about the work of Konrad Lorenz on imprinting, a system in which birds form a close relationship with the first largish object that moves around and makes noises. Biology had arranged that this was usually their mother, but Lorenz sometimes arranged for this object to be him. This worked just as well, and Lorenz writes of geese and other birds that became imprinted on him.

With the idea of imprinting and his observations of the profound effects of separations of children from their parents, Bowlby conceived the theory of attachment. It is that human infants are biologically programmed to keep close to their caregiver, while she or he protects and cares for them. Just as being suckled with milk when young is a physiological attribute of being a mammal, so attachment is its equivalent psychological attribute.

Bowlby's collaborator, Mary Ainsworth, recognized that the attachment relationship could occur in a number of styles, which she and her colleagues characterized in terms of what happened when infant and mother separated and then rejoined. First a mother and child would be observed together in a room. Then the mother would leave. A few minutes later she would return. In one style, called secure attachment, if the mother were absent for a while, the infant would be distressed, and when she returned there would be a joyful reunion. In avoidant attachment, it was as if an infant had come to think the mother was not available; when the mother returned after a departure, the child adopted an attitude of withdrawn independence and would not greet her. In ambivalent attachment, it was as if the child had found the mother unreliable. With her return after an absence, the child would be furiously angry with her.

With these styles (within which there are variations) it is as if from a whole range, emotional responsiveness in the first important relationship, a style has been selected as substance.[18] Character is built on this foundation, and the child carries this schema of relating into adulthood.[19]

A psychological analysis of character

Although there are numerous examples in fiction of escape from terrible childhoods, I can't think of good fictional examples of how character emerges from the formative experiences of childhood attachment. For this, we can look to fiction's sister art, biography. We can thus trace a line from biography as written by Plutarch, via Shakespeare's ideas about the emotional bases of character, and back to biography again,[20] where we find a brilliant book *The hidden genius of emotion*, which takes insights of attachment into biography. In it, Carol Magai and Jeannette Haviland-Jones depict the character of three men, each the inventor of an influential school of psychotherapy. One is Carl Rogers, founder of the counseling approach to psychotherapy. The second is Albert Ellis, founder of rational-emotive therapy, one of the tributaries of cognitive behavioral therapy. The third is Fritz Perls, founder of Gestalt therapy, a dramatized version of psychoanalysis.

The core idea of Magai and Haviland-Jones's book is of preoccupying emotional themes: the idea that in our relationships, and in our lives more generally, one set of emotions becomes predominant, and forms an emotional style of character which, because of its one-sidedness (which we all have), sets a pattern, which affects how others relate to us, and which tends to be accompanied by a distinctive set of life problems.[21] Because, almost inevitably, one has restricted one's emotional repertoire in one's first close relationship, one has to deal with implications of that restriction, which tend to lead into particular avenues of adult relationship and preoccupation.

Magai and Haviland-Jones took attachment theory and other modern theories of how emotions work, and wrote emotion-based biographies of Rogers, Ellis, and Perls, for each of whom there was autobiographical and other biographical material available, as well as their scholarly writings, to see if, in this material, they could discern clues to character. They also used the first film that had been made about psychotherapy,[22] in which each therapist meets and works for half an hour with a client, Gloria, who had recently separated from her husband. In the film the character of each therapist fairly leaps from the screen: Rogers listens respectfully to Gloria. Ellis lectures at her. Perls more-or-less bullies her.

Here, I'll sketch one of the character studies: that of Carl Rogers. He was the fourth of six children, in a well-off fundamentalist Christian family. He was so unwell as a child that his parents worried that he might not survive, and gave him a great deal of attention. The family was warm, but certain emotions such as anger were forbidden. Soon after university, Rogers began a long and for the most part happy marriage, and an extraordinarily successful career in which he founded a new kind of therapy based on listening with understanding and empathy to his clients without trying to interpret what they were saying. In his autobiography he wrote that he was shy, professionally a bit of a lone wolf, but someone who enjoyed close relationships. People found him gentle and remarkably lacking in anger, but some colleagues in the psychiatric profession found him to be "an irritant of monumental proportions." He moved to new positions several times in his career, probably to escape professional conflicts.

Magai and Haviland-Jones write this:

> it appears that Rogers's primary attachment relationship was secure, versus avoidant or ambivalent. Yet, his interactions with other social partners could be fractious . . . Rogers could also be painfully shy, and yet he was drawn to people and even did group encounter therapies. He often made others the center of his existence. He was also often in conflict with others, but he was not a particularly "angry" or hostile man (p. 57).

Magai and Haviland-Jones propose that Rogers developed a core relational schema in which he longed for close relationships, but in which there was a great deal of shame, derived probably from his fundamentalist Christian upbringing, with a mother always ready to point out shortcomings. After the paradise of a warm and protected infancy, there was disillusion when he started school and also became the object of sibling teasing and competition. The longing for closeness never left him, but neither did his shyness. In his non-verbal patterns of interaction, Rogers shows a good deal of shame, in aversions of the eyes, and in speech with hesitations, "ums," and "ers." In his work, Rogers pioneered a therapy based on providing for his clients an atmosphere of secure relatedness.

In the film with Gloria, Magai and Haviland-Jones (experts in the analysis of facial expressions) note that Rogers's expressions as he talked with Gloria indicated a lot of interest but his eyebrows, slightly slanted upwards towards the middle of his brow, suggested sadness. Implicitly he invited Gloria into a protective relationship that could include talk of intimate matters. In this she avoided the shame of self-criticism, and took the opportunity Rogers always offered to his clients, to move towards greater self-acceptance. Gloria said about the session: "I felt my, uh, more lovable, soft, caring self with Dr Rogers. And, uh, I even felt more free openly, even about sex, and I was surprised by that."

When, after the session, Rogers spoke to the camera to sum up, he said he felt pleased by how it had gone. Magai and Haviland-Jones draw attention to a particular moment in which Rogers said: "When I'm able to enter into a relationship, and I feel it was true in this instance . . ." His voice rose with the last few words, and Magai and Haviland-Jones comment:

> He was being spontaneous here and the excitement and proud pleasure mounted. At the height of this juncture, the configuration of his face changed into a more open and unguarded one, and at this point we see the only "pure" prototypic interest expression (brows raised and arched)

of the whole film. Furthermore, what happened next is even more revealing. The raised brow lasted only a flicker of a second before the muscles controlling the outer brow were drawn into play to pull the outer corners down, thus creating the sad brow with the oblique configuration (p. 90).

Rogers had an instant of excitement and pleasure in what he had accomplished, but it was one on which the emotional organization of his character would not allow him to dwell. It is shameful to express too much self-satisfaction, and one must certainly never feel pride: the expression was quickly inhibited by shame and the face resumed its usual slightly sad look.

Marcel Proust had put a comparable idea like this:

> The features of our face are scarcely more than expressions that have been made so often that they have become fixed by habit. Nature, like the catastrophe of Pompeii, like the metamorphosis of a nymph, has immobilized us in a habitual movement (À la recherche du temps perdu, Vol. II my translation).

What about Rogers's antagonisms with psychiatrists and other professional colleagues? Here, Magai and Haviland-Jones suggest that he drew on a repertoire of self-righteous exclusiveness that derived from his religious upbringing. He tended to treat outsiders with reserve, sometimes even with contempt.

Magai and Haviland-Jones thus map out a new area of understanding character – as in the best fictional studies of character from Dante, through William Shakespeare, to Jane Austen, George Eliot, and Virginia Woolf – as one that emerges in interaction with others, and then shapes later interactions. As John Keats said, we shouldn't think that we humans live in a vale of sorrows, but in a vale of soul-making. How else could a soul be made, asks Keats, but "in a world like this?"

Attachment is generally the first love. Most literary love stories are about second love. Magai and Haviland-Jones's book about the formation of character around attachment and family culture to create habitual movements of established emotions might have much to offer fiction writers in the bridge from first to second love.[23]

Relationships with books

It takes a certain generosity to engage with a new person. In the same way, it takes a certain generosity to enter into a relationship with a poem, short story, novel, play, or film. One needs to trust the author. Then, it seems, one is able to take in the author's creations: one opens one's mind and allows them to enter one. I.A. Richards's students who were reluctant to enter in to John Donne's poem that starts "At the round earth's imagined corners blow" (see Chapter 3), showed how careful people are with their reading. As Rebecca Wells-Jopling pointed out in 2009, we may need to be careful, because we don't want to take in attitudes and thoughts that might cause havoc in our inner worlds. I remember many years ago, when I was staying in an apartment in a high-rise building, reading a short story by Roald Dahl (some of whose writing I like) that upset me so much that I took the book to the building's rubbish chute and threw it in there, to be rid of it for ever. I can't remember the title. It may have been a very good story.

It is, moreover, not just the author to whom we relate. I think in fiction that we form our strongest relationship to a character, perhaps a narrator, then perhaps to an author. As I explained in Chapter 2, the best metaphor for our relationship with a fictional story is friendship. Friends affect us. They change us. And just as we are careful whom we choose as friends, drawing as Virginia Woolf reminded us (in her 1924 talk at Cambridge) on our abilities to judge character, so we are careful what we read and what literary characters, or what narrators, we become mentally involved with.

Although we may be perfectly able and willing to imagine life in ancient Greece 2500 years ago, or even life on a moon of Alpha Centauri, when it comes to extending ourselves into the mind of certain fictional characters, we may be neither able nor willing. The Roman poet Terence said "*Homo sum: humani nihil a me alienum puto*" (I am a man: nothing human is alien to me). This statement, by a former slave who must often have felt the absence of human empathy in others' dealings with him is very striking. Is it, perhaps, a bit overstated?[24]

Characters as friends
In fiction, readers engage with the characters, and wonder what they are up to. It may even be that when we read fiction, theory-of-mind is a matter of constantly considering in our own minds the range of characters' next possibilities of action, including mental actions of thoughts and emotions. In this way, what characters do becomes recognizable, but also sometimes also satisfyingly surprising.

Writers of fiction sometimes find that their characters do things that they (the writers) don't seem to control. Marjorie Taylor, Sara Hodges and Adèle Kohányi published a study based on interviews with 50 fiction writers to explore this phenomenon. The writers ranged from published professionals to people who had not yet published anything. All but four reported some experience of characters exhibiting autonomous agency. Writers who had published their work had more frequent and more detailed reports of the phenomenon, which suggests that it is associated with expertise. Taylor and her colleagues also found that, as compared with the normal population, writers more frequently reported that they had imaginary companions as children. Writers also scored higher than the average of the ordinary population on tests of empathy.

The conclusion about characters taking off on their own is also supported by analyses of 52 *Paris Review* interviews with distinguished writers, who included 14 Nobel Prize winners.[25] Maja Djikic, Jordan Peterson, and I, found that 30 of 33 *Paris Review* interviewees who were asked a question about whether they made new discoveries in the course of writing said that they did, and these discoveries frequently included characters behaving in ways the writers had not expected.

E. M. Forster's talks of this in *Aspects of the novel:*

> The characters arrive when evoked, but full of the spirit of mutiny. For they have these numerous parallels with people like ourselves, they try to live their own lives and are consequently often engaged in treason against the main scheme of the book. They "run away," they "get out of hand": they are creations inside of a creation, and often inharmonious towards it; if they are given complete freedom they kick the book to pieces, and if they are kept too sternly in check, they revenge themselves by dying, and destroy it by intestinal decay (p. 64).

It is not, therefore, only we readers who imagine ourselves into the minds of characters as we run the simulation that is a literary story. Writers do something of the same; possibilities suggested by the contexts of action take precedence over other influences in how character is imagined. Our theory-of-mind, in other words, is theory-of-mind-in-certain-compelling-social-situations.[26]

Valentine Cadieux made the observation (in 2008), that it's not just that what she calls "intractable characters" have autonomous agency, they open up new perspectives. Without the character's particular traits and proclivities, the author might not have access to the possibilities the characters realize. Cadieux suggests that for writers, intractable characters are extensions of their own character that they would otherwise be unable to reach, "possibly even that these personality extensions may help us transcend the habitual limits, say, of being an agreeable person, or a graceless person, or a loud or quiet person."[27]

The character of Mr Darcy

Pride and prejudice is about the relation of love to the pride one takes in one's character, restricted as it has become at the time of early adulthood.

An important premise of any love story is that to start with one doesn't know much about the other person. Elizabeth Bennet is the daughter of an affectionate but silly mother and a clever but sardonic father. To her potential love object she brings beliefs, hopes, and expectations of her own self. In *Romeo and Juliet*, Romeo falls in love with Juliet as a result of mere visual appearance, by mere projection. In *Pride and prejudice* Elizabeth starts from a position of nursing her own pride, since the first thing Darcy does is to say something cruel. Her love grows as she comes gradually to know – as the readers also come to know – more about Darcy. Darcy is a character who himself changes in the course of a novel. Let us look first at Jane Austen's initial depiction.

To let us know she is thinking about character in the opening chapters of *Pride and prejudice*, Austen has her characters make several comments. "One cannot know what a man really is by the end of a fortnight," says Mr Bennet in Chapter 2. Then, in Chapter 4, Jane Bennet describes Mr Bingley (the new tenant of Netherfield Park), as "sensible, good humoured, lively, . . . with such perfect good breeding," to which Elizabeth, her younger sister, replies: "He is also handsome . . . which a young man ought likewise to be, if he possibly can. His character is thereby complete."

The central topic of the opening chapters of *Pride and prejudice* is the character of Bingley's friend Darcy. The two men were friends, says the narrator in Chapter 4, "in spite of a great opposition of character."

At the beginning of *Pride and prejudice* the character to whom we become closest is Elizabeth. Austen contrives this, I think, by having Elizabeth be likable, affectionate to her sister Jane, perceptive and witty in her inner life. Austen also arranges that she is in trouble at the beginning of the book. If there's someone we don't know well, we can sympathize when that person is in difficulties.[28] Jane Austen knew this principle. At the dance, Jane Bennet is singled out by the eligible Mr Bingley. He dances with her . . . twice. Jane is gratified and – says the narrator – "Elizabeth felt Jane's pleasure." But we readers are not moved in the same way, because we don't yet know Jane Bennet. By contrast, Elizabeth feels hurt by Mr Darcy, when he says to Bingley of Elizabeth (loudly enough for her to overhear): "She is tolerable, but not handsome enough to tempt *me*." In Chapter 5 Elizabeth says: "I could easily forgive *his* pride if he had not mortified *mine*." At this stage in the novel, we don't know much about Elizabeth but, because she is in trouble, we can feel for her.

As is the way in nineteenth-century novels the character of Darcy is developed for readers in three principal ways. First there is a description by the narrator. Chapter 3 depicts the dance and the narrator says: "Mr Darcy soon drew the attention of the room by his fine, tall person, handsome features, noble mien; and the report which was in general circulation within five minutes after his entrance, of his having ten thousand a year."

Second, comes action. Darcy refuses to dance with anyone except, out of a forced politeness, with the sisters of his friend Bingley. And thus, says the narrator: "His character was decided. He was the proudest, most disagreeable man in the world." As if to reinforce this judgment, comes the action that seems to define Darcy's character, his slighting remark about Elizabeth. Action is important as the basis of plot. Aristotle said that plot is the means by which we understand actions and their effects. From at least the time of Shakespeare, actions became not only the means by which plot is forwarded, but the determiners of incidents, which in turn function to illustrate character. Such is Darcy's action in speaking slightingly of Elizabeth.

Third, in ways of depicting character, there is commentary by others. Thus, in Chapter 5, Elizabeth's friend, Charlotte Lucas, says of Darcy that because he has family and fortune, "he has a *right* to be proud."

In *Pride and prejudice,* written at the beginning of the nineteenth century, inwardness of character, which became central to Virginia Woolf in the early twentieth century, is only beginning to be depicted. In this novel, inwardness is glimpsed only occasionally in Darcy, but it contributes strongly to the character of Elizabeth. We readers catch a glimpse of her inner thoughts as she considers to herself how Bingley's sisters were "not deficient in good humour when they were pleased," but that being rich and used to associating with people of rank, they "were conceited . . . entitled to think well of themselves, and meanly of others." So whereas Charlotte is in awe of the condescension that riches can afford a person, Elizabeth is critical.

As with Shakespeare, we are caught up in a counterpoint between shadow and substance. Darcy and Bingley's sisters behave in a proud way.

Do they have a right to do this? Does Darcy's outward action proceed from an inner pride that is justified, or does it proceed from substance which, as Mrs Bennet asserts, is "horrid?"

The novel of social explanation
The inventor of detective fiction is usually taken to be Edgar Allen Poe with his short story, "Murders in the rue Morgue." The genre requires that a crime has been committed, but not just a crime: an act that is mysterious. Then a person in the role of detective appears – a person who also typically has a somewhat mysterious quality – to work out by sheer application of brainpower what happened to cause the seemingly inexplicable event, and thus to put things right again in the world.[29]

In *Pride and prejudice* – well before Edgar Allen Poe – Austen invents a story-line of this kind in the domain of the social rather than the forensic. The mysterious event is of an apparently well-brought-up young man saying something rude about a young woman loudly enough for her to hear it. Austen then sets in train a round of discussion of this event – which is the opening phase in the depiction and understanding of Darcy's character – as to what the explanation of this rudeness might be.

There are, of course, innumerable puzzles in literature, for instance the question of how Oedipus might have known who his mother was, or how Tom Jones (in Henry Fielding's novel of the same name) could come to know who his mother was. But (I submit) puzzles of the kind Austen explores are different.[30] Austen conceived a novel based on social explanation, in which a solution is reached by means of conversation. Might one say that Austen invented the novel of social explanation?

Only through discussion among the novel's characters, and by further incident, is Darcy's rude behavior understood, and indeed the explanation that gradually emerges underlies the growing understanding between Elizabeth and Darcy. So whereas in a forensic detective story, one feels a curiosity that is gradually satisfied and sometimes an amazement at the detective's acumen, in Austen's story of social detection, with his or her gradual understanding of the character of Darcy, the reader feels a certain respect and love for him, that grows in something like the same way that Elizabeth's love grows.

The deeper point is that the character of others, and even of our selves, is always imperfectly known. The fact that in some genres of fiction the character of one or more characters is hidden, and needs to be discovered by a detective, is an allegory of the situation we always are in. Austen, more than writers of detective fiction, situates this issue where it properly belongs, in the world of coming to know others, and ourselves.

Austen doesn't ask us to feel for Darcy what Elizabeth feels. Austen suggests it without saying it, in the manner of *dhvani* (as explained in Chapter 3). She suggests to us a world – a dream world now 200 years old – and invites us to imagine ourselves into the spaces in the conversations about Darcy, and later in the book, in the conversations between Elizabeth and Darcy. So as Virginia Woolf put it: "Jane Austen is thus a mistress of much deeper emotion than appears on the surface. She stimulates us to supply what is not there . . . something that expands in the reader's mind" (p. 148).

5

Emotions

Figure 5.1 Close-up from Sergei Eisenstein's *The battleship Potemkin*, showing the ship's doctor holding his glasses, folded to make a lens, over a side of meat on which large maggots can be seen with the naked eye. Source: RIA Novosti/Topfoto.

Such Stuff as Dreams: The Psychology of Fiction, First Edition. K. Oatley.
© 2011 K. Oatley. Published 2011 by John Wiley & Sons, Ltd.

Emotions: Scenes in the Imagination

In the mind

If you watch Sergei Eisenstein's film, *The battleship Potemkin*, about the mutiny in 1905 of the crew of the *Potemkin*, or consider some of its shot-sequences (one of which I'll describe in a moment), you get an interesting glimpse of how the emotions of fiction are constructed in the mind. Eisenstein made *Potemkin* in 1925 as a patriotic political film for a Soviet audience, but he also made it to explore effects of juxtapositions of film shots with each other.

The film begins with sailors on the battleship getting out of their hammocks. Then you see a side of meat hoisted up from the hold, evidently for the sailors to eat. Everyone can see the meat is rotten, and the sailors start to complain. The ship's doctor is summoned.

Potemkin was made in the era of silent movies, so things that characters say are displayed as captions. About five minutes into the film one of the sailors says (in a caption): "The meat could crawl overboard on its own." Then come five shots in a sequence that lasts eleven seconds. Here is a summary (with the approximate duration of each shot in parentheses).

1. Group shot: Side of meat on the left of the screen with, in the middle and on the right, a row of sailors' faces scowling slightly and looking away from the meat (one second),
2. Group shot: Doctor, on the left of the screen, regards the meat and removes his glasses, while on the right a sailor looks on (four seconds),
3. Close up: Doctor's hands fold his glasses to make a double-lensed magnifying glass (two seconds),
4. Ultra close up: Doctor's eye seen through the folded glasses that have been made into a magnifying glass (two seconds),
5. Close up: Doctor's hand holds his folded glasses (magnifying glass) over the meat on which, without the aid of the magnifying glass, dozens of large maggots are seen to crawl (two seconds; the still at the head of this chapter is from this shot).

Although this is the movies, the principal movements take place not on the screen but in the spaces between the shots: in the minds of the audience.

Principally at issue is not the sequence of action, but the flow of viewers' emotion. With this in mind, let us look briefly at three moments in the development of the language of film.

In the earliest films, a static camera recorded the movements of actors, as if the camera were in front of a play performed on stage. The first distinctive development of film was composition from different shots and, in 1903, *The great train robbery* was made in this way. It's considered a landmark. It's a 12-minute film of shots taken at different times and spliced together, made by Edwin Porter, who is generally credited with the invention of film editing. Such editing now involves selecting which shots to include from an array that is many times more than the number in the final film. Editing involves, too, arranging the shots in order. Thus film becomes a language with the two functions identified by Roman Jakobson of selection and combination. In *The great train robbery,* the second shot (which lasts just over a minute) is an exterior shot of a train stopping at a water tower, of it taking on water and then, as the train sets off again, of robbers boarding it. The next shot is of the interior of the train's baggage car, in which the robbers shoot and kill the guard. Viewers experience these two shots as a narrative sequence, and don't think that they were taken at different times, and don't think that the interior of the baggage car isn't a train, but a film set. Emotionally, a shocking event is depicted, a shooting, and the audience is caught up sympathetically in it.

Second, at some time in the 1920s, Lev Kuleshov did the following. He obtained a shot (taken some years previously) of the expressionless face of a famous male film star. Then he edited together a sequence in which a shot of a plate of soup was followed by this shot of the actor's face, then a shot of a girl playing with a teddy bear followed by the same shot of the actor's face, the a shot of a dead woman in a coffin followed by the same shot of the actor's face. Viewers were said to have been moved by the film star's great acting, his hunger for the soup, his happiness at seeing the girl with the teddy bear, and his deep sorrow as he looked at the dead woman. This has become known as the Kuleshov effect.[1] Emotionally, the audience becomes involved in what they think the actor is feeling.

Third was Eisenstein, who was for a short time a student of Kuleshov.[2] The sequence of five shots (above) from the *The battleship Potemkin* is typical of Eisenstein's work. This sequence could not have been seen in ordinary life by a human observer, because each shot is taken from a different position and no-one could move instantaneously between these positions. Thus it is not naturalistic. It was carefully conceived by the director and editor, and meanings are constructed by the viewer. Eisenstein called the effect "montage," laying one image upon another, so that meanings that were not present in any of the individual shots would be constructed from the juxtapositions.[3] This is an advance on seeing the actor's emotions in the Kuleshov effect. Emotionally, we audience members experience the disgust in ourselves.

The realization that film has its own language, and is not just a version of what you could have witnessed if you had been at the scene, has been shown in a striking way by Sermin Ildirar and her colleagues who studied a group of people who lived in a remote area of Turkey and had never before seen film or television.[4] The researchers compared the understanding of these people with that of people who had five years' experience of viewing film and television, and with those of people who had ten years or more of such viewing. The participants were shown clips that included elements of the language of film, such as jump cuts (two juxtaposed shots of the same subject from different camera positions), pan (in which the camera swings so that a scene moves sideways across the screen), establishing shot (in which a shot is used to establish a context, for instance of an exterior of a building which is followed by a shot of actors inside the building), ellipsis (leaving out something from a sequence of action or plot), and parallel montage (shots of things on the same topic but occurring in different places to imply a relation among them).

Everyone in the study could understand the meanings of ellipsis and parallel montage. The viewers with no film experience and those with only five years experience could not, however, understand the meanings of jump cuts, panning, and establishing shots. Those with ten or more years' experience of film and television could understand the meanings conveyed by all the techniques. So film is a language. It has taken time to develop,[5] and it takes time to learn.

When learned, however, by film-makers and film-viewers, the language of film enables sequences in which the relationships between the images are exactly those required by the *syuzhet* (the discourse structure) of the film. The camera will have been in exactly the right place at exactly the right moment to record each necessary event in a plot, and to suggest a flow of emotion. Thus, as *The battleship Potemkin* begins, we glimpse something of the lives of sailors on a battleship, start to feel some sympathy for them. Then, in the eleven-second sequence that ends with the shot of maggots on the meat, sympathy gathers and we viewers feel disgusted, for ourselves and at the plight of the sailors.

A view of disgust

It's generally accepted that the dreams of fiction are about the emotions. One could almost say they are all about the emotions. Why are emotions so central?

We often recognize people's emotions from expressions of their face and voice, and from gestures and actions. The facial expression of disgust is distinctive, and it is reported to be recognized all round the world.[6] It is made by contracting the *levator labii* muscles on either side of the nostrils, which wrinkle the nose and raise the upper lip. Look in the mirror, imagine something disgusting, and you may see yourself making the expression. You might think, then, that to portray disgust in a film, nothing would be easier than to have an actor make this expression. But the idea of fiction, the idea of film, and indeed the idea of how we recognize emotions is far more interesting.

In prose fiction, on the stage, and in film, although characters are depicted as having emotions, their emotions are not really the issue.[7] If a film-maker were to show an actor making a facial expression of disgust, we would think the character was disgusted. How much better for the audience-member to feel the emotion. That was, in part, the point of Kuleshov's experiment with the actor's immobile face, the bowl of soup, the child playing, and the dead woman. Even more so, it was the point of Eisenstein's montage in the scene from *Potemkin*. It is we, members of the audience, who feel the emotions of a successful fiction film.

Research on disgust goes back to before the era of the movies. Charles Darwin observed and wrote about it in *The expression of the emotions*. He described how, during his voyage on the *Beagle*, a native of Tierra del Fuego touched with his finger some preserved meat he was just about to eat. Finding the meat was soft, the man made an expression of disgust. Darwin records that although the man's hands seemed clean, this quite put him off his lunch. A more recent study, using neuro-imaging, has shown that a brain area involved in recognizing facial expressions of disgust is the same as that involved in experiencing disgust.[8] So when we recognize disgust in others we do often so by creating, or simulating, the experience of disgust in ourselves. It wasn't just the fact of someone touching his preserved meat that put Darwin off his lunch. It was his own feeling of disgust, which mirrored that of the man who touched the meat.

Another touch is that disgust at the sight of something one would refuse to eat – for instance maggot-ridden meat or something someone else has touched – has been found to be exactly the same reaction as that of moral disgust, rejection of an unacceptable or unjust action by another.[9] This connection between disgusting food and unfairness was one that Eisenstein was happy to suggest. By means of juxtapositions, the medium of film has become particularly good at suggesting connections between objects, people, and emotional ideas.

In watching a film, or indeed engaging with any fiction, we experience a flow of emotion in relation to events. It is we who put these events together, constructing them into something meaningful to ourselves, and experiencing the resulting emotions.

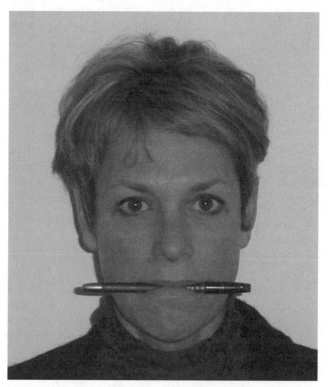

Figure 5.2 Photo used in an experiment by Paula Niedenthal and her colleagues (2009, p. 1128, figure 3) to show participants how to hold a pen in the mouth in a way that would prevent them from making facial expressions that mirrored emotion states corresponding to words they read. When they held a pen in this way, they were less accurate in making judgements about words for emotional expressions that they were asked to read. From Niedenthal, P.M., Winkielman, P., Mondillon, L., & Vermeulen, N. (2009). Embodiment of emotion concepts. *Journal of Personality and Social Psychology, 96,* 1120–1136, figure 3, p. 1128.

Empathy and identification

When we see someone smile, we tend to smile back. When we see someone frown we, too, tend to frown. This is called mirroring, a kind of imitation, and it is related to the idea of mirror neurons that I discussed in Chapter 1. Mirroring has been found experimentally to occur across a range of emotions. For instance, when adults looked at facial expressions of happiness or anger, they spontaneously made facial expressions of their own, which mirrored the expressions they saw. It has been found, too, that when people read words that indicate emotional expressions such as "smile," "cry," and "frown," they activate in themselves the facial muscles for making the corresponding expressions.[11] Experiments of this kind indicate that recognition of an emotion in someone else, and also when we read about it in a story, or see something of emotional significance in a film, typically involves mirroring. Mirroring involves empathy. We can recognize emotion by activating our own comparable experience and expression of a similar emotion.

Empathy – feeling with another person – is central to social interaction. Although the term is only about 100 years old, Adam Smith (250 years ago) included its characteristics in the more capacious term he used, "sympathy," which he thought was the glue that held society together.

In modern times, and on the basis of recent research on brain imaging, empathy has been described as involving: (a) having an emotion, that (b) is in some way similar to that of another person, that (c) is elicited by observation or imagination of the other's emotion, and that involves (d) knowing that the other is the source of one's own emotion.[12]

The findings on empathetic mirroring of emotions suggests a perspective on perceiving others' emotional expressions not as states that one simply sees out there in the world, as one might see a tree or a lamp-post, but as empathetic ways of attuning to others. Empathy did not develop recently in human beings. It is an ancient characteristic of social mammals.[13] It is central to social life.

Alvin Goldman has described two routes to empathy. The first is the simple case of recognizing an emotional expression. This, he says, involves low-level mind-reading, that is to say, attributing a certain emotion to the person who has made an expression. Recognition is based, he says, on being able to feel (simulate) the corresponding emotion in oneself (as in mirroring).

As Ludwig Wittgenstein put it:

> We see emotion . . . We do not see facial contortions and make the inference that he is feeling joy, grief, boredom. We describe the face

immediately as sad, radiant, bored, even when we are unable to give any other description of the features.[14]

In other words, mind-reading presents us immediately with experiences of a kind that are relevant to our interactions with others, not of components of facial muscle movements.

When we see a smile on the face of the person we are with, we tend to feel happy and smile back, disposed to cooperate. When we see tears, we tend to feel sad, and are prompted to help. When we see a frown, we often begin to feel angry, prepared for the possibility of conflict with the other. When we hear someone's cry of alarm, we usually feel frightened ourselves. In each case we experience an empathetic emotion that affects us and configures a relationship with the other person.[15] Think of it like this. For a stage performance, an actor learns a script, a set of words. The actor's job is to use the words and depict character-emotions that support certain relationships with other characters. In ordinary life, something like the inverse happens. Emotions provide us with scripts not of words but of relating – in happy cooperation, in sad disengagement, in angry conflict, in shared fear, and so on – and we supply fitting words in our interactions with each other. The words that Titania says in *A midsummer night's dream* to Bottom the weaver (who has been turned into an ass), after she has had the falling-in-love juice dropped into her eyes (which I discussed in Chapter 1, see page 2) are an example.

When one does not directly see or hear another person's expression of emotion, Goldman says a second route to empathy is used, which he calls high-level mindreading: imaginative empathy. The process has two parts. One part is that, by simulation within ourselves we infer what emotion the other person is feeling and we impute it to that person. The second part, which occurs at the same time, is that, because of the simulation, we feel a corresponding emotion in our self, in a way that can make for social coordination. This imaginative mindreading can be based on a wide variety of information about the other. It can occur both in the moment during an interaction, and over the longer term as one forms mental models of people we know.

Information from which we build mental models of others is of much the same kind when it derives from what we ourselves observe or imagine of a person, when it's information offered us by friends in conversation about people we know, and when it's offered by fiction writers about a character.[16] In fiction the mental models we build of characters shape our attitudes to them. A skilled author can help us build better mental models of fictional characters than we can sometimes build of people we know in everyday life.

The experience of emotion in fiction

When we read fiction or watch drama we want to be moved. When we read a piece of non-fiction, perhaps about genetics or history, we want to be informed. At least that's a first thought.[17] It's not a complete thought because we also often feel involved and moved when we read non-fiction. So let me see if I can put this intuition better. In fiction, as well as in genres like biography, emotions are critical; we engage with issues because they are emotionally important to us, having to do with people, with intentions, and with outcomes. The emotions we experience are not primarily those of the characters, they are our own, in the contexts we imagine. In non-fiction, the issues with which we engage may include people, intentions, and outcomes but they can be more various, and need not have our own emotions at the center.

How do we understand emotion? There is fair agreement in psychology that it is typically a process in which some event or person (in the outer world) is related to a concern or a purpose (which is inward).[18] Emotion is that process in life by which events become meaningful to us. Often it brings the events to consciousness.

Can we see in more detail how emotions are prompted in fiction? Gerald Cupchik, Peter Vorderer, and I, asked participants to read extracts of short stories from James Joyce's *Dubliners,* and we classified readers' emotions as fresh emotions (which occurred as they read), and emotional memories (which derived from memories that occurred to them as they read). Emotions of both kinds were experienced. Comparably, when people have been asked to read short stories and have been asked to mark the margin with Ms, Es and Ts (for memories, emotions, and thoughts, as described in Chapter 3), almost everyone has marked at least some Es, fresh emotions, as well as some memories that had emotional components.[19] How do the different kinds of emotions occur? In the next sections, I suggest they occur in four main ways.

Emotions of identification
Empathetic understanding of others' emotions is important in day-to-day social life and, with a small modification; it is carried into the world of fiction, where it has the name of identification.[20]

Here is the modification. In everyday empathetic mind-reading we see or imagine what the other is feeling and at the same time can feel a corresponding emotion our self. In fiction, the first move is to put aside our own goals and plans, and to insert, instead, the goals, plans and actions of a character (as indicated by the author) into our own planning processor. In the second move, with the goals and plans we have taken on, we experience our own fresh emotions in the circumstances of the character's actions and their effects.

The planning processor is the process by which we arrange our lives, and undertake actions. I might say to myself: "I'll finish writing this paragraph, and then make a cup of coffee." In reading a piece of fiction we withdraw from the immediate world, but after we have suspended our own goals, plans, and actions, we make the processor available to the goals, plans, and actions, of a protagonist in the story. The author tells the reader what plans and what actions to enter into the processor. Empathetic identification occurs when we insert the character's goals, plans, or actions, into our own planning processor, and we come to feel in ourselves the emotions that occur with the results of actions that we perform mentally as if in the place of character.[21]

Tom Trabasso and Jennifer Chung did an experiment that shows how this kind of identification works. They asked 20 people to watch two films, Alfred Hitchcock's *Vertigo* and Ridley Scott's *Blade runner*. Twenty viewers were randomly assigned to two groups. As they watched, each film was stopped at 12 points. At each of the film's stopping points, the ten viewers in one group were asked how well or badly things were going for the film's protagonist and for the antagonist. The purpose of this was to indicate viewers' sense of success and failure of the plans of the protagonist and of the antagonist. (The viewers' ratings agreed with the experimenters' analyses of the characters' actions and their effects as they watched the films.) At each of the film's stopping points the people in the second group of ten viewers had to indicate what emotions they themselves felt, and at what intensity. When things went well for a protagonist or went badly for an antagonist (as rated by the first group of viewers), the second group of viewers felt positive emotions, such as happiness or relief. But when (as rated by the first set of viewers) things went badly for the protagonist or well for the antagonist the second set of viewers felt negative emotions such as sadness, or anger, or anxiety.

This second set of viewers is us: readers and audience members. We feel happy or relieved when a liked protagonist is doing well. We feel sad, or angry, or anxious, when an antagonist is succeeding.[22]

Trabasso and Chung found just the basics. Their results are evidence of the close connection between fiction and games, because they apply, as well to watching sports. When we enter a piece of fiction or a sport in this way, we experience some excitement and enjoyment, some happiness at the success of the protagonist of a story or of our team, and some sadness and anxiety at the success of the antagonist or the opposing team. Literary art does not typically forego this effect. Instead, art elaborates it. In *Vertigo*, one of the films used by Trabasso and Chung, the protagonist, Scottie, is played by James Stewart, a product of the Hollywood star system. He has been cast in this role because he is likable and, at the beginning of the film, he is in difficulties. It is easy to identify with him. Scottie has been a detective and he has taken early retirement because he was involved in a traumatic incident in which a colleague fell to his death. Now he has a phobia for heights. He is asked by an old college friend to follow the friend's wife, Madeleine, who has started to behave strangely and thinks she is possessed by a dead relative. So the movie might seem to be a pastime movie, with a mystery motif.

But *Vertigo* is not just another pastime movie. It is, I think, a work of art. As the film gathers momentum we find that Scottie has characteristics that are more questionable than those generally seen in a pastime protagonist. He becomes obsessed with Madeleine. Then he starts to act coercively, and indeed becomes rather repellent. So, as we identify with Scottie and take on his goals, plans, and actions, we start to find ourselves in imagination acting in ways that are contrary to those in which we usually act. Are we, ourselves, capable of being obsessed by a friend's spouse, of becoming coercive? Since we continue to identify with Scottie, the answer is yes, in our imagination.

In almost every action movie, and in many works of literary fiction, we can find ourselves experiencing emotions of identification, becoming vengeful, for instance, on behalf of a protagonist who has been harmed. So, yes we are capable of such destructive feelings. One of the differences, I think, between the pastime and the work of art, is that with a simple action movie we feel angry, and the end of the story is that our vengeance is satisfied. We have run a schema of habit, not much different than putting on our clothes in the morning. In art, by contrast, our conception of our selfhood can change, for instance towards understanding in ourselves certain potentialities that we might not normally admit to ourselves, which we might think belong only to others. We discover that we too, as members of the family of human beings, are at least mentally capable of emotions that are not very creditable.

Here is how it works, I think. A very basic emotional process engages
the reader with plans and fortunes of a protagonist. This is what often
drives a plot and, perhaps, keeps us turning the pages, or keeps us in our
seat at the movies or at the theater. It can be enjoyable. In art we experience
the emotion, but with it the possibility of something else, too. The way we
see the world can change, and we ourselves can change. Art is not simply
taking a ride on preoccupations or prejudices, using a schema that runs as
usual. Art enables us to experience some emotions in contexts that we
would not ordinarily encounter, and to think of ourselves in ways that
usually we do not.

Emotions of sympathy

A second way of prompting fresh emotions in the reader is for the author
to provide what is called a pattern of appraisal, a pattern of events capable
of causing emotions.[23] According to this idea, which goes back to Aristotle's
Rhetoric, emotions are caused by appraisals of events of a kind that might
concern people. Particular emotions are caused by particular patterns: so
happiness arises with successes or reunions with friends, sadness with
losses, anger with frustrations and deliberate hurts by others, fear and
anxiety with danger.

As well as identification one may, therefore, experience an emotion in
relation to an appraisal pattern by sympathy. In modern usage, sympathy
is generally taken as separate from empathy (feeling with), and usually
means feeling for someone in their predicament. The idea is that we understand the emotion-producing events (predicaments) from the way they are
depicted by a writer as occurring to a story character. We recognize the
predicament, and feel sympathetic emotions for the character.

As I discussed in Chapter 4, with people one does not know it is easy to
sympathize if they are in difficulties. In Kate Chopin's "The dream of an
hour," we don't know Mrs Mallard to start with, but we learn in the first
sentences that she has a heart trouble, and that she is told news of her
husband's death. It is easy to feel sympathy for her.

The best account that I know of the sympathetic emotions of fiction is
by Ed Tan, in relation to film which, says Tan, seems to be deliberately
constructed as a machine that prompts us to feel emotions: tender emotions in a love story, fear in a thriller, anger in an action film, and so on.
For Tan, these are witness emotions. We feel them because the film-makers
first clothe us in invisibility and then take us, as if by magic, to witness a

scene with emotional implications, then another, then another. We are like those time travelers transported to another era: we can see what is going on but we can't affect it in any way. We appraise the set of events leading to a falling-in-love, or a conflict, or a wrong that must be avenged. We enjoy seeing what will happen.

According to this idea the process has two parts. One is the construction by writers or film-makers of events (predicaments) liable to cause emotions in the characters. The second is that we readers and audience-members appraise these events, and recognize what emotions they would cause. Because we are witnesses, our emotions are witness emotions. Nico Fridja (whose theory of emotions is the one on which Tan bases his work) put the idea to me like this. We were standing, I remember, in a restaurant in Pittsburgh, a long way up and looking down at traffic below. "Imagine there was a car accident," said Nico. "You are both fascinated and afraid for the occupants of the car. But you don't feel as if you're in the car, and you don't feel as you would if your children were in it."

This kind of account needs, I think, to include the idea that certain kinds of events – accidents, fallings-in-love, fights and other assaults, betrayals, injustices, falls from grace, sufferings of loss – have strong fascination for us. This is one of the reasons why film and television are heavily populated with such events. With each such incident, we want to know more. They are the stuff not only of popular fiction but of media news-stories. Perhaps such events are clashes of the gears in the smooth running of society, and they are fascinating because we want to know how things will turn out.[24]

In the theory of sympathetic emotions, our enjoyment of a fictional story derives from entering a narrative world in which we feel for those who suffer certain events. But we're immunized from harmful effects of the events on our own person or on loved ones. By following the story, we achieve the satisfaction of narrative closure. When we read "The dream of an hour," therefore, our attention is attracted first by the death of Mrs Mallard's husband. We recognize that news of it will cause grief to Mrs Mallard, and it does. We read on because as social beings we are interested in what happens to people generally and, with death's breach of the fabric of everyday life, we want to know how this emotion-eliciting event will affect those who are involved. With sympathetic emotions we develop a concern for the character and her or his fate.

Here is how George Eliot, from the generation before Kate Chopin, put it.

The greatest benefit we owe to the artist, whether painter, poet or novelist, is the extension of our sympathies. Appeals founded on generaliza-
tions and statistics require a sympathy ready-made, a moral sentiment
already in activity; but a picture of human life such as a great artist can
give, surprises even the trivial and the selfish into that attention to what
is apart from themselves, which may be called the raw material of moral
sentiment . . . Art is the nearest thing to life; it is a mode of amplifying
experience and extending our contact with our fellow-men beyond the
bounds of our personal lot (p. 192–193).

Literary emotions
Emotions of identification and sympathy are fresh emotions. They occur
as a result of events in the story. But often, too, fiction prompts in us emotions that derive from memories of our own lives.

The best theory of how remembered emotions affect us in fiction comes,
I think, from India. Whereas in Western poetics the central term is *mimesis,*
in the parallel tradition of Indian poetics, emotions are central. This theory
is presented by Abhinavagupta, whose exposition of the idea of *dhvani*
(suggestion) I introduced in Chapter 3.[25] In this theory, a distinction is
made between *bhavas,* everyday emotions, and *rasas,* literary emotions. The
term *rasa* is a metaphor from the flavor of food. It means the experience
of emotion in a work of literary art.

The Indic theorists argued that in a play, an actor enacts specific emotions by gesture, tone of voice, and so on, and thereby *rasas* are prompted
in the audience. The idea is the same as the one discussed in relation to
sympathy, of a story or drama presenting patterns of appraisal that specify
particular kinds of emotion. The Indic theorists argued that there are nine
fundamental emotions, *bhavas* and *rasas,* as follows:

Bhava	Rasa
sexual delight	the amorous or erotic
laughter	the comic
sorrow	the pitiable or tragic
anger	the furious
perseverance	the heroic
fear	the terrible
disgust or disillusion	the odious or loathsome
wonder	the marvelous
serenity	the peaceful

These theorists held that each work of literary art should focus on one *rasa,* and offer as a plot a series of patterns of appraisal focused on that emotion. The West has the comparable idea of genres: love stories, comedies, tragedies, and so forth. Even when based on one *rasa,* plots typically pass through sequences of other emotional states, as well as transitional phases such as apprehension and bewilderment.

In the theory of *rasas,* emotion-based genres are important in that each gives rise to a particular range of implications, and possibilities for suggestion, *dhvani.* So, for instance, in a love story (based on the *rasa* of the amorous), in a scene between two people who are mutually attracted, one may ask the other, "Do you have everything you need?" and this can carry implications it would not have in a story of the heroic.

Rasas differ from everyday emotions in that we can experience them with deeper insight. As the Indic theorists put it, our understandings of our everyday emotions are often hidden from us because our eyes are covered with a thick crust of egoism. Among other reasons that the Indic theorists give for the priority of *rasas* over everyday emotions is that they can bring to awareness memories from a wide range of past lives. Modern Westerners might take this to mean that in fiction we experience emotions remembered from our own experience and – because of our awareness of our evolutionary and cultural kinship – with the rest of humanity. Bringing a range of experience to a piece of fiction can also occur by seeing a lot of dramas and reading a lot of novels.

A Western theory of *rasa*-like literary prompting of emotions is by David Miall and Donald Kuiken, who propose that insightful emotions – they call them self-modifying feelings – can occur when two elements come together. One element is in properties of a text, for instance in its defamiliarizing qualities. The other element is personal, for instance a remembered emotion. Miall and Kuiken liken the process to metaphor, in which one thing can become something else. Similarly, they say reading can produce "metaphors of personal identification that modify self understanding" (p. 221), by which they mean one emotion can become another, and thereby can be experienced in a new way. They give an example from Sophocles's *Oedipus Rex.* The emotion that Sophocles thought was most in need of therapy was shameless *hubris* (arrogance). Audience members would have some remembered experience of it. In the play it can be modified (metaphorically transformed) in the mind of the audience member by the emotions that Aristotle identified as central to tragedy, first by fear for oneself, and then by pity for the protagonist. What can thus happen, say Miall and Kuiken, is that:

Remembered feeling . . . does not remain merely replicative; what began as remembered feeling may become fresh feeling. Either the original feeling is modified, or limitations of the original feeling are shown in such a way that a fresh feeling is created in its place. In several previous studies, we have provided evidence of the modifying power of feeling, in particular showing how aesthetic feelings, i.e., moments of defamiliarization in response to foregrounding, instigate an affectively guided search for alternative interpretations that, in turn, shape subsequent understanding (p. 229).

In 2008 Miall wrote a chapter in which he pointed out that *rasas* have a timeless quality. *Rasas* are, as it were, the emotions of humanity. So, if I may modify *rasa* theory in the light of his proposal: writers and performers offer us appraisal patterns for certain emotions. Prompted by defamiliarization, we bring our selves and our past experience to these patterns and we actively encourage our selves to experience the literary emotions in imagination. A remembered emotion is now experienced in a new context, so the range of our experience of it is increased. In turn we may focus on the text, on a memory, and on the timeless quality of the emotion in a way that can take us out of ourselves. It is, perhaps, the movement among such states that enables us to change our understanding of the emotion in the text we are reading and in ourselves.

Rasa theorists have stressed the importance of bringing an educated sensibility to literary art, and they have also stressed art's morally educative properties. Rather than art imitating life, they thought that an ethically ordered life should imitate well-constructed art. To the idea of *rasa,* we can add Miall and Kuiken's proposal: in self-modifying feelings we use the literary emotions prompted in us by the text to explore possibilities of promoting new understandings and changes of these emotions within ourselves. Even in such genres as tragedy, enjoyment can occur of understanding and the construction of sensibility and responsiveness to others.

Comparable ideas are expressed in Konstantin Stanislavski's *An actor prepares,* narrated by Stanislavski as he imagined himself to have been when he first trained as an actor. He is taking classes with a well-known director who, in the book, is himself 40 years later in his role as Director of the Moscow Art Theatre. The Director observes that at the beginning of rehearsals for a new play, actors' performances have an energy in them as the actors recognize with a shock the situation their characters are in. But as rehearsals continue, performances often become tired, merely behavioral. It is at this point that Stanislavski makes his famous recommendation, that actors recall memories from their own lives, of emotions that are comparable to those of the characters in the play, and draw on these emotions as raw material for their performances.

It is not a long step from Stanislavski's formulation for actors in rehearsal[26] to the idea that audiences and readers also experience emotions mediated by memories, in their own personal enactments of stories. Patterns of emotional appraisal provide cues for memory: so that we can bring emotions forward in time and apply them to new contexts, so that they may be better understood and perhaps modified.

Another idea that fits with the idea of *rasas* is that of Marcel Proust who proposed that for the most part we don't fully engage in our experience. It may happen too quickly, or we may just not think about it. Proust thought that it is rare for an experience to connect with its meaning, but that when this occurs, for instance by connecting the pattern of a memory to its meaning, the conjunction can create a deeply moving understanding. Proust's famous instance was depicted in a passage in *Du côté de chez Swann*, the first book of his novel *À la recherche du temps perdu*. Proust's narrator, Marcel, as an adult, had come home one day and was persuaded by his mother to sit with her and take some herbal tea and a Madeleine cake.

> And then, mechanically, oppressed by a dispiriting day and the prospect of the next day being miserable too, I carried to my lips a spoonful of the tea in which I had moistened a piece of Madeleine cake. At the very instant that the mouthful of tea mixed with cake touched my palate, I trembled, attentive to the extraordinary thing that was happening to me. A delicious pleasure had entered me, isolated, without my having any idea of its cause. It had immediately made life's vicissitudes indifferent, its disasters harmless, its brevity illusory, in the same way that love works by filling me with a precious essence: or, rather, this essence was not in me, it was me. I stopped feeling mediocre, mortal, living a life of contingency. Wherever could it have come from, this powerful joy? (p. 44, my translation).

Marcel spends the next two and a half pages of the novel trying to discover the origin of his profound joy. He tries more spoonfuls of tea, without success. It was clear, he said, that the truth wasn't in the tea, but in himself. For a long time, he strains after a solution, but gets nowhere, feeling something indistinct stirring within, then nothing again. Then suddenly a memory occurs, of drinking tea with his Aunt Leonie, when he was a child.

His joy was not a reliving the taste of the tea. It occurred because of a return of memories from childhood, a state and a time that he had not understood when it was happening. But now his childhood with its meanings started to unfold for him like those Japanese pieces of folded and dried paper that are put into a bowl of water so that:

> . . . as soon as they are immersed, they form into shapes with color, they differentiate, become flowers, houses, people, distinct and recognizable, and in the same way, now, all the flowers that had been in our garden and those in M Swann's park, and the good people of the village and their little houses, and the church, and the whole of Combray and its neighborhood, all assumed form and solidity, emerged, town and gardens, from my cup of tea (p. 47, my translation).

The taste of tea in adulthood, as Marcel sat with his mother after a dull day, had summoned a moment from the past, and with it a seed of meaning, which now he could bring to his childhood, a meaning that became the basis for his novel. This was the source of his joy.

This idea connects, too, with my discussion in Chapter 3, of Keats's idea of poetry being "almost a Remembrance" of how a sense of profound meaning can occur when a writer offers words (to the language layer of the mind) that the reader makes his or her own because they seem perfectly to correspond to a sensory impression or piece of understanding (in the intuitive layer of the mind).

In the *rasa* theory of literary emotions, our enjoyment of a fictional story derives first from recognizing patterns of emotions that we have experienced ourselves (in life or literature) in a new context. We project ourselves imaginatively into this context, and experience the emotions in a way that enables us to understand them more deeply, and in the process perhaps to make some changes in ourselves.

Relived emotions

If you read Kate Chopin's "The dream of an hour" and marked it with Ms, E's and Ts (as I suggested in Chapter 3), you may have experienced an M (memory) when Mrs Mallard looked out of her window, and said "Free." Perhaps, at this point, you recalled a memory in which you said something secretly to yourself, with a sense of relief about some event. Perhaps, when reading the story, you found yourself reliving some aspect of the emotion of a memory.

The best approach I know of how this kind of remembering is discussed by Gerald Cupchik.[27] It is the idea one of the properties of works of art is that they can prompt emotions at a certain distance – called an aesthetic distance – neither too close so that they overwhelm us nor too distant so that they don't affect us.

Thomas Scheff has taken this idea and proposed that in the ordinary world we don't always experience our emotions because sometimes they happen at the wrong aesthetic distance. Sometimes they are too close, for instance, emotions of grief or other losses, emotions of shame that we can't admit to ourselves or others, emotions perhaps of frustration or hatred about matters we can do nothing about. These emotions are "under-distanced." So we remember some aspects of the events that gave rise to them, but in a way that their emotions are not properly assimilated into our autobiography, or into our understanding of ourselves. Huge emotions at the under-distanced end of the scale of relived emotions are among the symptoms of post-traumatic stress disorder, when whole lives are over-turned, as for instance, from being in military combat, or being in a civil disaster, or being criminally assaulted or raped. In this syndrome, people suffer flashbacks and nightmares, but can't tell a coherent narrative of the events.

Another way of not assimilating emotional experience is to block it out altogether. Emotions can then be "over-distanced," and effects of this kind can occur, for instance, when a person has been very hurt in a relationship and vows never to be hurt in that way again. The person often accomplishes this by cutting him- or her-self off from relationships altogether, and hence from most emotions. You probably know such people, who can often seem cut-off, unresponsive, cold.

The function of drama and other kinds of fiction, says Scheff, is to enable us to relive, and hence assimilate, emotions from our past which, although they are not fully conscious, can continue to have serious effects on our lives, and particularly on our relationships. Fiction, with characteristics that are more controlled than those of everyday life, enables us to re-experience such emotions at what Scheff calls an optimal aesthetic distance. In Scheff's treatment, the job of the writer is to present emotionally significant events at an aesthetic distance that enables us to recognize them, experience them, and assimilate them to ourselves.[28]

In the theory of relived emotions, a fictional story is enjoyable because it is therapeutic. Therapy derives from a moving forward in our sense of ourselves, and of being able properly to experience emotions that have been problematic for us. Our experience of emotions as we read or watch a piece of fiction, then, says Scheff, is a reliving of the emotion from our own past at a better aesthetic distance. When we cry at the fates of Romeo and Juliet, says Scheff, really we are re-experiencing a loss of our own with which we have not come fully to terms. Perhaps, at the play, our experience of sadness allows us to make a small further step in assimilating our loss.

Conclusion on elicitation of emotions

The four means described (above) of prompting emotions (fresh emotions of identification and of sympathy, and emotional memories as literary emotions and relived emotions) were originally put forward as competing theories of how emotions arose in fiction. It is now clear that they are not different theories, but different means a writer can use to prompt emotions. For instance, in the study of fresh emotions and emotional memories (by Cupchik, Vorderer and me, mentioned above) we chose passages from James's Joyce's short stories that were either of emotional themes, or of dense description. We instructed participants either to feel what it was like to be the protagonist (identification) or to feel sympathy for the protagonist (sympathy). In response to the emotional passages, we found that fresh emotions and emotional memories occurred about equally often, but with the descriptively dense passages, identification prompted readers to experience more fresh emotions, and sympathy prompted them toward emotional memories. Fresh emotions and emotional memories do not therefore occur because of alternative theories, but as different processes during reading.[29]

If we put the theories from the foregoing sections together, we see that we are not just in a single state when we read,[30] indeed some writers set us into several different emotions at the same time. Writers vary the aesthetic distance of the text, by defamiliarization and in other ways. Readers focus now on this aspect, now on that, in the manner described by Roland Barthes (discussed in Chapter 3). So, with emotions as experienced freshly in identification or sympathy, and with emotional memories experienced as *rasas,* or relived at a better aesthetic distance, we can see that we move into and among several possible states.[31] In this movement we make our own juxtapositions, and we experience emotions in ways that are not just those of ordinary life. Emotions experienced in fiction can sometimes prompt changes in our understanding of these emotions, and enlarge our sense of our selves.

In the spaces of metonymy

Emotions in ordinary life typically occur with juxtapositions, for instance of an expectation with an event. Fiction therefore uses such juxtapositions. In prose fiction, juxtapositions can occur at the levels of words, paragraphs, and scenes.[32] In film, they can occur at the levels of image-parts (of objects or persons), shots (as I discussed at the beginning of the chapter), and scenes.

At the lowest level of words and image-parts, Jane Austen uses a juxtaposition in the first sentence of *Pride and prejudice*: "a single man in possession of a good fortune" is juxtaposed with "must be in want of a wife." It is striking and defamiliarizing.[33] In the sequence from *The battleship Potemkin* that I discussed at the beginning of this chapter, the closing image of the sequence is a juxtaposition of the doctor's hand holding his glasses that have been folded into a magnifying glass, with dozens of large maggots that are easily seen without magnification. In both the prose piece and the film, there is an emotional shock.

At the level of paragraphs and film shots, if we think back to Shakespeare's "Sonnet 27" (discussed in Chapter 1) and consider the first eight lines (the octave, in which the poet makes a mental journey to his loved one) and the last six lines (the sestet, in which the poet imagines what his loved one might be doing) as separate paragraphs, their juxtaposition produces one of the moving effects of the sonnet, a longing on which is superimposed a jealous suspicion. It's the juxtaposition that gives rise to the poet's anxiety and insomnia. In the sequence from *The battleship Potemkin,* a shot of the doctor folding his glasses to make a magnifying glass is juxtaposed with a view of the doctor's eye through the folded glasses, which in turn is juxtaposed with the shot that contains the maggots. The magnifying glass is unnecessary. It's an attempt at obfuscation. An emotionally disturbing question is: what else in plain view in Russian society of 1905 is being obfuscated?

At the largest level, most striking piece of literary juxtaposition that I know is from the "Down at the cross: Letter from a region in my mind" by James Baldwin, published in 1963.[34] Here is the defamiliarizing passage.

White Americans find it as difficult as white people elsewhere do to divest themselves of the notion that they are in possession of some intrinsic value that black people need, or want. And this assumption . . . is revealed in all kinds of striking ways, from Bobby Kennedy's assurance that a Negro can become President in forty years to the unfortunate tone of warm congratulation with which so many liberals address their Negro equals. It is the Negro, of course, who is presumed to have become equal (p. 102).

The juxtaposition is between the schema of the white majority and that of the black minority.

In *The battleship Potemkin,* the scene with the maggots is juxtaposed with the next scene in which the battleship is back in port, where a mutiny begins. Not only can details be juxtaposed, but emotionally significant questions can be suggested.

The extraordinary property of juxtapositions and of gaps – between words, between film shots, between scenes, between schemas – is that what fills the gaps is the reader's or audience member's mind. In these gaps, the imagination can expand.[35] In them emotions – whether of identification or of sympathy, or of *rasas* or relived memories – as well as thoughts associated with them, can grow and be experienced, sometimes in new ways.

I don't think this effect has been put better than by Anton Chekhov who wrote in a letter to his friend and patron, Alexei Suvorin, that in his short stories he counted "on the assumption that [his readers] will add the subjective elements that are lacking in the story."[36]

Whereas metaphor (including allegory, dream, and simulation) is the very basis of literary art, one can argue that what Jakobson called the other pole, metonymy, might be even more basic in how the brain works, in how we feel, how we imagine. Whereas metaphor seems to depend on mental processes of symbolization, mapping, and comparison, that may in turn depend on the mind's language-processing layer, metonymy seems to depend on principles of association that power our more basic, intuitive mental processor.[37] This power includes that of suggestion, *dhvani,* by which a word or concept frames a range of relevance, and to which literary understanding in both metaphor and metonymy is closely linked. It is the intuitive processor that is, perhaps, the generator of our subjective experience.

More or less deliberately, in the process of creation, a writer or filmmaker draws on his or her own set of resonances and inner associations, and explores ways of externalizing them into concrete images and scenes that may be juxtaposed in ways that resonate with readers and audiences.

In a letter of 27 February 1818, to John Taylor, John Keats said: "Poetry should surprise by a fine excess, not by Singularity." He meant that poetry should exaggerate a bit – draw attention – but it should not be weird.

When the reader makes the creative connection, there may be an emotion of surprise, and also a sense of aptness, which can be profound, sometimes sublime. How does this occur? One possibility is that the words connect several intuitions (in the intuitive-associative layer), and thereby juxtapose intuitions had not been connected before, in a way that seems right.[38] The words articulate a relation between the intuitions, and this constitutes the insight. With it one can hold on, also, to the words that make that connection.

Exploration and projection

One of the most cogent ideas to have emerged from the Romantic theory of art, which started with such writers as Coleridge, is that of Robin Collingwood. In *The principles of art,* he says art IS the exploration of emotions.

First Collingwood cleared away ideas of what art is not. It is not, he says, mere craft, because craft is technique. Certainly an artist has to perform skillfully, but craft on its own is not art because it is without innovative exploration, which is necessary to art. In making a chair, or making *lasagne,* one pretty-much knows the end product before one starts. One might even have a set of drawings, a formula, or a recipe. Second, said Collingwood, art is not persuasion because, as with making *lasagne,* persuasion has an intended result in which what's intended is not physical but social. A work of art is not the result of a particular intention, prescribed in advance, to affect an audience in a particular way. Third, said Collingwood art is not amusement or entertainment, which he describes as "A device for the discharge of emotions in such a way as they shall not interfere with practical life" (p. 78). Entertainment has valid purposes as do crafts and persuasions but, said Collingwood, art proper is different. It is fundamentally an exploration, the results of which are not known in advance. In particular it is exploration of emotions. So, said, Collingwood, imagine this man:

> At first he is conscious of having an emotion, but not conscious of what this emotion is. All he is conscious of is a perturbation or excitement, which he feels going on within him, but of whose nature he is ignorant. While in this state, all he can say about his emotion is: "I feel . . . I don't know how I feel." From this helpless and oppressed condition he extricates himself by doing something which we call expressing himself. This is an activity which has something to do with the thing we call language:

he expresses himself by speaking. It also has something to with consciousness: the emotion expressed is the emotion of whose nature the
person who feels it is no longer unconscious (pp. 109–110).

This is the artist, who explores by expressing it, in a language – perhaps of
words, or painting, or music – what the meaning might be of this emotion,
which perturbs and impels but is not yet understood.

If the language in which the artist expresses himself or herself is that of
words, what the reader then does is to take in these words through the
language processor of the mind, to create pathways that connect them to
his or her associative-intuitive layer, and thus take part at the same time
both in some of those emotions and in the exploration of their
meaning-in-a-language.

Collingwood's idea is about the artist. He's less good on the reader or
viewer, but if we take the ideas about imagination and the elicitation of
emotions that I have been discussing, I think it's possible to complete this
part, too. What the reader or viewer does is to project meanings into the
work of art, not any meanings but choices from a family of meanings that
the work suggests.

Here is a demonstration of how this happens, from a cartoon film made
by Fritz Heider and Mary-Ann Simmel. In a paper published in 1944 they
discussed the effects of this film on viewers. The sole contents of the film
were a triangle, a somewhat smaller triangle, a small circle, and five straight
lines in the form of a box with a kind of flap; the triangles and circle moved
around, and went in and out of the box. The viewer, who was asked to say
what he or she saw, started by talking about the movements of the triangles
and circles, but then could not help seeing these marks on a screen in terms
of actions of agents with intentions, for instance movements of chasing,
and of characters entering and leaving a house or room.

In a follow-up to this study, Nicola Yuill and I remade this film. Our
version lasted 87 seconds, in five scenes. When we showed the film, we
stopped it at the end of each scene to ask our participants what had happened, and (except at the end) what they thought would happen next. The
numbers, 0s, 5s, 10s and so on (in the diagram on the next page) show how
many seconds had elapsed in the film when each position was reached, and
the boxes round these numbers indicate the end of each scene, where the
film was stopped for viewers to make judgements.

In a first experiment we confirmed what Heider and Simmel found that,
to start with, participants used impersonal verbs like "move" to describe

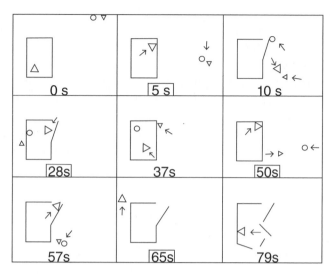

Figure 5.3 Drawings of stills from Oatley and Yuill's (1985) remake of Heider and Simmel's cartoon film; the arrows did not appear in the film, but represent the directions of movement of the triangles and circle.

what happened and what they thought would happen next. At 50 seconds into the film, three quarters of the verbs viewers used were of personal intentions (such as "escapes"), interpersonal intentions (such as "chases"), or mental states (such as "loves"). One intention for our version of the film was to make it ambiguous in three distinct ways, and in a second experiment we gave different groups of viewers three different titles for the same film. The viewers who were given the title "The householder," described a story of a robbery: the small triangle distracted the large triangle who came out of his house, and the circle went into the house to steal something valuable. For the viewers who were given the title "The anxious mother," the large triangle was seen as a mother trying to keep her child (the circle) from going out to play with the small triangle. For the viewers given the title, "The jealous lover," the big triangle was seen as someone who sees his/her lover (the circle) coming past with a new beloved (the small triangle) and tried to keep the lover in the house, but the lover eloped with the new beloved.

The cartoon film involved selection (of the triangles, the circle, and the straight lines) and combination (correlated movements of the large and small triangles and the circle, the arrangement of straight lines to appear as an enclosure). The actions – robberies, escapes, elopements – were suggested, but they were enacted in the minds of the viewers. To tell the story of what they saw in the film, viewers used emotion words: anger at having something stolen, anxiety about a child, jealousy of a lover. In the film's final sequence, as the small triangle and circle ran away, the large triangle was seen to hit the walls of the house, to shatter it in despair.

In relation to emotions, literature can depend on whole series of contexts created by juxtapositions, that invite metaphorical transformations in which one emotion can become another. But it's not just protagonists' emotions that are involved. It's the emotions of the reader or audience member.[39]

Perhaps the principal reason why emotion is so important to fiction is that it is the touchstone of consciousness. By externalizing certain elements of mind into a book or other kind of object in the outside world – which is what art does – a growth of feeling and consciousness[40] is enabled, both in the author and in the person who engages with the created artwork. As Susanne Langer has put it:

> The emergence of . . . "feeling" in the broadest sense, or consciousness . . . [was] a crisis in natural history as great as the emergence of life from physicochemical processes; the . . . crisis may not have been a "crisis" in the ordinary sense of a single, more or less cataclysmic, event, but a vastly distributed, protracted process taking eons to develop. As it did so, however, "life" in another than physical sense originated with it – "life" as the realm of value. For value exists only where there is consciousness. Where nothing ever is felt, nothing matters (p. 165).

Fiction has been often thought of as a creation of the writer. Really it's a joint creation of writer and reader (or viewer), the joint creation of an imaginary, but conscious, world that has emotion (or feeling in Langer's sense) at its center.[41] Emotion in human beings is that process in which events are related to purposes and hence to meanings. What a writer does is to offer cues, or suggestions, so that the reader or viewer can start up and sustain scenes in imagination, and experience for him- or her-self meaningful emotional effects of their juxtapositions. How a writer makes such suggestions is the subject of the next chapter.

6

Writing Fiction

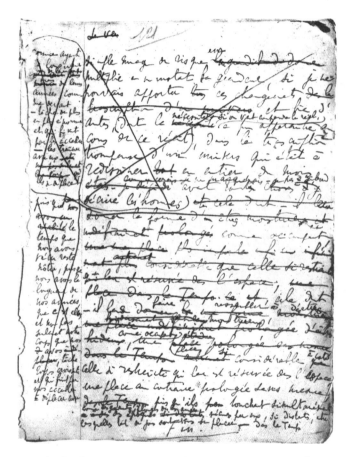

Figure 6.1 The final manuscript page of Marcel Proust's novel *À la recherche du temps perdu*. Source: Bibliotheque Nationale, Paris, France/Giraudon/The Bridgeman Art Library.

Such Stuff as Dreams: The Psychology of Fiction, First Edition. K. Oatley.
© 2011 K. Oatley. Published 2011 by John Wiley & Sons, Ltd.

Writing Fiction: Cues for the Reader

Early writing

The first writers of fiction lived probably in Sumer, in Mesopotamia, about 5000 years ago. They were scribes. Their usual duties were to externalize memories of commerce into writing, as well as to promulgate laws made by rulers. The script they used is called cuneiform, triangular marks made with a pointed stick on wax-covered boards that have not survived, and on clay tablets that would be baked, some of which have survived. At some point, one or some of these scribes must have started to write down some of the stories that people told orally.

The most famous of these ancient stories is *The epic of Gilgamesh*. The version I cite is not from the Sumerian, but is a translation of a more com-

Figure 6.2 Fragment of a clay tablet in cuneiform from *The epic of Gilgamesh*. © The Trustees of the British Museum.

plete later version in the same script in a Semitic language, Akkadian, also called Old Babylonian. It starts like this.

> He who saw the Deep, the country's foundation,
>   who knew the proper ways, was wise in all matters!
> Gilgamesh, who saw the Deep, the country's foundation,
>   who knew the proper ways, was wise in all matters!
> He explored everywhere the seats of power [1]
>   . . .
>
> He came a far road, was weary, found peace,
>   and set all his labours on a tablet of stone
> He built the rampart of Uruk-the-Sheepfold,
>   of holy Eanna, the sacred storehouse.
>
> See its wall like a strand of *wool*,
>   view its parapet that none could copy!
> Take the stairway of a bygone era,
>   draw near to Eanna, seat of Ishtar the goddess
> That no later king could ever copy!
>
> Climb Uruk's wall and walk back and forth!
>   Survey its foundation, examine the brickwork!
> Were its bricks not fired in an oven?
>   Did the seven sages not lay its foundations?

Here, in the most charming way, the writer acknowledges the readers and listeners. Andrew George's beautiful translation puts it like this: "See," says the writer, "the wall of the city, mount these steps, draw near to the temple." Perhaps for the earliest listeners, the city of Uruk was present. But even for them, as the story begins to unfold in a few words, they could not physically do what the story teller suggests in the time it takes to read or hear the invitation: "Take the stairway, draw near to the temple, climb the wall, survey its foundation, examine the brickwork." For later readers and listeners, this literary device still works. We start to create glimpses of the city. The device of taking us mentally round the stairways and walls is beautiful, and it sets up a relationship between the person telling the story and the person who will create it in imagination.

Four devices of fiction

How does one write a piece of fiction? The first thing, as I heard Ursula LeGuin say at an interview in Toronto, is that you have to have read at least one book. Translated, this means that you have to have some kind of mental model of the kind of thing you want to write. Most writers think about what they might write for a while. Some nurture an idea for years. Some think about it at the bus stop. Some make notes. In his interview for the magazine *Paris Review,* Georges Simenon explained how, before starting to write a Maigret novel, he would sketch notes on the back of an envelope about the story's characters and their family relationships.

What one has to do, when writing fiction, is not just to have a dream for a book or story. It's too easy for this to remain vague. One has to elaborate its details, its characters. One has think how to offer such details and characters to someone else so that they can start up their version of the dream.

One approach is to start with Tom Wolfe's essay "The new journalism," in which he proposed that what is exciting in modern journalism has been imported from fiction. "Journalists," said Wolfe, "began to discover the devices that gave the realistic novel its unique power variously known as its 'immediacy,' its 'concrete reality,' its 'emotional involvement,' its 'gripping' or 'absorbing quality.'" What are these devices, and how did Wolfe use them in his own non-fiction magazine article entitled "Radical chic," on the occasion when the celebrated composer Leonard Bernstein, an advocate for civil rights, invited members of the Black Panthers (a Black Power group of the 1960s) to his elegant Manhattan apartment. One of the devices is that Wolfe asks readers to imagine themselves into the mind of Bernstein: "Wonder what the Black Panthers eat here on the hors d'oeuvre trail?" thinks Bernstein. "Do the Panthers like little Roquefort cheese morsels rolled in crushed nuts this way, and asparagus tips in mayonnaise dabs?" (pp. 413–414). To grumble that Wolfe couldn't possibly have known what went on in Bernstein's mind would be petty. It was vivid journalism; the device was straight from fiction.

Wolfe proposed that the power of the new journalism derives mainly from just four devices. The first is to use scene-by-scene construction, rather than giving descriptive historical sequences of the kind that might be found in memoirs and histories. The technique is as old as Gilgamesh. It's mandatory in the theater and cinema, but important, too, in print fiction. The second device, which Wolfe thought involved the reader more completely than any other, is realistic dialogue. The third device is to use third-person point of view, so that each scene is presented through the eyes of a character, and to do this in such a way (as with the extract about Bernstein above) that the reader experiences the scene as if from inside the mind of the character. The fourth device is to depict status life, which, said Wolfe:

has always been the least understood. This is the recording of everyday gestures, habits, manners, customs, styles of furniture, clothing, decoration, styles of traveling, eating, keeping house, modes of behaving toward children, servants, superiors, inferiors, peers, plus the various looks, glances, poses, styles of walking and other symbolic details that might exist within a scene. Symbolic of what? Symbolic, generally, of people's status life, using that term in a broad sense of the entire pattern of behaviour and possessions through which people express their position in the world or what they think it is or what they hope it to be (p. 47).

What Wolfe is talking about here, I believe, is the set of behavioral indicators or, to use Shakespeare's term, the shadow, of character.

Fiction and non-fiction are usually distinguished by whether a story has been imagined or reported. For many purposes that distinction is critical: one does not want to read in the newspapers material that has been fabricated.[2] But the issue for a psychology of fiction is different. It is about what a deeper conception of the essential properties of fiction might be. The view I propose is that narrative enables the reader, hearer, or watcher to construct and maintain a mental simulation, a dream of social happenings, and here, I think, a fiction writer can do well by taking account of Wolfe's four devices, which I discuss in the following sub-sections.

Device 1. Scene-by-scene construction
Unlike some of the English novels of the eighteenth century that took the form of memoirs, or histories, with long linking passages, Jane Austen used scene-by-scene construction in *Pride and prejudice* much as Wolfe would recommend. Here is how this device works in the novel's first five chapters. Between its brief opening and closing passages by the narrator, Chapter 1 is the scene of Mr and Mrs Bennet's conversation in their house. In Chapter 2 the scene is again in the Bennet house a few days later, with Mr and Mrs Bennet and their daughters. At the beginning of Chapter 3, Austen lapses into the narrated history of how Bingley could not come to dinner when he was invited by the Bennets, but after a page another distinct scene is depicted: the assembly room in Meryton, where the much-anticipated dance is in progress. The last page of Chapter 3 is a new scene: the Bennet women at home after the dance, recounting to Mr Bennet the events of the evening. In Chapter 4 the scene changes to an intimate conversation between Jane and Elizabeth Bennet, followed by three paragraphs of the narrator's observations of the reactions to the dance of Bingley, of Bingley's

sisters, and of Bingley's friend Darcy. In Chapter 5 the scene is a visit by the Bennet women to the nearby house of their friends the Lucas family.

Scene-by-scene construction, in a novel, play, or film, enables, on a larger scale, the same kinds of effects as shot-by-shot construction in the sequence from *The battleship Potemkin,* with which I started Chapter 5. That is to say, it allows for juxtaposition. Juxtaposing the scene of Chapters 1 and 2 of *Pride and prejudice* allows Mr Bennet's refusal to pay a call on the newly arrived Mr Bingley to be closely followed by the reader being told that he does go to visit. Next, the juxtaposition between Chapters 2 and 3 allows the Bennet women's excitement in anticipation of meeting Mr Bingley and his party to be followed by a scene of meeting, of the fulfillment of the excitement in Bingley's interest in Jane, and of the crushing of enjoyment for Elizabeth in Darcy's shame-inducing snub. The juxtaposition between Chapters 3 and 4 is between a scene of the dance itself and its effects on Jane. The juxtaposition between Chapters 4 and 5 is the contrast between the dance's joyful effects on Jane and its mortifying effects on Elizabeth.

When we read, we make mental models of each scene.[3] This helps our understanding of events and it is essential to running the mental simulation of the story. Writers do well to assist readers in this. In ways that may not occur with a history, metonymic juxtaposition of scenes carries far more than mere temporal sequence. Most importantly it carries causation, but it also carries the emotional flow of fulfillments, contrasts, commentaries, echoes . . .

Device 2. Dialogue

By the time stories were recorded in writing, dialogue was already prominent. Dialogue may be the most distinctive aspect of fiction, the hinge between its imaginings and the everyday worlds we inhabit. Not very far into *The Epic of Gilgamesh,* there is some dialogue between Shamhat, a temple priestess and Enkidu to whom she makes love for six days and seven nights, an experience that transforms him from being a wild man into a civilized human being, where "civilized" means capable of living in a city. Then she invites him to accompany her to Uruk, where he will meet Gilgamesh.

In his discussion of the four devices of fiction that he says are central to making writing vivid, Wolfe argued that what he calls "naturalistic dialogue" has a critical place.

In *Gilgamesh,* the conversation between Shamhat and Enkidu is cooperative. The two take turns. She offers an invitation, he replies by accepting.

Everyday conversation is usually cooperative in this kind of way. It tends to follow rules that make for mutual understanding. These rules were formulated by Paul Grice and they are known as Grice's maxims: be truthful, be informative, be relevant, be clear. For a conversation to work, the people who converse must cooperate in these ways. Each must want to be understood, and must want to understand the other. Wolfe asserts that a writer must make dialogue realistic and for his piece "Radical chic" he says he went to the Bernsteins' party with his notebook, wrote down as much as he could, and that his article includes these transcriptions.

But for fiction, Wolfe's idea that dialogue should be realistic gives a false impression. As Sol Stein put in his book of advice to writers, *How to grow a novel*,[4] "Our native language is not dialogue."

My most important realization from reading Stein was that in fiction dialogue better not be realistic. He points out that if, in a novel or a play, you were to write conversation as cooperative in the way that occurs in ordinary life, no-one would read it. In fiction, says Stein, the turns each person takes in conversation must not proceed straightforwardly. Instead, responses of one character to what another has said should be oblique. They should perhaps be adversarial, even non-sequiturs.

One can think of literary dialogue, then as like a series of knight's moves in chess, not straight but with sideways hops.

Several thousand years ago, the writer of Gilgamesh, had not quite realized this, but two hundred years ago Jane Austen did. Here is an exemplary piece of dialogue from the first chapter of *Pride and prejudice*. Mrs Bennet's main concern in life is to get her daughters married advantageously. She informs her husband that a young man of good fortune has taken Netherfield, a large house nearby. Mr Bennet replies:

"What is his name?"

"Bingley."

"Is he married or single?"

"Oh, single, my dear. To be sure! A single man of large fortune, four or
    five thousand a year. What a fine thing for our girls!"

"How so? How can if affect them?"

"My dear Mr Bennet," replied his wife, "how can you be so tiresome?
    You must know that I am thinking of his marrying one of them."

"Is that his design in settling here?"

"Design! Nonsense, how can you talk so?"

The first exchanges are cooperative enough: Mr Bennet asks two questions, to each of which his wife replies helpfully. But with his next utterance, Mr Bennet leaps off to one side. Mrs Bennet is talking about a matter which, to her, is of utmost concern. But Mr Bennet is cantankerous; his intention is to inveigle her into utterances that he can pretend not to understand. Here we see, in perfect form, the novelistic apparatus of dialogue.[5] Mrs Bennet says that the arrival of the rich new tenant at Netherfield Hall will be "a fine thing" for their daughters. Mr Bennet asks how it can affect them.

Conversation in ordinary life is cooperative, either for the social purpose of maintaining relationships or for the practical purpose of accomplishing some task that requires the achievement of increments of agreement about what to do or how to do it. By contrast, literary dialogue has two entirely different purposes.

The first purpose of literary dialogue is to further the plot. In *Pride and prejudice* this purpose is reflected in the plot-line of Mrs Bennet's plans to get her daughters married. Mrs Bennet informs her husband of the arrival of Mr Bingley, and tries to persuade her husband to go and visit him, to begin an acquaintance. We readers use this to build our simulation of this novel: Mr Bingley is rich and eligible, a suitable piece of property for one of the Bennets' daughters.

The second purpose of literary dialogue is to offer readers sequences of utterances from which they understand the characters who are speaking. Cooperation between speakers can interfere with the depiction of character. Hence it's often best if fictional characters do not agree when they talk to each other. The key to Mrs Bennet's character is her preoccupation with getting her daughters advantageously married. The key to Mr Bennet is that he married his wife for her beauty, but now he is irritated by her "mean understanding, little information, and uncertain temper." The best he can generally manage when he is with her is to tease her. To the extent to which interlocutors' intentions are different, it is a skill the writer must develop to offer dialogue that depicts what each is up to, and this is aided by the jumping movement similar to the knight's-move across the board of social dialogue.

Whereas in ordinary life people maintain relationships with each other, in fiction, the writer (or narrator, or character) has to maintain a relationship with the reader. In ordinary life, people only occasionally, and probably unintentionally, indicate their character when they converse. They are busy being cooperative. In fiction, let's say from Shakespeare onwards, the goal of depicting character and showing how characters differ from each other has become critical. In fiction, characters differ in their goals, in their plans, in their preoccupations, in their . . . character. It is by means of the idea of character that literary authors seem able to form intimate relationships with their readers.

Device 3. Point-of-view

The idea of seeing a scene or a whole story through a particular pair of eyes, which is Wolfe's third fictional device, has been discussed from at least the time of Henry James. Such ways of seeing can be thought of as perspectives. The usual heading for this idea is point-of-view.[6] Usually three distinct perspectives are discussed, and a writer needs to choose among them.

The first perspective is first-person point-of-view. The writer becomes a character-narrator in a story, writes of "I" and "me." The reader understands events from within the narrator's mind. Marcel, in Proust's *À la recherche du temps perdu,* is an example.

The second perspective is called third-person omniscient point of view. It is used by Austen in *Pride and prejudice.* In it, the pronouns "he" and "she" are used when characters' utterances and actions, and sometimes their thoughts, are being depicted, but the author-narrator knows more than any character. Thus, we readers might learn, apparently directly, the thoughts of several characters. The perspective, really, is from somewhat above it all.

The third perspective is called third-person point-of-view proper. In it, the writer uses pronouns "he" or "she," but depicts only what can be perceived and realized from the mind of one character. This was the method advocated by Henry James. Wolfe's idea of making scenes vivid tends towards adopting this perspective.

Device 4. Status life

According to Wolfe status life is the least understood technique of fiction and journalism. Wolfe gives a long list (above) of means by which people convey their status life. Status is, of course, a thoroughly researched issue in both psychology and sociology, but status life is not just status. The best translation of Wolfe's idea into social science is perhaps in Erving Goffman's *The presentation of self in everyday life.* James Baldwin's "Down at the cross: Letter from a region in my mind" (from which I cited some lines in Chapter 5) beautifully exemplifies it.

Fiction writers indicate how people present themselves in everyday life (consciously and unconsciously) to depict character. In my view, one of the most accomplished practitioners of this kind of depiction was Anton Chekhov. I am going to discuss his famous short story *"The lady with the little dog"* at some length later this book.[7] The story is about a man, Dmitri Gomov who, at a seaside resort meets a young woman, Anna Serguyevevna, whom he has seen walking with her little dog. They are both married to other people, but they begin an affair. A third of the way into the second part of the story, come these two brief paragraphs just after the protagonists, Gomov and Anna, have made love for the first time.

"It is not right," she said. "You are the first to lose respect for me."
There was a melon on the table. Gomov cut a slice and began to eat it slowly. At least half an hour passed in silence.

Here is an ideal piece of fictional dialogue: an utterance and a failure to reply. It's also an ideal observation about status life. Like the metonymic methods used by Eisenstein in the shot-sequence from *The battleship Potemkin,* that I discussed at the beginning of Chapter 5, Chekhov uses metonymy. It's a double metonym. In one metonym – Anna's distress is juxtaposed with Gomov cutting himself a slice of melon – character has, in Henry James's words, determined incident. The second metonym is that the small gesture of eating a slice of melon is a metonymic part-for-whole figure (synecdoche) that points to the status life and character of Gomov. He's just made love with a woman in whom he is interested. They have been close. He has achieved his desire and is, perhaps, in a state of warm post-coital satisfaction. He is not impatient. He senses that this pleasant affair will continue. He turns to something else that will satisfy him. The thing to which he turns is trivial, and it serves to indicate his boredom with life.

In the gap between the two paragraphs, we readers are invited to think: "What's going on here?" It's not explained on the page. It is we who are in a position to wonder what is happening between these two paragraphs, between these two characters, and to think what might happen next between them.

In books of advice to writers we are often told to give our characters some distinctive physical trait or quirk. This helps, so the advice books say, to make the character distinctive and memorable. Sometimes this works beautifully, as it does, for instance, with Robert Louis Stevenson's depiction, in

Treasure island, of Long John Silver as a man with only one leg, who often had a parrot sitting on his shoulder. Tom Wolfe in the brief excerpt I cited of his characterization of Leonard Bernstein (inside Bernstein's mind) in "Radical chic" is less subtle, with an eye to satire, but it's still effective. In some pieces of fiction, one can more-or-less see that writers have thought about a bit, and come up with some slightly weird quirk or trait to give to their character. The model, I think, should be something more like Chekhov.

Expertise

In the psychology of creative writing, the theory of inspiration has been largely replaced by the theory of expertise. To attain expertise is to become accomplished at something, and it has been found that this is open to us if we choose what to concentrate on, in relation to what we know of our abilities and interests. When we do concentrate in order to become good at anything – cookery, parenthood, understanding movies, writing novels – really good so that people say "I don't know how she (or he) does it," we must put in a lot of time.

Expertise has become an important concept in cognitive psychology. The word signifies both an approach and a group of findings on how skills are attained.[8] A principal conclusion of this research is that to become an expert you need to devote some 10 000 hours to problem-solving in the domain of your interest. It's not simply a matter of putting in the time. The person who aspires to expertise needs to be devoted to acquiring new knowledge and procedures: to aim for targets that are beyond current abilities, to set problems and try to solve them. These matters need to become passions. Variations must be mastered; mistakes must be made and learned from. In *Ulysses,* James Joyce has Stephen Daedalus discuss Shakespeare, about whom he says: "A man of genius makes no mistakes. His errors are volitional and are the portals of discovery" (p. 156). But writers need not be geniuses. For all of us, an imperfect draft or a piece that did not come out right can be a portal of discovery.

Laboratory studies of writing

One of the methods of the study of expertise has been to ask people to think aloud while they are performing a skill. Using this method, the thinking-aloud of experts can be compared with that of novices, so that models can be made of expert knowledge and procedures. With a model one can understand the experts' knowledge, and take some of it on oneself, in one's own progress towards expertise. The classic research on expertise in writing was by John Hayes and Linda Flower who asked novice writers (Grade-12 high-school students and first-year undergraduates) and experts (professional journalists) to think aloud while they performed writing assignments. Here is an example of a think-aloud: the numbers indicate utterances, and the dashes indicate silences of two seconds or more. Utterances 12 and 13 made it into this writer's draft:

> Oh, bleh!—say it allows me (10)—to use (11)—Na—allows me—scratch that. The best thing about it is that it allows me to use (12)—my mind and ideas in a productive way (13) (p. 1109).

The cognitive model that Hayes and Flower developed was that writing has three phases:

> In planning . . . the writer generates ideas and organizes them into a writing plan. In sentence generation, the writer produces formal sentences intended to be part of a draft. In revising, the writer attempts to improve a draft" (p. 1107).

The model contains the idea that writing has a goal, to solve an ill-defined problem, which is something like: "What am I trying to do with this piece of writing?" As the writing proceeds, the plan of how to solve this problem changes, sometimes radically. Previously unsuspected sub-goals and methods are discovered and developed. It's a process of solving multiple constraints, which include adapting existing knowledge of the topic, assimilating research, the conventions of writing and vocabulary, understanding how the world works, memories (of incidents, principles, and people), and solving the rhetorical problem of engaging the reader.

Hayes and Flower found that in all three phases there were substantial differences between novices and experts. In the planning phase, the experts gave more consideration to their readers and produced a more elaborate set of inter-related goals than did novices. Here is a typical difference (this one is not from Hayes and Flower). If you are a teacher and you give a Grade-12 student a writing assignment in class, he or she will typically start immediately and continue to write until you say " Stop." By contrast, if you are an editor and you say to a journalist that there is a rush on, and could he or she write a brief piece and complete it in an hour, he or she may well first say something that I should not repeat here. Then he or she may well spend half of the available time without writing anything at all, but thinking about the first sentence because a reader who doesn't take to the first sentence of an article is not going to read the second. Hayes and Flower found that in the phase of sentence generation, the sentence-parts produced by experts were 50% longer than those produced by novices. In the phase of revision, novices did not change much, and typically their changes were at the word and phrase level. Only 12% of their alterations changed the meaning of what they had written. Experts changed far more, and made three times as many alterations that changed the meaning of what they had written.[9]

Expertise and memory
One of the earliest studies of expertise, which helps us to understand why it is important, was made of by Adriaan de Groot in which he compared chess players who were at the master level (as he was himself) and players who were relative novices. Among de Groot's studies was to set out 20 pieces on a chess-board from a game that had been played, and have players look at the board position for five seconds. He would then swiftly remove the pieces, and ask the players to replace them. Experts could do this, making perhaps a mistake with one piece. Novices could correctly replace only about seven of the pieces. This result reflects on the psychological concept of short-term working memory.

Does de Groot's experiment mean that chess experts have a working memory with larger capacity than chess novices? Not at all. Everybody's short-term working memory holds somewhere around seven items. The difference was that experts had learned so much about chess that when they saw a board position from a game that had been played, they recognized and could easily remember configurations of pieces, for instance "fianchetto on the King's side." This is part of a standard opening position in chess. It describes the position of six pieces in a particular part of the board. Psychologists call this a chunk. The chunks with which a novice works are single pieces in single positions. When a chess master looks at a 20-piece chess position, he or she has a schema for chess and remembers, as chunks, four or five configurations each with certain developments or variations. When they are given five seconds to look at 20 pieces placed on a chess board in random positions, master chess players do no better than the novices at replacing them.

Short-term working memory is verbal (for instance the contents of consciously verbalized thoughts as they go through our minds when writing), and also visual (for instance the layout of a scene). The idea of working memory is that it is the means by which we hold something in mind consciously while we think about it: a mental space for the manipulation of ideas.[10]

The skill of writing depends on short-term working memory.[11] The results, discussed above, on expertise of writers, are important because it becomes clear that the more experienced one is, the larger and more sophisticated are the chunks (objects) that one can hold in mind and manipulate.

Long-term memory is also important to writers. Books by skilled writers such as E.M. Forster, in his *Aspects of the novel* and Frank O'Connor in his *The lonely voice* can be thought of as externalizations of some of some of their long term memory about writing. Linda Flower and her colleagues have shown how writers bring three kinds of knowledge from their long-term memory into their writing: topic knowledge, schema knowledge, and constructive knowledge.

As to topic knowledge, several studies have shown that the more elaborate a writer's knowledge of the subject of the piece, the better he or she can write on that topic.[12] As to schematic knowledge, based on the idea of "schema" that Bartlett established from his studies of remembering, writers are likely to have created elaborate schemas into which they have compiled information about books they have read, about genres, about characteristics of different points of view, and so forth. As to constructive knowledge: this is the set of procedures that the writer has developed including those for how to create settings, dialogue, character, and so on. Constructive methods must be flexible enough to take advantage of opportunities that emerge unexpectedly during the development of a piece.

The attainment of expertise involves conscious and deliberate effort, but unconscious factors of authors' personalities also enter into their writing.[13]

I have already mentioned some of the way in which this happens, for instance, Jane Austen's playfulness but also her hatred of the arrangements of society in her time. Ian Lancashire has gone further, into the very structure of texts. He discusses for instance, Shakespeare's quirky attitude to dogs, which appeared as a schema that recurred throughout his works in clusters of images.[14] Thus, in metaphors for human greed and flattery, dogs represent fawning and obsequiousness, but also the dangerous and the ungoverned. Here is this schema (as pointed out by Lancashire) in *Richard III*, when Queen Margaret speaks to Buckingham of Richard.

O Buckingham, take heed of yonder dog.
Look when he fawns, he bites; and when he bites,
His venom tooth will rankle to the death (1, 3, 756).

Further idiosyncrasies occur in the writers' cultivation of their memories. A recent psychological finding is of a type of long-term memory[15] that has some of the characteristics of being rapidly cued and of enabling manipulation of concepts in a way that is comparable to short-term memory, but without short-term memory's limitations of capacity. This kind of memory is constrained to the specific domain that an expert has developed. It takes a great deal of work to establish it, and it lasts only as long as the expert maintains his or her skills. An expert writer can read a draft he or she has written, load it up into this specialized long-term working-memory which includes fluent language generation processes, so that ideas and the sentences that represent them can be mentally manipulated.

If we think back to Andy Clark's idea of the mind as a hybrid, we can see, first of all, that the verbal layer is very dependent on short-term working memory in the moment-by-moment processes of reading, thinking, and writing. Long-term working memory may include a process in which longer lasting connections are generated between the verbal and intuitive layers. In writing this might be the process in which knowledge of style, tropes, and literary sentence generation is drawn on, to elaborate the dream of a story. It will be accompanied by generation of sentences as verbal instructions of how to start and maintain the dream, by means of event structure, discourse structure, and suggestion structure.

Good writing is therefore not – as novices sometimes think – doing a mind dump: emptying contents of the mind onto paper. It needs to offer readers a set of cues to start up and run the simulation-dream of the story world with its characters and incidents. This simulation needs, too, to involve the reader emotionally. As David Olson and I have shown, the fiction writer's job is to offer cues: of what is said in dialogue, of thoughts in characters' minds, and of observations and descriptions by a narrator. Used together, they enable the reader to create the distinctive fictional imaginings of selves, their projects, and their interactions. Consider how Jane Austen, towards the end of the first paragraph of Chapter 3 of *Pride and prejudice*, handles her characters' thoughts, when the prospect is announced of Bingley bringing a large party to the forthcoming dance. "Nothing could be more delightful!" she writes. "To be fond of dancing was a certain step towards falling in love." These two sentences are in free indirect style, newly invented in Jane Austen's time. This style is a cue to the reader to imagine himself or herself into the minds of the Bennet girls in their anticipation of the dance. It is because they are not tagged as belonging to any particular character, these thoughts float free, in a dreamy way. They can be thoughts in the mind of the reader, who thereby becomes an intimate part of the scene.

One of the useful aspects of externalizing a story onto paper is that a writer can read what she or he has written, and the writing will start up and sustain for him or her, the dream with its emotional aspects. In this process the writer is necessarily doing what Barthes called a writerly reading.

Flaubert's writing practice

Given the antiquity of written stories, and the centrality of stories to the world's great religions, it is surprising that the first explicit theory about how to write prose fiction seems to have been formulated only about a century and a half ago. According to Pierre-Marc de Biasi, it was formulated by Gustave Flaubert.

Flaubert's *Madame Bovary* is widely regarded as one of the world's great novels, and his "A simple heart" as one of the great short stories. Flaubert's published output was not large, but he deliberately preserved some thirty thousand pages of notes and drafts, which he thought would show people his elaborate process of creation.

De Biasi explains that the process consisted of five phases.

First, came a plan – an idea really – which would change as the process continued. Once he had the plan, Flaubert would daydream around it. He would imagine his characters and their psychology. He would imagine key scenes, choose locations, and perhaps do some research such as reading, visiting places, interviewing. At this stage, although he might write some indications of the idea, he would not write much. Instead he continued his mental work until he could see the story in his mind's eye.

Second, Flaubert wrote what he called scenarios. His invention of how to do this was one of his innovations. Scenarios were not drafts. Hardly anything in them would reach the final version. Scenarios were intermediates between the plan and the next stage which would be a draft. They were not designed for the reader, but were instead, notations designed for him, the writer, to prompt his own further thoughts, reminders of what he had considered and of ideas he had had. In a scenario, many implications of the story could be developed. Its directions could be explored. A scenario would contain some of the main lines of the narrative in a very schematic way, with semi-formed phrases, and with names and places signified by x, y, z.

Flaubert's third stage was to write what we might think of as first drafts, except that there were usually a number of them, first, second, third, etc. These can be thought of as expanded drafts, because there was far more in them than would reach the final form of the piece. In them, however, for the first time in the process, sentences and paragraphs started to take shape in forms that might perhaps reach the reader. In this way, multiple possibilities continued to be explored, with many corrections, and many insertions between the lines and in the margins. At this stage Flaubert might do more location work, less to check for accuracy than to see scenes through the eyes of each of his characters.

Only in the fourth stage, did Flaubert start to think about style. He began to produce drafts that approached the form that the reader would see. We can think of them as refining drafts, because in them a page in an expanded draft might be reduced to a phrase. Large parts of the expanded drafts were simply deleted. At this stage also, the text was subjected to the test of reading aloud. Further drafting occurred until everything fitted together, like a musical score, to be heard by an imagined reader.

Fifth, a final draft was produced, which could be sent to the publisher.

Flaubert argued that style is a way of seeing the world, and that style and content are inseparable. He thought that prose should be like verse, incapable of being paraphrased. It took him five years to write *Madame Bovary*, starting in 1850. He thought the novel was a genre that had just been born, that it awaited its Homer, perhaps himself. Tony Williams cites Flaubert's writing style of this new genre of the novel:

> would be as rhythmical as verse, as precise as the language of science, and with the undulations, the humming of a cello, the plumes of fire, a style that would enter your mind like a rapier thrust, and on which finally your thoughts would slide as if over a smooth surface" (p. 167).

Williams goes on to quote Flaubert's idea that in the creation of a work of art, the artist recapitulates human history:

> At first, confusion, a general view, aspirations, bedazzlement, everything is mixed up (the barbarian epoch); then analysis, doubt, method, the

arrangement of the parts, the scientific era – finally he returns to the initial synthesis executed more broadly (p. 167).

To see some his methods at work, let us look at a small part of how he wrote his short story, "*Un coeur simple*" (A simple heart). It took him six months – from mid-February to mid-August, 1876 – at least some of which time, as we are told in his correspondence, he was in his shirtsleeves, writing through the night. What was he doing all this time? He was going through the stages described above. We can get a glimpse of his method in action from an account of Raymonde Debray Genette who describes how, still preserved from Flaubert's work on the story, are "three plans or résumés . . . three scenarios, a subscenario, two [expanded] drafts, two [refining] drafts, and the copyist's manuscript." She discusses those parts that concern the final paragraph of the story.

The first plan was entitled "Perroquet." It was of "a woman who dies in a saintly fashion . . . Her parrot is the Holy Spirit." Flaubert's thought was that the Holy Spirit is usually represented by a dove, but why not by a parrot? It's an ironical idea, one that educated people might find comical.

The story is about "housemaid Félicité . . . envy of all the good ladies of Pont-l'Evêque." She extends her love to two children of her widowed mistress, a nephew who goes to sea, and a parrot, all of whom are taken from her by death. The story's last two pages describe the feast of Corpus Christi, in which the sacrament is carried through the streets of the village, and stops at highly decorated outdoor altars, to one of which, beneath her window, Félicité has donated her parrot, now stuffed. The procession pauses beneath the window of the room in which she lies dying. Here is my translation of the story's final paragraph.

> As a vapour of blue incense rose up into her room, Félicité flared her nostrils, and breathed it in with mystical sensuality; then she closed her eyes. Her lips smiled. The movements of her heart slowed down, one by one, each time more vague, more soft, like a fountain running dry, like an echo fading away; and, as she exhaled her last breath, she thought she could see, as the heavens opened to receive her, a gigantic parrot hovering overhead.

Debray Genette shows how Flaubert had to solve three substantial problems to achieve this paragraph. First, it had not to be a cliché, and it had to go beyond his own previous scenes of death such as that of Emma Bovary. Second, it needed to suggest the bodily process of dying. Third, it needed also to suggest the sacredness of the death of a saintly person. The following derives from Debray Genette's account.

A critical moment (in writing his story) occurs for Flaubert in the second scenario, which is crossed out with an X. In it Flaubert tries out the idea of Félicité as a saintly person with the phrase: "the acceleration of her chest of this heart (*coeur*) which had never beaten fr [sic] anything ignoble." A critical word is "heart" (*coeur*), but Flaubert seems not to recognize its significance at this point. Here is one of the reasons why it is so important to externalize one's thoughts onto paper: they can be revisited.

Then, in the first expanded draft, there are 60 lines that form the basis of the final six-line paragraph. Debray Genette points out that, for this last paragraph in this draft there are two rough columns (see Figure 6.3, a transcription of part of this 60-line section). Although the classification is not exact, the left hand column includes bodily descriptions such as "she closed her eyes" and "her smiling face," whereas right hand column includes many images such as "like a statue in a tomb . . . the vibrations of a string which has been plucked" that Flaubert will eliminate. It is in this draft that Flaubert has the thought that will be the key to his final paragraph, perhaps suggested by the word "heart" (*coeur*) that he wrote in the second scenario. It is the exact word – the *mot juste* – that unites the two aspects of Félicité's death, partly bodily, partly spiritual. In this draft Flaubert writes a sentence that he joins by a long line from the phrase "The movements of the heart" in the right hand column to "slowed down" in the left hand column 14 lines further down. Here is the beginning of the sentence including the joining line and deletions:

"The movements ~~jerkings of her heart~~ of the heart ——————— slowed
down, one by one, slower, each time ~~each time farther apart~~ softer . . ."

He can now also give his story a title: "A simple heart" (*Un coeur simple*).

Flaubert was carried forward during the six months he took to write "A simple heart" by interests that were very personal: his own childhood, the nature of maternal love, how ordinary people are often better than members of the bourgeoisie (such as himself), and the relation of the profane to the sacred. But he also took his own advice – to remain impersonal, not to write himself – and the final paragraph is beautifully balanced. It is still faintly ironical in Flaubert's characteristic style, but also intensely moving, with a lovely ambiguity that remains unresolved, without moralization, but putting to the reader the question of what to think about Félicité, and about the meaning, in the world, of people like her.

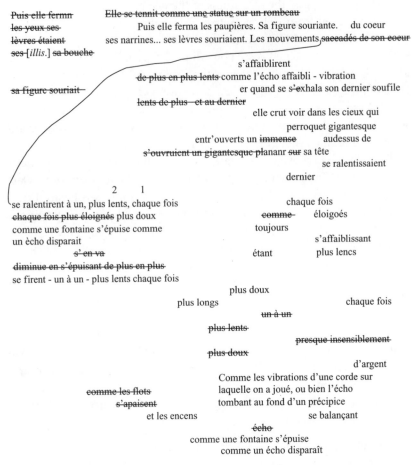

Figure 6.3 Illustration derived from an article by Debray Genette (2004), to show a transcription of a small part of Flaubert's work on the last paragraph of "A simple heart." In J. Deppman, D. Ferrer and M. Groden (Eds.), *Genetic criticism: Texts and avant-textes* (pp. 69–95). Philadelphia: University of Pennsylvania Press, after illustration on p. 90.

Writers' theories

When people first have the idea of writing fiction they often have the theory that they have something in their heads that they can put down on paper, and the theory that others will be interested in it. Learning to write often involves giving up both these theories. Perhaps the most important insight from Flaubert's practice of writing is that a story is not usually in one's head before one starts writing. A piece of worthwhile fiction only emerges from thinking, and more thinking. Writing fiction is that process in which imaginative thinking is augmented by externalization onto paper or onto a computer screen, in such a way that what is written prompts further thinking. Flaubert's "scenarios" – writings that were specific beyond the initial idea but which were not drafts – had the sole function of prompting more thoughts. They are a brilliant idea.

And if one writes a piece of fiction, will anyone be interested? We can think of this as the matter of the rhetorical: how the writer addresses the reader. With practice a writer learns to transfer priority from the writer's thoughts to the question of how the reader might be invited towards his or her own thoughts, feelings, and understandings.

Only when works of literature, film, or theater, have been carried through processes of iterated thinking and rhetorical suggestion might one expect them to become more than ephemeral. Only then, will a writer have seen deeply enough into an imagined dream world to depict its intimate workings for someone else. Only then will the writing be able to have effects for readers that might become the readers' own. These effects are the subject of the next chapter.

7

Effects of Fiction

joking   flustered

desire   convinced

Figure 7.1   One of the slides of Simon Baron-Cohen's *et al.*'s (2001) test of adult empathy and theory of mind (Autism Research Centre, Cambridge, England), as used in Raymond Mar *et al.*'s study of effects of reading fiction as compared with non-fiction. This test, the Mind in the Eyes test, is available on the internet, at http://glennrowe.net/BaronCohen/Faces/EyesTest.aspx. This is item no. 3 on the test on the web site.

Such Stuff as Dreams: The Psychology of Fiction, First Edition. K. Oatley.
© 2011 K. Oatley. Published 2011 by John Wiley & Sons, Ltd.

Effects of Fiction: Is Fiction Good for You?

Truth and fiction

At least since the time of classical Greece people have wondered whether fiction was good for you. Plato thought it was not. He banned poets from his ideal society. He thought that the world we see is one of mere appearances, and likened us humans to prisoners in a cave shackled to a bench, staring at a wall. Behind us is a fire and, between our backs and the fire, people come and go. But we can't really see what is happening; we see only the shadows of these people projected onto the wall. The shadows are appearances. Our task, said Plato, is to break our shackles, and stumble out from the cave into the daylight.

Truth does not exist in this world, says Plato, only shadows. Fiction (he and Aristotle called it poetry) is a copy of appearances, a shadow of a shadow, so it takes us even further from the truth. Not only that but, because it can affect people emotionally, it's destructive of our rationality.

I believe, as did Plato, that truth is not simply in surface appearances, but I don't agree with him about fiction. In this book, I propose that for the social world, fiction can bring us closer to truths of our human condition. These are not truths of analytical reasoning of the kind in which Plato was primarily interested, nor truths of the kind that physicists seek. Fiction offers very particular kinds of truth, of what we human beings are like, and what we are up to in our interactions with each other. Although Plato is scathing about fiction, he doesn't acknowledge that, in his own writings, he uses fictional devices. He uses metaphors such as the one of prisoners in a cave. He uses allegories (dream worlds): his book *The republic* is a utopia.[1]

His principal device in his philosophical writings is dialogue in which his protagonist, Socrates, potters about in the marketplace, goes to a drinking party (*symposium*), and so on, in order to chat to people about truth and how to approach it. Craftily, he depicts this search for truth in story form.

When people talk about fact and fiction, they imply that fiction is deficient, because it's imagined. But the contrast between fact and fiction is not always helpful. The essential fact about fiction is that it is about selves in the social world. To put this same fact in terms used by Jerome Bruner, narrative fiction is about human intentions and their vicissitudes.[2] The question then arises as to whether reading and thinking about this topic in short stories and novels, or seeing and thinking about it in dramas, can improve our understanding of the people we know, and of ourselves, in the day-to-day world in which we live.

In this chapter, I describe some of the work of the research group in which I work (Maja Djikic, Raymond Mar, Jordan Peterson, and myself), and the work of others, in gathering evidence about whether and how fiction affects its readers and watchers, including evidence about whether reading is good for you and how, in the domain of the human social world, it might exhibit truths.

Effects of reading

The invention of the Greek writing system was an important step in the history of fiction. For perhaps two thousand years after their invention, writing and reading were specialized skills, the province of scribes. Barry Powell has explained how written Greek originated. It was probably invented by a scribe who spoke and wrote in the West Semitic language, Phoenician, and also spoke Greek. This person seems to have taken Phoenician letters, added some, and mapped them to Greek speech sounds to produce the first alphabet composed of straightforward representations of both consonants and vowels. Written Greek offered a new departure. It was the door to literacy for a much wider section of the population.

Greece was unusual in that it was without a specialized profession of scribes. It was unusual, too, in that a work of fiction, Homer's *Iliad,* was the reference work of the culture. Powell suggests that written Greek may have been invented to take dictation from oral versions of the *Iliad.* Since those times, literacy has been both the starting point and center of education. Without becoming literate, it is difficult to take a full part in the modern world.

What effect does the ability to read and write have on the mind?[3] Among the first to show empirically that reading – not just fiction but anything at all – has important cognitive effects were Keith Stanovich and Richard West. They first needed a simple method by which they could assess how much people read in their daily lives. They devised the Author Recognition Test: a list of names, some of which are of authors and some of which are of people who are not. A person taking the test checks the names of all the authors he or she recognizes. A score is derived by summing the number of names correctly recognized and subtracting the number the person thought were authors but were not. The test works because people who read a lot immerse themselves in the world of books, not just by reading them, but by discussing them, reading reviews, visiting bookshops, and so on. Scores on this test have been found to agree closely with scores derived from more time-consuming methods such as daily activity diaries and behavioral observations of when and how much people read.

Next Stanovich and his colleagues measured skills such as vocabulary, general knowledge, verbal reasoning, and so on. They predicted that the more people read, the better they would be at these skills. First they had a control for (that is to say subtract out the effects of [see Chapter 2, note 35]) other factors such as people's IQ (general intelligence), social class, and the level of their education, all of which contribute to these skills. But when they had controlled for these factors, they found, still, that the more people read as measured by the Author Recognition Test, the more they knew, and the better they knew it. Scores on this test did not predict everything. For instance they did not predict people's abilities at verbal reasoning in such forms as syllogisms.

The big insight that our research group reached (others have reached it too) was that fiction is about a relatively specific area of knowledge, of selves in the social world. A striking finding about expertise (discussed in Chapter 6) is that taxi drivers with expertise of how to find their way about in London had an enlarged hippocampus (a part of the brain concerned with spatial knowledge).[4] Our research has been mainly on how reading fiction might enlarge people's knowledge of selves in the social world. Our group has even found that certain brain areas are involved.[5]

I have presented the psychology of fiction in terms of guided dream, or simulation. One of the uses of simulation is that if you learn to pilot an airplane, you may find it worthwhile to spend time in a flight simulator. Learning in an actual airplane is essential, but a good deal of the time aloft nothing much happens. In a simulator you confront a wider range of experiences and try out in safety how to respond to critical situations.[6] The skills you learn transfer to flying an actual plane. If we engage in the simulations of fiction, do the skills we learn there transfer to the everyday social world?

Understanding others

To see how much fiction people read, Raymond Mar devised a method that derived from Stanovich and West's Author Recognition Test. He modified it to include authors of fiction and of non-fiction, as well as names of non-authors. With this it was possible to see who read predominantly fiction, and who read predominantly non-fiction. Mar and his colleagues[7] then reasoned that if fiction is a kind of simulation of selves and their vicissitudes in the social world, people who read more of it would be better at theory-of-mind, and more accurate at perceiving what goes on in social interactions, than those who read mainly non-fiction books.

To measure social abilities Mar and his colleagues used two tests. One was the Mind in the Eyes Test, which can be thought of as a measure of empathy, or an adult measure of theory-of-mind.[8] When a person takes the test, he or she looks at photographs of people's eyes, as if seen through a letter-box, as in the photo at the head of this chapter, and chooses which of four mental states the photographed person is in, for instance: "joking," "flustered," "desire," "convinced." In the second test, the Interpersonal Perception Test, participants are asked to view 15 brief video clips of ordinary people in interaction, and to answer a question about each one. For one clip, the question is: "Which of the two children, or both, or neither, are offspring of the two adults in the clip?"

We found that the more fiction people read, the better they were at the Mind-in-the-Eyes Test. A similar relationship held, though less strongly, for reading fiction and the Interpersonal Perception Test.

One might think that this result might have been due to people with a certain kind of personality being more interested in the social world and, therefore, also more interested in reading fiction. In a second study, to test this possibility, Mar and colleagues again used the Mind in the Eyes Test as an outcome, and measured readers' personality.[9] In this second study we confirmed the frequent finding that women read more fiction than men. We also found that people, who were high on the personality trait of Openness to Experience and those who were drawn to fantasy, read more fiction. We did not, however, find that other personality traits, or indeed other individual differences of any kind were associated with reading more fiction. The most important result from this second study was that when we controlled for all individual differences we still found that the more fiction people read the better they were at the Mind-in-the Eyes Test. The result indicates that better abilities in empathy and theory of mind were best explained by the kind of reading people mostly did.

The stereotype of people who read a lot is that they are lonely and socially isolated. In this second study (the one in which we also measured personality) we looked into this question. We found that reading fiction was not associated with loneliness,[10] but was associated with what psychologists call high social support, being in a circle of people whom participants saw a lot, and who were available to them practically and emotionally. Loneliness and low social support were, however, associated with reading predominantly non-fiction. Insofar, therefore, as the stereotype of readers being socially isolated is accurate, it applies more to non-fiction readers than to fiction readers.

This relationship between reading fiction and social abilities is not, however, entirely straightforward. For instance, in 2008 Willie van Peer reported a study of university students of science and of the humanities on a measure of emotional intelligence.[11] There was considerable scatter, but on average the science students had higher emotional intelligence than the humanities students, the opposite of what was expected; van Peer indicts teaching in the humanities for often turning people away from human understanding towards technical analyses of details.[12]

In his PhD thesis, Raymond Mar did another follow up, with an experimental design. He used a fiction story and a non-fiction piece from the *New Yorker,* and randomly assigned people to read one or the other. After reading, the people who read the fiction story did better than those who read the non-fiction piece on a test of social reasoning, though not on a test of analytical reasoning.

How are associations between reading fiction and better social abilities to be explained? The members of our research group think it is a matter of expertise of the kind I explained in Chapter 6. Fiction is principally about the problems of selves navigating in the social world. Non-fiction is about – well – whatever it is about: selfish genes, or how to make *boeuf bourguignon,* or whether climate change will devastate our planet. Readers of fiction tend to become more expert at making models of others and themselves, and at navigating the social world,[13] and readers of non-fiction are likely to become more expert at genetics, or cookery, or environmental studies, or whatever they spend their time reading. Raymond Mar's experimental study on reading pieces from the *New Yorker* is probably best explained by priming. Reading a fictional piece puts people into a frame of mind of thinking about the social world, and this is probably why they did better at the test of social reasoning.

Changing ourselves

But what of ourselves? Are readers affected in themselves by what they read? This was the question behind a different kind of study in our group, led by Maja Djikic.[14] We randomly assigned people to read either a short story or a version in a non-fiction format based on the events of the story. Before and after participants read the text, we measured their personalities using a standard personality inventory. The story we chose was by Anton Chekhov "The lady with the little dog," which I introduced in Chapter 6. It's the story of a love affair, and of how the feelings of the two protagonists for each other come, to the surprise of both of them, to be much more important than anything else in their lives.

The non-fiction styled version of the story was written by Djikic in the form of a courtroom report of divorce proceedings. It has the same characters, all the same events, and some of the words, of Chekhov's story. It was composed to be exactly the same length and exactly the same level of reading difficulty as Chekhov's story and – importantly – the readers of the non-fiction styled courtroom transcript found it just as interesting, though not as artistic, as Chekhov's story.

We found that the personalities – the way people saw themselves – of those who read Chekhov's story changed more than those who read the courtroom account. The changes in personality were not large, but they were measurable, and they were in different directions for different readers. They were mediated by the emotions that readers experienced while reading.[15]

What happened, we believe, was that the engagement with art in Chekhov's story had two kinds of effect, which we call an identification effect and a transcendent effect. The first of these was that as people read the Chekhov story, we think they experienced empathy with the two

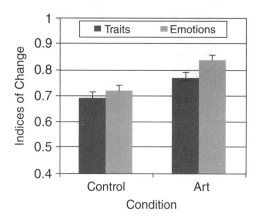

Figure 7.2 Results of the study by Maja Djikic *et al.* of comparing change of personality traits and emotions as a result of reading either Chekhov's short story, or a version in a non-fiction style of a court-room transcript.

protagonists; they identified with them, so that each in his or her own way became affected by them. Or perhaps as they entered mentally into these people's lives and thoughts, they started to compare their own lives and decisions with those of the characters. (I discuss the range of readings of this story further in Chapter 8.) The second effect (a general effect of art, we believe) is that, in the Chekhov story, people were taken out of themselves, out of their usual ways of being and thinking. The art of the story acted as something that was beyond themselves (transcendent), and this helped to loosen up the habitual structures of selfhood.[16]

An objective basis for fiction

With the studies of high levels of empathy and theory-of-mind in readers of fiction, and the possibility that people can change their personalities a little by reading fictional art, the research group in which I work has taken two steps, I believe, towards establishing an objective basis for believing that fiction can – potentially at least – be good for you.

It is reasonable, if one is a member of the literary world, to take the view that literary art is important whatever psychologists may say. But in a time when evaluation of what goes into educational curricula, a time when health outcomes of various activities, from watching television to running marathons, are eagerly researched, we believe that our results are steps in an important direction.

These results can also start to counter misgivings of certain scientists and policy makers that fiction might be perfectly pleasant, but that it is no more than a pastime. If it can be shown, in more studies, that fiction can improve our understanding of other people and of ourselves, this would indicate its value beyond the merely enjoyable. Our results indicate that fiction is best characterized by its typical content – selves and their vicissitudes in the social world – and that these matters are not straightforward of understanding. It argues, too, against an idea held by many psychologists that fiction is of no value because it's a set of arbitrary descriptions without procedures for establishing whether the descriptions are reliable or valid.

Our results indicate that fiction is not, in general, a failed attempt at behavioral description (in contrast to descriptions derived from controlled psychological studies). Instead it is a set of mental simulations. Since our empirical findings indicate that fiction does relate to measures of certain social abilities and to possibilities of change of personality, these findings help to validate the procedures of fictional simulation.

In the minds of others

The finding by Raymond Mar and colleagues that people who predominantly read fiction had better empathy and theory-of-mind than those who predominantly read non fiction, raises the question of the relation of reading to theory of mind in childhood.

Theory-of-mind in childhood is measured by tests that derive from the study I described in Chapter 2, of Maxi and where he might look for his chocolate when it had been moved while he was out of the room. The question of whether fiction contributes to children's theory-of-mind has been researched.[17]

Joan Peskin and Janet Astington chose a group of published children's picture books. From these they created two sets of books. In each case the stories, actions, and pictures were the same, but in one set the experimenters pasted into the book text that had a lot of mental state language ("he felt," "she thought," etc.). In the other set the pasted-in text had no mental state language. Children were assigned to one kind of book or the other, and over four weeks in school, teachers and research assistants read the children about 70 such books. The children who encountered the books with a lot of mental state terms used more such terms in stories they dictated to a scribe. But it seems that they were probably using the terms without fully understanding them, because children in the group who heard the stories without mental state terms had better comprehension of theory-of-mind. It seems that children in this second group were affected by the gaps: they had actively to construct their own inferences about what characters were thinking and feeling. Thereby they reached better understandings of these issues.[18]

Another experiment on the importance of inferences when reading fiction was reported by Marisa Bortolussi and Peter Dixon.[19] In collaboration with a student, Maria Kotovych, they found that when readers of a short story, "The office," by Alice Munro had to pick up the writer's indirect suggestions that concerned the first-person narrator in the story, they understood the narrator better than when direct information about the narrator was substituted into the story. Bortolussi and Dixon suggest that a relationship is built between narrator and reader and that, as in a conversation, we readers are constantly making inferences about what the narrator is intending, thinking and feeling. In conversation, we enjoy making such inferences because they contribute to our relationship. The same goes for fiction. In ordinary life and in fiction, the models we form of others as we exercise our theory-of-mind are actively constructive. It's not just a matter of being told this or that about a person.

In a kind of re-run in children of the finding in our research group that reading fiction by adults was related to theory-of-mind, Raymond Mar, Jennifer Tackett and Chris Moore found that exposure both to stories that were read to them, and to movies (though not to television), predicted four- to six-year-old children's theory-of-mind.

The idea of self-improvement

The idea that we might understand ourselves through fiction goes back, in the West, at least to the time of Plato and Aristotle. Norman Holland says this:

> Most theorists seem to insist that art and literature do two somewhat inconsistent things. Horace in his *Ars Poetica* put them simply and directly: prodesse and delectare. [Where delectare means] to delight – we turn to literature for enjoyment. Theorists usually translate Horace's other term, prodesse as "to instruct" or "to teach" or "to enlighten," and it is what justifies the enjoyment. "A poet should instruct, or please, or both" (p. 354).

But the idea that literature might instruct and enlighten has come under suspicion. Part of the devastation of World War II was the failure of German citizens, one of the world's most highly educated populations, to prevent their nation's slide into Nazism.[20] George Steiner has famously asserted: "We know that a man can read Goethe or Rilke in the evening, that he can play Bach and Schubert, and go to his day's work at Auschwitz in the morning"(p. 15).[21]

People have wondered why education – the humanities, literature, visual and musical art – did not enable the people of Germany to avoid slipping into a moral morass in which they thought some people in society were fit, while others were fit only to be exterminated. There are now well-informed historical accounts of Germany's adoption of Nazism.[22] An effective propaganda campaign based on the new media of radio and film persuaded many people to see Hitler not as a criminal but as a good person who would lead their country to greatness. Apart from propensity to violence, nationalism, and anti-Semitism, Nazism was marked by hostility to humanitarian values in education. From 1933 onwards, the Nazis replaced the idea of self-betterment through education and reading by practices designed to induce as many as possible into willing conformity, and to coerce the unwilling remainder by justified fear.

In *The fragility of goodness* Martha Nussbaum pointed out that for Plato the route to goodness was a life of contemplation, seeking certainties of ideals in a world of thought, beyond the one in which we live from day to day, insulated from its shocks. By contrast, she argues, day-to-day life is full of accidents, and this makes goodness fragile. So where do we find analyses of life as affected by accidents? It's in literary fiction. Nussbaum points us towards Aeschylus, Sophocles, and Euripides, and says:

> Greek tragedy shows good people being ruined because of things that just happen to them, things they do not control . . . Tragedy also, however, shows something more deeply disturbing: it shows good people doing bad things, things otherwise repugnant to their ethical character and commitments, because of circumstances whose origin does not lie within them" (p. 25).

Plato's descendants are the scientists, who strive towards ideal truths that transcend individual human cognition. No informed person would wish to argue against inferences drawn validly from empirical science, including science in the domain of psychology. But complementary to such inferences, as Nussbaum argues, are understandings from literary fiction, whose truths are relative to the reader, and point to vulnerability rather than Platonic self-sufficiency as the center of our humanity. Rather than the ordinary world being a shadow of an ideal (as Plato argued), our earthling world is where the action really is. Human action is seldom ideal, and human knowledge is never certain. In a life marked by accident and imperfection, what we understand is provisional. Fiction portrays the imperfect, and the provisional.[23]

In *Poetic justice*, Nussbaum starts with Adam Smith's idea of the "judicious spectator" who can mentally enter the plight of another person. She argues that this ability to identify with others by means of empathy or compassion is developed by the reading of fiction. This ability is, she says, essential to any true idea of justice, because one has to be able to think oneself into the circumstances of people who have been harmed in society, and one has to be able to think of these people in their individuality. The individuality of each person is among the goods that fiction can offer us. One way in which psychologists might like to think about this is in terms of the actor-observer discrepancy, of how we tend to see others and ourselves in different ways. For instance, if I see someone walk across a room and nearly trip over a child's toy that has been left on the floor, I tend to think that person is clumsy. If I walk across the room and almost trip in exactly the same way myself, I tend to think that it's because the toy shouldn't have been there. This set of ideas derives from Fritz Heider, who formulated attribution theory about how we try to understand the behavior of others and ourselves in terms of its causes. Fiction enables us to overcome the actor-observer discrepancy. The great writers –William Shakespeare, Jane Austen, Gustave Flaubert, George Eliot, Leo Tolstoy, Virginia Woolf – enable us to understand character both in terms of personality and by being inside the character and then, perhaps, to practice this same kind of understanding in ordinary life.

From the time of the Epicureans and Stoics, as Brian Stock has shown in *Ethics through literature,* reading has been seen in the West as important to self improvement, and it has included narrative. Until after about 1455, when printed books were invented in Europe by Johannes Gutenberg, reading was an activity of a tiny minority, among whom were monks. Stock points out, however, that from antiquity, throughout medieval and Renaissance times, and up to the present, there were always two aspects to it. He calls these the ascetic and the aesthetic. In Stock's usage, the ascetic does not indicate self-denial; it indicates concern with how to become ethically a better person, in one's relationships with others. By contrast, the aesthetic indicates reading for pleasure, although this kind of reading can also have ascetic qualities.

Stock shows that the tradition that developed with such readers and writers as Augustine, Petrarch, and Montaigne, was of ascetic reading in a way that one would enter a state of calmness with one's book, exclude the outside world and take in the words, and then a second phase of contemplation and reflection, to incorporate the meanings as parts of oneself. He points out, too, that this account parallels in many ways the practices of meditation in the East, which of course, also aim at self-improvement. I see the results presented in the foregoing sections as having a continuity with this tradition.

Can fiction have beneficial effects?

Nothing I have said so far implies that all fiction is worthwhile. In *Experiencing narrative worlds,* Richard Gerrig described how fiction can enable us to believe certain things too easily. Coleridge was misleading when he said that that artistic literature requires a "willing suspension of

disbelief." Often it's the opposite. Gerrig has proposed that fiction transports us into imaginary worlds, and in some cases in such worlds our
judgment can err. Sometimes we can too-easily believe things that are
untrue. This is a harmful effect.[24] I imagine we can all think of novels, films,
and plays that are biased, that is to say composed around an idea that is
false or that seeks to induce contempt for alternatives. In addition, many
people are convinced that certain kinds of fiction, for instance that which
dwells on violence or that which portrays certain kinds of sexuality, can be
actively harmful, especially to young people.[25]

The fiction about which I have been writing in this book is not of a kind
that is thought to be generally untrue or generally harmful. By reasoning
backwards from the effects that have been found of improved social abilities of empathy and theory of mind in readers of fiction it's possible,
perhaps, to indicate what it is about fiction that is likely to have beneficial
effects. Four themes can be inferred: exploration of the minds of others,
investigation of relationships, dynamics of interactions in groups, and
grappling's with the problems of selfhood.[26]

Understanding others, entering their minds
In Chapter 2, I introduced the idea that, within their first two years, children experience themselves as agents in the world and experience others
also as agents. By the age of four, with theory-of-mind, they can infer some
of what others are thinking and feeling, and know something of their own
minds. People form models of others (and themselves). They use these
models in their interactions with others.

This kind of model is like a wristwatch, a model of the rotation of the
earth and the procession of sun, moon, and stars, across the sky. Often it
isn't possible to see sun, moon, or stars, and so a wristwatch is convenient
for knowing the time, actually more accurate than any direct observation
of heavenly bodies. With watches to tell the time humans can coordinate
with others. So it is with theory-of-mind. With the models people make of
each other they can tune in to what others are thinking and feeling.

Questions of understanding what others think and feel, either in the
immediacy of an encounter (theory-of-mind), or over the longer term of
a relationship (character), are among the most central issues of human life.
And, although we humans are good at both of these kinds of understanding, we are not that good. *Pride and prejudice* can be thought of as about
the problems of coming to know other minds, coming to know them in
order to love them, coming to love them because one knows them.

George Eliot put it like this: "We are all born in moral stupidity." Understanding that others are also selves is something we have to discover, as Dorothea came, in *Middlemarch*, to discover that the man she had married "had an equivalent centre of self, whence lights and shadows must always fall with a certain difference" (p. 243).

It is in fiction, with its range of social contexts, and its range of character, that we might hope to improve our understanding generally. As Proust has put it:

> Only through art can we escape from our selves and know the perspective of another on the world, which is not the same as our own, and which contains views of landscapes that would otherwise have remained as unknown as any there may be on the moon (*À la recherche du temps perdu*, Vol. VIII, pp. 257–258, my translation).

Perhaps most importantly, understanding others as like oneself, with the same kinds of emotions and hence the same rights, has contributed hugely to society. Lynn Hunt has shown that the establishment of human rights has been strongly affected by literary art. We now think of human rights as universal, but Hunt shows that 300 years ago the idea that all humans have equal rights was scarcely present in European society. It had to be invented. By the end of the eighteenth century a change had been accomplished. Hunt offers three landmarks. In the American Declaration of Independence (of 1776) we read: "All men are created equal . . . with certain inalienable Rights, that among these are Life, Liberty and the Pursuit of Happiness." In the French Declaration of Rights of Man and Citizen of 1789, the first article is: "Men are born and remain free and equal in rights." Now, in our present age we have a Universal Declaration of Human Rights, written in 1948, in the shadow of the Nazi era. Its first article is: "All human beings are born free and equal in dignity and rights."

The full establishment of these principles in society world-wide is still some way off, but important steps have been taken. Slavery is no longer tolerable. Torture is no longer accepted as a legal procedure. In many countries women and ethnic minorities are now, like everyone else, equal before the law.

Hunt's finding is that invention of the idea of rights, the declarations of rights, and the changes in society that have followed them, depended on two factors. One was empathy, which depends, as Hunt says, on "a biologically based ability to understand the subjectivity of other people and to be able to imagine that their inner experiences are like one's own" (p. 39). The other was the mobilization of this empathy towards those who were outside people's immediate social groupings. Although Hunt does not attribute this mobilization entirely to literary art, she concludes that the novel contributed to it substantially. "Reading novels," she says, "created a sense of equality and empathy through passionate involvement in the narrative" (p. 39). Many novels contributed. One on which Hunt concentrates was Samuel Richardson's *Pamela* (1740) written by a man and inviting empathetic identification with a woman of humble social class. Hunt quotes from *Pamela*:

> . . . he kissed me two or three times, as if he would have eaten me. – At last I burst from him, and was getting out of the Summer-house; but he held me back, and shut the Door.
>
> I would have given my Life for a Farthing. And he said, I'll do you no Harm, Pamela; don't be afraid of me. I said I won't stay! You won't, Hussy! Said he. Do you know who you speak to? I lost all Fear, and all Respect, and said Yes, I do Sir, too well! – Well may I forget that I am your Servant, when you forget what belongs to a Master.
>
> I sobb'd and cry'd most sadly. What a foolish Hussy you are! said he: Have I done you any Harm? – Yes, Sir, said I, the greatest Harm in the World: You have taught me to forget myself, and what belongs to me (Richardson, p. 23).

Pamela and other novels of the middle of the eighteenth century were hugely successful and enthusiastically discussed by a rapidly growing reading public. Through fiction, readers entered into emotions of ordinary people, says Hunt; and then she says: "Human rights grew out of the seedbed sowed by these feelings. Human rights could only flourish when people learned to think of others as their equals, as like them in some fundamental fashion" (p. 58).[27]

Understanding relationships
A second theme in potentially beneficial effects of fiction is in understandings of relationships. It is not accidental that the most common stories worldwide are, as Patrick Hogan has shown, stories of the emotions of relating, stories of love and anger. It isn't that we spend most of our time in incidents of this kind; it is that there's always more to understand about these issues. They are critical to what is most important to us, but their

implications are often a bit beyond our mental reach and this is where simulations (dreams) of the kind that fiction offers can come in.

The understanding of relationships in fictional simulation is less like a wristwatch and more like a weather forecast. When we read, hear, or watch a weather forecast, it comes from the output of a computer simulation. Weather is the outcome of many processes in interaction. We are quite good at understanding one process at a time, for instance that when a mass of cold air meets a mass of warm air precipitation is likely because the cold air cools the warm air to the point at which its water vapor condenses to form rain or snow. But in order to know whether it will rain tomorrow, this process has to be set into interaction with atmospheric pressure, humidity, the influence of the surrounding geography and so on.

In *The epic of Gilgamesh*, Gilgamesh has become a tyrant, and Enkidu is wild. It is only through relationships that either can move forward. In Shakespeare's "Sonnet 27," the implication is that, if one has a loved one, the person should be known – that's part of what love is –but what if aspects of other are not known? In Chekhov's "The lady with the little dog," it might seem that the kind of relationship that would develop between a man and a woman, alone, on holiday, in a seaside town, would be completely predictable. We seem to know all the necessary factors. But Chekhov shows that perhaps we do not.

Dynamics of interaction in groups

Thirdly among themes that can be enlightening, there are questions of what people do in families, in political maneuvering, or when a number of people are confined together in other kinds of group. Jane Austen gives us an instance, in Chapter 3 of *Pride and prejudice,* of the dance at the Meryton Assembly Room. Some of those at the dance, like Jane Bennet, enjoy the interactions. Others like Darcy are full of disdain for the proceedings. Whatever is going on? In novels we can ask such questions.

The hope in fiction, as Aristotle says, is to discover not the history of what happened, but principles of what is possible. We do not ask whether Darcy really did say, "She is tolerable." We can ask whether the scene that Austen prompts us to imagine is enlightening about how people behave in groups.

Problems of selfhood

The fourth theme of fiction that can potentially prompt self-improvement is in understandings of the self. Just as we can make models of others, we can make models of ourselves. Indeed, it is a model of this kind that we call our "self." Although, in Western society, we tend to think of our self as autonomous, the source of our thoughts, feelings, and decisions, really, as Charles Cooley pointed out, our self isn't really autonomous. It's self-in-relation-to-others.

In Kate Chopin's "The dream of an hour," Mrs Mallard experiences a flood of self-realization, that she is free of the constraints of her marriage. Chopin is careful to point out that this is not a matter of the particular relationship of Mr and Mrs Mallard. The issue is more general. Mrs Mallard thinks of the "powerful will bending hers in that blind persistence with which men and women believe they have a right to impose a private will upon a fellow-creature." Thus, Mrs Mallard felt, her selfhood had been distorted by her marriage.

Cooley's most famous concept was the "looking-glass self." (It's the appearance, in social science, perhaps of Shakespeare's idea of shadow, or behavior, as reflection in a mirror.) At about the same time that Cooley coined his idea, across the other side of the world, Chekhov used it in his short story "The lady with the little dog." Towards the end of the story of the affair between Gomov and Anna, Chekhov writes this: "He came up to her and patted her shoulder fondly and at that moment he saw himself in the mirror." Gomov glimpses himself as others might see him.[28]

In one's life among people, one wants to be seen by them in something like the way in which one sees oneself. How, then, can one present oneself in everyday life? And what if one's self is defined by others in a way that is disdainful or condescending? Here is an issue that I discussed in Chapter 5, to which James Baldwin points in "Down at the cross: Letter from a region of my mind."

The concerns of fiction

I don't think the four potentially beneficial themes that I have indicated (above) define fiction. I do, however, think that some conceptualization of this kind might help us come closer to the psychology of fiction. We can think of fiction as centered on themes and preoccupations that are essential to our lives as social beings, depicted in the form of imaginative simulations, waking dreams.

Transportation, persuasion, indirectness

Perhaps it is narrative (the style of fiction) as compared with exposition (the characteristic style of non-fiction) that is responsible for some of the effects that have been found in reading fiction. Allan Eng asked participants to read a two-page passage of either narrative or expository prose that had the same content and the same level of reading difficulty. Subjects marked the margin with an M whenever a memory occurred. After reading, they wrote summaries of these memories. Memories of those who read the narrative, as compared with the expository version, were significantly more vivid, and more often involved the reader as actor or observer in a detailed scene, rather than being reports of events or semantic memories. Narrative, the native mode of prose fiction, can prompt vivid images.

A term that has come into use in relation to getting lost in a book is "transportation." According to Melanie Green and Tim Brock, transportation is a state of immersion in a story. It can involve the experience that Csikszentmihalyi calls "flow" (discussed in Chapter 3) of being totally engaged in what one is doing. It involves attention, imagery, and emotion.[29] Green and Brock found that the extent of our transportation into a narrative world predicted the extent to which readers' beliefs became consistent with beliefs and evaluations in the story.[30] This is the basis of their approach to narrative as a means of persuasion.[31] Green has also found that labeling a story as fact or fiction had no effect on the extent of transportation that occurs. With P.M. Mazzocco and other colleagues, Green found that some people were more easily transported than others, that a narrative was more effective at inducing transportation and persuasion than a purely rhetorical argument carrying the same information about a minority group, and that high transportation and changes of attitudes occurred because the text induced empathy for the people of minority status.

In researching other effects of narratives, Terre Satterfield and her colleagues offered people the same information about effects of a planned hydroelectric system on a river's salmon population in either a narrative or a didactic format. They found that people who received the information in a narrative format were better able to evaluate the issues, and better able to apply what they had learned in a complex policy judgment.[32]

An important way of thinking about fiction is that it depicts roles – people as lovers, parents, helpers, criminals – and these roles can be either attractive or not. Such roles enable us to imagine ourselves into them, to feel sympathy for them,[33] and see what it is like to be a certain kind of person. This line of thinking led Frank Hakemulder to his PhD thesis which, strikingly, he called *The moral laboratory*. He had Dutch university students read either a chapter of a novel about the difficult life of an Algerian woman, or an essay on women's rights in Algeria. Those who read the fictional piece said they would be less likely to accept current Algerian norms for relationships between men and women than did those who read the essay.[34]

Hakemulder has also investigated a practical application of the idea of role taking in a fictional form called Forum Theatre.[35] A play in this format is performed twice in one session. The first time is much as it might occur in an ordinary theater. The second time, spectators are invited, by an actor called the Joker, to come onto the stage and play the roles of some of the characters. Thus within a performance a spectator-turned-actor might forego a path towards self-destructive actions and, instead, choose an alternative. In their newly imagined roles, different courses of action are explored. By taking part physically, on the stage, moreover, participants have an experience of being in situations that are alternatives to what they are used to, and of seeing what these roles feel like.

Hakemulder tested the effects of Forum Theatre plays staged by Enter-Growth's *Palama*, a project of the International Labor Organization, in Sri Lanka. The project had an explicit aim: to change the predominantly negative beliefs about business in rural Sri Lanka. In his evaluation of this project, Hakemulder measured transportation both in those who took a role in the play when invited by the Joker and in audience members who just watched. He found that, both cases, the extent to which people felt transported predicted their changes of beliefs towards the possible benefits

Figure 7.3 Logo of Enter-Growth's Palama group, which gives Forum Theatre performances in Sri Lanka. The logo is by Enterprise for Pro-Poor Growth of the International Labour Organization.

of taking part in some kind of commercial activity and earning a living thereby.

Persuasion is essential to every practical decision that involves others, from national politics to making a personal choice that affects a family. Among important issues are distinctions of persuasion from coercion, of persuasion that carries useful information from persuasion with false or self-interested information, and of persuasion that is candid from persuasion that is surreptitious. The surreptitious for instance, is discussed by Patrick Hogan in *Understanding nationalism*. He argues that certain universal story themes (introduced in Chapter 4) – the heroic in which a hero defeats evil enemies, and the sacrificial in which a large sacrifice is needed to save society – seem to have been particularly effective in recruiting people to nationalistic dispositions, without them being fully aware of the effects.

Related to the psychology of persuasion and enculturation is, of course, the psychology of advertising and propaganda. In a related way, many action stories and romances come in this category. Robin Collingwood, whose book *The principles of art* I introduced in Chapter 5, regarded such genres as action and romance as non-art, because they are not explorations. They follow formulae, and their writers intend to induce particular kinds of emotion. If successful they are entertaining. That's their intention. But they are not art, and they are not – in my view –the kinds of works that are likely to increase understanding of ourselves or others, at least when the formula of the genre is adhered to in the usual way.

But art – I'll offer a criterion –does not recruit people to believe or act or feel in a particular way. Søren Kierkegaard put it like this:

> The indirect mode of communication makes communication an art in quite a different sense than when it is conceived in the usual manner . . . To stop a man on the street and stand still while talking to him, is not so difficult as to say something to a passer-by in passing, without standing still and without delaying the other, without attempting to persuade him to go the same way, but giving him instead an impulse to go precisely his own way (pp. 246–247).

Maja Djikic and colleagues found that people changed in their personalities as a result of reading Chekhov's "The lady with the little dog," and that these changes were not all in the same direction. Each person changed in his or her own way.

In general the intention of political discourse is to persuade towards a particular view or course of action. Literary art is not without political purpose: its forms are adapted to our deeper purposes of understanding others in their individuality and of understanding ourselves. But these forms – I'm trying to say this as persuasively as I can – are in a different register than those designed to persuade towards particular beliefs and actions. Among the practices that Kierkegaard called indirect, one is psychotherapy of a certain kind. One, I think, is the relationship of love. Another – the subject of this book – is fiction: fiction as art.

In fiction that is art, one is not programmed by the writer. One starts to explore and feel, perhaps, new things. One may start to think in new ways. And as one feels and thinks, one often wants to talk about these matters with someone else. This is the subject of the next, and last, chapter of this book.

8

Talking About Fiction

Figure 8.1 Picture used by Literature for Life. Photo courtesy of Literature for Life.

Talking About Fiction: Interpretation in Conversation

Orbits of discussion

To talk about fiction is almost as important as to engage with it in the first place. Works of art are surrounded by orbits of discussion. Often, to start with, the discussion is by experts, for instance in reviews in newspapers or magazines. In educational settings discussion that surrounds a work will have been directed by teachers who have themselves been taught by experts who had distinct views about how we should think about what we read. But more and more it is coming to be realized that the important discussion of fiction is between friends, colleagues, and relatives.

One of the best books on talking about fiction is *How to talk about books you haven't read*. The author of this book with the teasing title is Pierre Bayard. The reason he puts it in this rather gross way is that even books we have read and films we have seen are retained only as fragments. Therefore we tend to discuss – can only discuss – small parts. Like a dream on waking, only a feeling and some fragments remain. So books we have read and films we have seen become a bit like books of which we have read reviews and films friends have told us about. Now here's a good part. When we discuss those parts of books and films that we noticed and that we remember, they can be augmented by the different parts noticed and remembered by people with whom we have the discussion. Thereby we can put fragments together, to make the books and films more whole.

A book Bayard has read is Frederic Bartlett's *Remembering*, which I discussed in Chapter 3. It was the basis of the new cognitive psychology. It demonstrated that we assimilate what we read to a schema of what we know, while retaining only salient details. We store these fragments in what Bayard aptly calls our inner library, which is entirely idiosyncratic. In it, items seldom coincide with items in the inner libraries of other people. And when we discuss books of fiction, not only do we exchange our impressions of fragments we have read with the impressions of fragments in the inner libraries of other people, but we re-introduce this material – fiction – about what people are up to in the social world, back into the social world of conversation and relationship.

Bayard proposes a rather good theory of reading and imagination. The question he asks is: how can we come to know, and to take in so that they become parts of us, the contents of books amid the formidable infinity of published material? He introduces an apt notation for the books he discusses: SB means "book I have skimmed," HB means "book I have heard of," and FB means "book I have forgotten." He offers, as someone to admire, the librarian in Robert Musil's *Man without qualities* (SB), who doesn't want to read any of the books in his library, but only to know how they relate to each other. He also suggests that we take seriously Paul Valéry (SB and HB) who advocated that we should avoid reading books because we can too easily get lost in their details, or find that they overwhelm us. Bayard goes on to point out that the fragmentariness of what we remember also holds for books we have written ourselves (FB).

When I read Bayard's book (which is so witty and engaging that I am sorry to say that I read the whole of it), I was delighted to find that he used some examples that were in my inner library. One is the fine scene in Graham Greene's *The third man* in which Holly Martins, author of pulp Westerns who is mistaken for a highbrow writer also called Martins, has to give a talk at a literary gathering in post-war Vienna. The subject on which he is asked to talk is the future of the novel. It's a topic he's never thought about. Another is a wonderful paper by anthropologist Laura Bohannan, which I did not know existed in anyone's inner library but my own, in which she tries to explain to a group of the Tiv (an ethno-linguistic group in West Africa) the story of *Hamlet*. The Tiv are very interested in stories, and the group is pleased when Bohannan offers to recount a story from her culture. But although they remain appreciative of her efforts, at every juncture they tell her she has it wrong. They tell her that dead people do not reappear, that the young Hamlet should leave affairs of state to elders, and that it is not wrong, but imperative, for a woman recently bereaved to marry again as quickly as possible, and so on. Bayard follows these episodes with scenes from David Lodge's *Changing places,* in which is introduced the game of Humiliation, as played in a group of literary people. To play the game you have to admit to not having read a famous book. The person with the most outrageous admission wins. *Steppenwolf,* anybody? *Oliver Twist? Hamlet?*

Bayard's book gets even better as it goes along. It turns into a literary version of Bartlett's theory, that our understanding is based on personal and cultural schemas that are partial, ever active, ever changing. And (resonating with my discussion of creativity in Chapter 3), towards the end of his book Bayard says:

"Who can deny . . . that talking about books you haven't read constitutes an authentic creative activity, making the same demands as other forms of art. Just think of all the skills it calls into play – listening to the potentialities of a work, analyzing its ever-changing context, paying attention to others and their reactions" (pp. 182–183).

Conversation and reading

As I explained in Chapter 4, most conversation is not practical. That is to say it is not about arranging how to do something. It's social, about maintaining our relationships. It's often about ourselves, our plans, and their outcomes. It's also about the characters, the plans, and the actions of other people. Fiction is about this same set of issues, so it is an extension of ordinary conversation. Books and films are also among the things we talk about with friends. Another important topic is emotion, also a frequent topic of conversation. Emotions occur with the outcomes of actions (in life and in fiction).[1]

Both emotion and fiction are about people and their doings. Both involve comparisons of what we feel and think with the opinions and judgments of other people in our social circle. This doesn't mean we are insecure. The reason is deeper. It is that we are social to our core. Knowing what others think and feel, including how they think and feel about what we think and feel, is always important for us, so conversation is essential to our very being. As Charles Cooley observed, our lives are lived in the minds of others. Although often we think of ourselves as individual, and even separate, unless we were in other minds, and unless others were in our minds, we would not be human.

As well as talking about books we haven't read there is, of course, the activity of reading. Elaine Duncan and I asked people to keep diaries structured like questionnaires of incidents of emotion that occurred in their everyday lives. We found that some 20% of such incidents were caused not by events in the immediacy of life, but by events at one remove, and these include memories, ideas in imagination, reading, going to the movies, and so on.

In follow-up research, I adapted the idea of daily diaries, and concentrated on reading, using the method I introduced in Chapter 3, of asking readers to mark Ms, Es, and Ts in the margins of a story, to indicate (in a diary-keeping kind of way) the occurrence of memories, emotions, and thoughts, as they read. For example, in one study, Mitra Gholamain and I asked members of reading groups to read a short story about the loss of a romantic relationship ("Bardon Bus," by Alice Munro). After they read the story, participants described the most significant of the memories they had marked with Ms, and also wrote an overall response to the story.

We then categorized people's most-significant memories according to Tom Scheff's scheme of aesthetic distance. (Scheff's theory of emotions of fiction as derived from memories relived at a better aesthetic distance was introduced in Chapter 5.) A memory was categorized as over-distanced when it lacked emotions (possibly because emotions were unconscious); it was under-distanced when it was all emotion and no reflection (when emotions were overwhelming); and it was optimally distanced when it combined emotion and thought in connecting the remembered event to the current self, as in the following example:

> I remember one day receiving a letter from a young man whom I had known briefly (and had quite liked). I had not heard from him since we graduated from high school. The letter arrived at a time when I was feeling quite alone and unhappy and unsure of what I wanted to do with my life. I had a four month old baby and was living again with my family having been away from home for a year. In the letter this young man expressed an interest in how and what I was doing and professed a "fondness" that he had held for me in school. The tone of the letter made it quite clear that he wanted and hoped to become a part of my life. I felt overjoyed, my hope renewed. I can remember to this day the sensation of my heart swelling and the feeling that all would turn out well in the end. And yet, these feelings were tempered by the reality of the changes that had occurred in my life namely the addition of a child.

The woman who wrote about this memory seems to have written it for herself, as well as for us. It's a lovely, reflective, piece.

In their overall responses to the story, people who had predominantly over-distanced memories tended to be over-intellectual, for instance only making judgments about the story's writing style. Those who had under-distanced memories tended to be over-emotional, for instance saying only whether they liked or disliked the story, or how they felt what a character felt. Those with optimally distanced memories, such as the one quoted above, tended to write overall responses that referred to emotions and contained elaborated thoughts about the story's meaning. We found, too, that when people engaged with a literary story such as "Bardon Bus," they tended to identify with a protagonist. The task for a writer is to offer a story to readers in a way that enables them to experience crucial parts of it at an aesthetic distance where they can experience their emotions.

Talking about books

I introduced Chapter 2 with a scene of from Judy Dunn's book *Children's friendships,* two friends playing at being pirates. Friendship involves theory-of-mind – understanding the thoughts and feelings of the other person – and, says Dunn:

> children who were early "stars" at mind reading and understanding feelings were particularly likely to develop friendships in which they shared exciting and elaborate pretend play, and long, connected conversations . . . Once a friendship begins to develop, the opportunities for the children involved to learn about what [the] other person feels and thinks increases markedly. It is through their creation of joint imaginary worlds, their extended conversations and their management of problems and disagreements that these opportunities arise (p. 65).

The boys who played at pirates would hardly have heard of pirates without meeting them in books or films. So fiction can become, and does become, a basis for shared worlds.

Many of us were introduced to fiction by having books read to us when we were children. Others had books introduced at school. And if, at school or university, we did courses in literature there were further introductions, as well as interpretations of poetry and prose fiction, at which we, too, had to try our hand in essays, usually careful to follow suggestions of teachers, as to what to read on the fiction in question. Typically we were taught the canon, the set of works chosen to exemplify what is best in our culture.[2]

As I discussed in Chapter 3, I.A. Richards did the experiment of giving undergraduates in his university English classes 13 poems from the canon, for instance by John Donne, Thomas Hardy, Gerard Manley Hopkins, Christina Rossetti, and others. Education in English literature, for several decades under the influence of Richards and the New Critics, then became teaching people not only what to read but how to read.[3]

Education in English literature followed a process of induction that occurs for students in any subject. But whereas in mathematics or biology, one needs to climb upwards through successively more complex understandings –and stand, as Robert Burton put it, on the shoulders of giants – in the matter of interpretation, the question is perhaps not so simple, because (as I have suggested) not only do works of fiction almost of necessity have multiple interpretations, but also because enjoyment of fiction involves making what we read our own.

Of late, therefore, under the influence of feminist and post-colonial critics who have made remarks about "dead white males," the question of who should choose the canon has become urgent. It is, of course, valuable to have experts on literature sort through, comment upon, and review works of fiction, in such literary periodicals as the *Times Literary Supplement* and the *New York Review of Books*. So many books are published each year that, without some guidance and suggestions, any ordinary person would be unable to sample them. I feel indebted not just to these periodicals, but also to the juries that evaluate books for the Man-Booker prize, the Pulitzer prize, and so on.

I have to admit, also, that in my education and reading, I do think that some books are more worth reading than others, that some plays work and others don't, that some films are boring while others are moving and thought-provoking. I own to being affected by F. R. Leavis, who has argued that some fiction is important, while other fiction is not worth the time it takes to read it.

A close friend of mine was an undergraduate in Leavis's group, at Downing College, Cambridge. I would sometimes go to Leavis's lectures, and occasionally I would join the group in the evenings, and listen to the discussions. Leavis encouraged an atmosphere among his students of engaged excitement and moral seriousness. I was a medical student at the time, taking courses with a lot to remember but not much to think about. The atmosphere that Leavis created was closer to what I'd come to university for. The sense I acquired, already germinating in my schooldays, and then encouraged by my propinquity with the Downing group, was that nothing else is quite as important as literature. It's like being infected with a chronic disease which, although it comes and goes, I've not entirely been able to shake off. My additional, and secret, thought – an indication no doubt that whatever this infection was, it had affected me dangerously – has been that the only really worthwhile thing to do in my work-life was to write a novel, and so I feel fortunate to have been able to do that.

Leavis's most influential book is *The great tradition*. It starts like this:

> The great English novelists are Jane Austen, George Eliot, Henry James, and Joseph Conrad – to stop for a moment at that comparatively safe point in history . . . it is as well to start by distinguishing the few really great – the major novelists who count in the same way as the major poets, in the sense that they not only change the possibilities of the art for practitioners and readers, but that they are significant in terms of

that human awareness they promote; awareness of the possibilities of life (pp. 9–10).

This last word, "life" is significant. Thus, said Leavis:

> As a matter of fact, when we examine the formal perfection of [Jane Austen's] *Emma*, we find that it can be appreciated only in terms of the moral preoccupations that characterize the novelist's peculiar interest in life . . . the same is true of the other great English novelists . . . they are all distinguished by a vital capacity for experience, a kind of reverent openness before life, and a marked moral intensity (p. 17).

Leavis could be combative and self-righteous. But when I contracted the infection of his group, I acquired with it the strong belief that up to the early years of the Twentieth Century, Jane Austen, George Eliot, Henry James, and Joseph Conrad were – indisputably – the great novelists in English. What has happened since, thank goodness, is that the range of novelists who are thought to be worth reading has been enormously widened. No longer just English or European or Russian or American, great novelists come from across the world.

I have enjoyed reading literary criticism, from Samuel Johnson to James Wood. But alongside the interpretations of texts for which I am grateful because many of them I could not have thought of myself, there has been another strain in the academy. It is of interpretations of texts that are only indirectly about the texts themselves. They are, instead, about political positions. The literary scholar David Miall put the problem they present like this in 2009:

> My problem with [this kind of] interpretation is that in literary scholar-ship it typically takes us away from the text itself to using the text as a specimen of some historical or cultural issue. Peter Rabinowitz has characterized this very effectively as the "Rule of Abstract Displacement." There are two steps to it. "The first step involves an act of substitution: according to this rule, good literature is always treated as if it were about something else." Its "real" meaning, that is, lies in something other than its ostensible, surface meaning. The second step is "an act of generaliza-tion," towards some proposition that is supposed to have universal value . . . I don't believe that most ordinary readers (outside the class-room) are engaged in interpretation, in this sense. Of course, there are other meanings to interpretation, and I wouldn't want to suggest they are without interest. It's the bypassing of the text itself that I want to point out.

The difficulty, as Miall points out, is that however interesting the displacing critic may be, the intention is to divert one from the text, towards the position (often ideological) for which the critic is arguing. The result is that, in reading the critic's piece, one is not so much enabled to think and feel about the text in a new way, one is being induced to vote.

The psychology of interpretation of texts by the range of ordinary readers (rather than the interpretation of texts as examples of political or ideological positions) can be thought of helpfully in terms of a phrase that Bill Benzon has proposed: "how texts work in the mind and brain."[4]

Reading groups

At a recent conference I heard someone (I wish I knew who) say: "The whole activity of interpretation has moved from departments of literature to reading groups."

The best book I know on reading groups is by Jenny Hartley and Sarah Turvey who conducted a survey, mostly in UK, but also world-wide. In 2000 they estimated that there might be as many as 50,000 reading groups in Britain and 500,000 in America. In their main survey, of 350 groups in UK, they were able to find both a range of types of group, and to depict what the typical group was like. About two thirds of reading groups were of women only, most of the rest were mixed, and just a few were of men only. A typical reading group tends to meet about once a month, and to read fiction rather than non-fiction. Amongst other results of their survey Hartley and Turvey came up with the three favorite reading group books among their 350 groups. These were as follows (with the number of groups that read each in parentheses): Louis de Bernières *Captain Corelli's mandolin* (81), Frank McCourt *Angela's ashes* (71), and Arundhati Roy *The god of small things* (58).

Figure 8.2   A meeting of a reading group. © Najlah Feanny/Corbis.

Hartley and Turvey depict a general sense of enthusiasm among members, with many people looking forward eagerly to the next meeting of the group. Here are two quotes: "We enjoy feeling totally free to express our own opinions," and "Discussions can be anything from profound to hilarious, but are always lively." The best observational study I know of reading groups is by Zazie Todd (2008).[5] She found that group discussions revealed:

> a search for a meaning within the book, and participants sometimes found quite different meanings, linking the text to their own emotional and autobiographical responses (p. 256).

Reading groups tend to be middle-class, but other types of group have also emerged. One type has become a program called Changing Lives Through Literature, for people convicted of crimes. The movement began in 1991 with discussions between Robert Waxler, a professor of English literature at the University of Massachusetts, Dartmouth, and his friend Robert Kane, a judge. They agreed that perhaps offenders could be sentenced to probation rather than jail on condition that they attended a seminar on literature.[6]

In 1996 Karen Thomson founded Literature for All of Us, in Chicago, based on reading circles for teenage single mothers. In this program, which by 2009 had reached 4500 people, weekly 90-minute book groups are facilitated by experienced leaders. Discussions of books that the groups read are followed by poetry writing exercises in which members complete a set of sentences with textual prompts such as "I am ...," " " I think that ...," and so on. A program in Toronto, based on the same principles, Literature for Life, was founded in 2000 by Jo Altilia who continues to direct it; by 2009 it had reached 1400 young people.

The website of Literature for All of Us has reported:

> Evaluations found significant developments in the use of critical thinking and problem-solving skills.

The director of Literature for Life has reported that many of the young women who have joined book circles "experience an increase in perspective-taking, empathy, and problem-solving as a result of their participation." A culture of literacy can begin to emerge, which also helps prepare children for school.[7]

In a study of reading groups that emerged with the rise of the women's movement in USA, Elizabeth Long found that middle class women accomplished a valorizing of themselves as women in these groups, in ways that were often devalued by society. There is no reason why this kind of effect should be confined to the middle classes.

As well as the face-to-face reading groups that meet in people's living rooms, there have been movements of larger numbers of people to discuss books, of which Oprah Winfrey's television-led reading group is perhaps the best known. In addition, on-line reading groups have become popular, and Barbara Fister describes how active on-line discussion among committed readers reveal much about how discussion can enrich the experience of reading. Fister studied a successful on-line reading group called 4 Mystery Addicts (4MA), which was founded towards the end of 1999 by four people who liked mystery stories, and wanted to share their reading experiences. It had 600 members, and 1500 to 3000 messages a month were posted by its members. Fister said that:

> Although many of these messages are marked "OT" for "off topic" and long-running inside jokes and personal observations pepper the daily diet of lively conversation, the focus is kept on books through three well-organized monthly book discussions and regularly scheduled opportunities to share reading experiences.

At the beginning of March 2010, I Googled 4MA and found it to be still active. At the same time, another long-running online group mentioned by Fister, named DorothyL (after Dorothy L. Sayers), also for readers of mysteries, was active with 1000–1800 posts per month. Online discussion groups also exist for books other than mysteries. For instance, The Valve is an active on-line reading and discussion group, the core of which is of people who are or were teachers of literature. And, since 17 February 2009, the *New Yorker* has been running an online book club for general literature. Another kind of online discussion which one can follow on the internet is *The golden notebook* Project. It takes the form of notes in the margin and conversations by seven women on Doris Lessing's *The golden notebook*.

Changes of interpretation
The idea that interpretation has moved from departments of literature to reading groups is very interesting, perhaps even correct. It would represent, I think, three kinds of movement, as follows:

Democratization. Interpretation was once, perhaps, the province mainly of teachers of literature who, equipped with interpretations of canonical works, would instruct others. But with the reading group movement, interpretation has become a matter for everybody.

Some empirical work by Marc Verboord and Kees van Rees has investigated this kind of democratization by asking what influences have affected what gets taught in literature classes in high-schools in Holland. They analyzed the content of textbooks on literature, and teachers' choices among these textbooks. They found that, over the last decades of the 20th Century, the way in which literary authors and their works were presented in textbooks increasingly came to be based on students' reading preferences rather than on a canon specified by literary experts. Over this period, too, teachers seem to have chosen those textbooks that were most responsive to students' preferences.

The variety of engagement. An implication of reader response theory is that the variety of responses to works of literature has become no longer a problem but a feature. This does not mean that interpretations by experts – literary critics and reviewers – are not valuable. One of the sources of their value is that what experts write, like the works on which they write, are the outcomes of having thought about something deeply. One of the founding principles of the *New York Review of Books* was to try and find reviewers who knew more about the subjects of books to be reviewed than the authors. None of us can be experts across the range of books in which we might be interested in this kind of way. This situation does mean, however, that we don't need to be constrained by the idea, which derives from an educational system directed towards student assessment, that there are correct kinds of interpretation, which are the only ones to be taken seriously.

Interpretation in conversation. Interpretations have become no longer pronouncements but contributions to conversations that can, in such contexts as reading groups, be parts of relationships.[8]

I have been a founding member of two reading groups, one in Edinburgh that ran for about three years, and one in Toronto that has run for 20 years. In both groups we read only novels – well pretty much only novels, although we've had a few lapses into short-story, memoir, and biography. Both of these groups were of friends. We have met, and continue to meet as a group, about once a month. Our current group has nine members (five women and four men), which for us is about right. In the group there is a wonderful variety of experience of works of fiction, so that things that I completely did not see in what we have read, or did not realize, or did not understand, are seen, realized, understood and thought about by other people in the group. Often we discuss character. The group discussion allows me to expand on what I have read. It's quite common in the group for someone to say: "Well, I didn't much like the novel, but the discussion was wonderful." At the same time, by relating what we read to our personal experience, the relationships among the members of the group, and our understandings of each other, are deepened and extended.

When reading groups really work
In reading groups that are working well, people talk about why a book touched them (or didn't), or how it enabled their feelings to change, or what they saw in it, or what part of their experience the book enabled them to articulate. Then, rather than the partial readings that Paul Bayard jokes about in *How to talk about books you haven't read,* each person sees and articulates something that others did not see, and an expansion occurs. The group and its members start to fill out their experience of a book towards wholeness in a way that is far more difficult to achieve on one's own.

In Chapter 3, I introduced Roland Barthes's idea that as one reads a piece of literature one may focus first on one aspect then another. This idea is useful, I think, for understanding what can go on in reading groups, because people in the group can represent – in what they say at any moment – any of these modes, and others can represent other modes. So (following the same order as in Chapter 3), a person may (i) talk about how some aspect of the text seems mysterious, and how the mystery might be solved, (ii) how something concrete in the text suggests a significant abstraction, (iii) how an action of one of the characters has a surprising effect or implications, (iv) how something in the text is productively ambiguous, (v) how certain cultural values – familiar or unfamiliar – are elaborated. All these are aspects that can be experienced as important and meaningful by some people on some readings, and less so by others. But, within the circle of friendship in the group, it is easy to acknowledge that things one did not find important in one's own reading, can nevertheless be so from another perspective.

Barthes's third mode is about actions. In this book I've taken an Aristotelian view and written of action in terms of plot. In a reading group the sequences of action are generally something about which everyone can agree, even when members might have missed something. The group generally, as it were, agrees on what the Russian Formalists called a novel's *fabula*, its event structure. This then provides a skeleton on which the body of discussion can be built.[9] With it in place, people can talk about their own experience, and they often do this in very different ways.

In addition to the modes set out by Barthes (above) I think two issues to which I have given priority in this book also become important in reading groups: character and emotion.

As to character, in the reading group of which I am a member, and as Todd found in her study, when members are unable to identify or sympathize with characters, they tend to complain about the book. Through identification and sympathy, a character, a narrator, or an author, is welcomed into the mind, and then can be spoken for to the others in the group. This can happen when there is something recognizable about a character, or the character's situation, or the arc of the character's trajectory through which a story articulates something of personal significance. With characters who are identified with, it is as if the friendship network of the group can extend itself, and invite that character to join the group. But, just as I. A. Richards found that some of his students were unwilling to allow certain poems to enter their minds, some people in the group are sometimes unwilling to allow certain characters or authors to enter their minds.

As to emotions, people in reading groups talk both about fresh emotions and emotional memories that occur when they read. Fresh emotions (discussed in Chapter 5) are of identification and sympathy.[10] People also discuss autobiographical memories of an emotional kind, prompted by what they have read. In a group of friends, as in the group of which I am a member, such confiding increases understanding of each other, increases intimacy. Particular people resonate with particular moods and emotional structures, in some books but not others. Emotions are very much part of group members' search for meanings in what they read. Sometimes people talk about how emotional meanings changed as they read. Some aspect of a book can resonate with current or predominant emotions or experience for a group member, and can articulate some aspect of an interpersonal situation that is important or unresolved. In this way, both the emotions that group members talk about, and the meanings they are seeking can be very different, but at the same time can be accepted by the membership of the group.

Talking of Chekhov

Anton Chekhov's "The lady with the little dog" is thought to be one of the world's great short stories. It is one of the pieces of literature that members

Figure 8.3 Anton Chekhov's house in Yalta in 1899: the place and year in which he wrote "The lady with the little dog." Source: RIA Novosti/Alamy.

of the research group of which I am part have studied and, in Chapter 7, I discussed how it can enable people to make small changes in the personalities. In this section, I offer an interpretation of the story, not as a pronouncement but as a contribution to the conversation in which I hope to have been taking part with you, the reader of this book. You might respond by thinking of something quite different that you see in Chekhov's story, or that you feel about it.

The story has four parts. The first starts with a man called Gomov, at the seaside resort of Yalta, on the Black Sea. There he meets a woman, Anna Sergueyevna, the lady with the little dog. They are both married to other people, whom they have left at home. They start conversing and going about together. In Part II, Gomov and Anna go to her hotel room. They make love. She feels terrible, and thinks herself a low creature for having done such a thing. But later the two feel close again, and they drive out before dawn to Oreanda, where they sit on a bench and look out over the sea. The end of the holidays come, and they go home to their spouses. In the third part, although Gomov has had affairs before, and expects to forget Anna gradually and pleasantly, he cannot stop thinking about her. He makes an excuse to his wife and travels to the town where Anna lives. There is an opening night at the town theater, and Gomov sees her there. In the interval, they talk briefly, and she promises to come to Moscow to visit him. In the fourth part, in Moscow, Gomov is utterly absorbed in his affair, and feels at odds with himself, as if everything people see of him is a lie, whereas everything that is true about him has to be kept secret. Anna visits Gomov in Moscow, from time to time, and for both of them these visits are disturb-ing. They hope they will be able to resolve their situation, but both know it may not be possible.

I'll now relate some of my experience of the story and ask you how you think and feel about it.

To start with, I identify with Gomov. I take on temporarily his character his interests in philology (as one might now say in literature and its psy-chology) and his aspiration to be an opera singer. Working in a bank feels stultifying, and the situation is made worse by being married to someone to whom he does not feel close, someone of whom he is frightened. So here, at the beginning of the story, is Gomov, not perhaps in serious difficulties, but in difficulties nonetheless. He has characteristics about which I feel uneasy, for instance the way in which he talks cynically about women. But in my identifying self, I can take on these characteristics, and for this story can also take on his purposes.

How do you feel about Gomov? Do you identify with him? Or do you, rather, distance yourself from him, and feel disapproving of his affairs, feel contemptuous of him being a roué?[11]

In Part II, I come to understand more of Anna. She has married young, because she wanted to get away from her family; she thought that surely "there is another kind of life." But, married, she discovers that although her husband may be a good man, she does not respect him. And, without quite knowing how, because she felt vaguely ill or just wanted to get away from him for a while, to be on her own, she came to Yalta, and has walked around "dizzily, like a lunatic." Now she has done this thing, had sex with a man she scarcely knows, made herself into "a wicked, low woman."

I find it easy to identify with Anna. She is attracted to a man who seems sympathetic and, for whatever reason, she wants to feel close to him. But in the first really strong emotions of the story, after she and Gomov have made love for the first time, Anna feels terrible; guilty, ashamed: not that she has betrayed her husband, but herself. I have a sufficient store of experi-ences of feeling guilty and ashamed that I empathize with her. Should she have kept her distance? Is she being taken advantage of, cynically, by a seducing man who wants what men want: sex?

My identification with Gomov comes under strain. In genre romance novels, there is nothing wrong with the male hero. Usually he is of the right age and a widower. Gomov is neither of these things. Worse than that, when Anna has her outburst of self-loathing, despite having recently been very close to her, Gomov is bored and irritated. She is having an affair – he thinks – what does she expect? He wants to spend his time with her pleas-antly, not with her making scenes. He cuts himself a slice of melon. He waits for her to calm down. Here, I think, something important happens in the story. I have identified with Gomov, and I continue to be so, but as that continues, because of him starting to behave badly, I am forced to look into myself –because I have gone along with Gomov. Am I, too, bored and irritated by Anna's despair; would I prefer to read more about the affair? Because I have gone along with Gomov, my conception of myself changes. I am capable of this too: selfishness, lack of sympathy. It's different from the way I like to think of myself.

Then, Anna and Gomov feel close, and continue to feel close.

If we identify with the protagonists, and take on their goals, who is the antagonist? In this story, I think, the antagonist is something like society, the arrangements of which, without our being able to think about them properly, seem to maneuver us into situations that, if we were able to understood them better, we might not choose.

Or perhaps that's not the right way to put it. Perhaps it's better to think that, particularly when we are young, we can become drawn to a person in a sexual relationship, which seems right at the time. Then without knowing how it happens, a relationship willingly entered into becomes a commit-ment, the commitment becomes a constraint, the constraint becomes a prison. Perhaps it's this hidden sequence –from sexual attraction to prison – that is the antagonist.

Gomov's wife and Anna's husband are antagonists of sort, but only in a shadowy way. They do little to thwart the protagonists, who have married people for whom they found it hard to maintain ongoing affection. Their marriages now prevent them by means of perfectly good, respectable, decent barriers, to attain the intimacy between them into which they feel drawn.

What about you in the scene after Anna and Gomov have made love? If your primary identification is with Anna, what do you make of Gomov's self-absorption, his failure to realize what a step she has taken?

In the early morning, after they made love for the first time, Gomov and Anna walk out to the town quay, and take a cab to Oreanda.

At Oreanda they sat on a bench, not far from the church, looked down at the sea and were silent. Yalta was hardly visible through the morning mist. The tops of the hills were shrouded in motionless white clouds. The leaves of the trees never stirred, the cicadas trilled, and the monotonous dull sound of the sea, coming up from below, spoke of the rest, the eternal sleep awaiting us. So the sea roared when there was neither Yalta nor Oreanda, and so it roars and will roar, dully, indifferently when we shall be no more.

This is one of the most moving passages I know in prose literature. Others agree. It's the scene with which Janet Malcolm starts the book of her pilgrimage to Russia to visit the places in which Chekhov lived and wrote.

I can imagine sitting on that bench, imagine sitting next to someone of whom I am becoming fond, imagine the tumult in Anna's heart, imagine Gomov's somewhat pathetic attempt to stem the sense of futility in his heart, to find the sense of intimacy and purpose which he has lacked in his life. And however important, however significant these or any other human matters may be, the waves of the sea will continue to break on the beach. The effect is moving, I think, because it is the perfect metonym. The monotonous dull sound of the sea, which I have heard many times, expands – part for whole – to the indifference of the natural world to our human concerns. It's an indifference that will include our own death, as our consciousness sinks into mere waves and particles of matter. What makes this scene seem, to me, especially moving is that in it Chekhov has found such right words that I can take wholeheartedly into my mind not just the situation, the couple, the bench, the sea below, but the very words themselves The effect is like a poem, in which the poet has found exactly the right words for some particular thought or feeling. It is what John Keats wrote, in his description of what poetry should be, when inwardness and expression meet, "almost a Remembrance."

In Part III the story moves to Moscow, and I receive some more insight into Gomov's character: character in the manner of a nineteenth-century novel. He likes Moscow. He likes the first snowfall. He reads three newspapers a day while saying that he does not read the newspapers as a matter of principle. He likes famous people visiting his house, he enjoys the round of dinner parties, he plays cards with a professor at the university club. I get the sense that he has been invigorated by his affair and, both externally and internally, he is in a state of wellbeing. He expects the memories of Anna to ebb pleasantly, as memories of this kind have ebbed in the past.

Now suddenly, the nineteenth-century fictional character fades and suddenly I enter Gomov's inner life, almost as if Virginia Woolf were depicting it. I read that Gomov would shut his eyes and see Anna looking at him from the corner of a room. I read that "she seemed handsomer, tenderer, younger than in reality; and he seemed to himself better than he had been at Yalta." I read that he would look at women in the street to see if they were her. I read that he is filled with intense longing. He wants to confide in someone, but there isn't anyone. The round of parties and socializing in which he takes part seems barbarous. He suddenly finds himself planning a journey to S., to the town where Anna lives. He does go there. He does succeed in meeting her.

I can remember occasions on which I was filled with this kind of longing for someone. On one occasion I was in my late teens, on holiday with my parents, at a place I liked, but I found it repulsive. All I wanted to do was to be with that certain person. Then, on another occasion, older now, in my thirties, I was in Canada and my wife's father died. My wife went back to England to attend the funeral, and to be with her mother. I could not go because of my work. I could think of nothing but being with her, and was visited by compulsive thoughts. Chekhov helps me to articulate those experiences.

What do you think of Gomov's longing?

In Part IV, Anna has started to visit Moscow, supposedly to visit a specialist in women's medical conditions. Now comes another startling and defamiliarizing passage, about Gomov's inner experience:

And by a strange conspiracy of circumstances, everything that was to him important, interesting, vital, everything that enabled him to be sincere and denied self deception and was the very core of his being, must dwell hidden away from others, and everything that made him false, a mere shape in which he hid himself in order to conceal the truth, as for instance his work in the bank, arguments at the club, his favorite gibe about women, going to parties with his wife – all this was open.

What a terrible rift within the self. What a terrible yearning. What an irony that the man who had conducted affairs that he had regarded lightly – in which he perhaps had left women heartbroken – is now himself completely overwhelmed. What do you think?

Now occurs something to make the situation worse: the passing of time. The antagonists – current commitments, convention, society – do not remit. As one is swept up in a passion of this kind, one does not see oneself properly. But Chekhov lets us know.

His hair was already going grey. And it seemed strange to him that in the last few years he should have got so old and ugly. Her shoulders were warm and trembled to his touch. He was suddenly filled with pity for her life, still so warm and beautiful, but probably beginning to fade and wither, like his own. Why should she love him so much?

Just as the sea at Oreanda had sounded monotonously, time was passing in that same impersonal way. We are not far now from the story's moving final sentence.

> And it seemed that but a little while and the solution would be found and there would begin a lovely new life; and to both of them it was clear that the end was still very far off, and that their hardest and most difficult period was only just beginning.

What do you think?

In a conversation or reading group one starts to see the variety of interpretations. But conversation is intimate. In one's identifications one discovers aspects of oneself, and confides in oneself. A novel or short story can also be a step to intimacy in one's conversations, rather as when two people confide, or when a patient recounts a dream in psychoanalytic therapy.

From conversation to conversation

It seems likely that fiction grew out of conversation – that very human cultivator of our relationships and of the models we hold about others – out of stories about what the teller had done and about exploits of people the hearers knew. In time such stories became carefully created narratives about the possibilities, the vicissitudes, and the emotions, of being human. In time, conversation became dialogue, one of the most characteristic contents of fiction. In this final chapter, we have returned to conversation, about the fictions – waking dreams of the imagination – that can become objects of shared attention, and joint participation, in our relationships.

Endnotes

Chapter 1

1. I have done a bit of mild research on William Shakespeare's use of the word "dream" and its variants in the Open Source Shakespeare Concordance. According to this source Shakespeare used the word "dream" 125 times in his plays and poems, the word "dreams" 46 times, and variants which include "dreaming," "dreamer," and "dreamt," 48 times. The first instance in the chronological series of plays that I can find in which "dream" is used to mean an alternative view of reality is when Valentine, one of the protagonists of *Two gentlemen of Verona* (thought to have been written between 1592 and 1593) says in an aside: "How like a dream is this I see and hear!/Love lend me patience to forbear awhile"(5, 4, 2175).

   All my references to Shakespeare are from Open Source Shakespeare, which gives his complete works, accessible at http://www.opensourceshakespeare.org. In the plays, lines are numbered from the beginning, rather than by act and scene.

2. Just as Virginia Woolf (1924) was exaggerating a bit when she said, in a phrase to which my sentence alludes, that character changed in 1910, so I may be exaggerating when I say that Shakespeare's idea of plays as models of the world came to him suddenly in 1594. Patrick Hogan has suggested to me that Shakespeare developed his idea more gradually.

   It is widely inferred that Shakespeare joined a travelling theater company as an apprentice actor and arrived with the company in London in the late 1580s. His first plays, written around 1590, perhaps in collaboration, were the three *Henry VI* histories, which were a success. Stephen Greenblatt (2004) brings what is known of Shakespeare's life close to the immense scholarship on

Such Stuff as Dreams: The Psychology of Fiction, First Edition. K. Oatley.
© 2011 K. Oatley. Published 2011 by John Wiley & Sons, Ltd.

Shakespeare's writing, to consider factors in his apprenticeship as a writer during the years before 1594. His training as an actor seems to have struck the young Shakespeare with the potentialities of the idea that on the stage an actor could give up his selfhood and become another distinct person (a character).

3. Some of Shakespeare's early plays seem very different from those that came later. Although Shakespeare is thought of as "for all time," *The taming of the shrew* seems now to be dated sexism, and *Titus Andronicus* a horror-play.

4. In *A midsummer night's dream*, Bottom says of the alternative world in which he was turned into an ass, and then loved by Titania: "I have had a dream, past the wit of man to say what dream it was: man is but an ass" (4, 1, 1767).

5. Paul Ricoeur (1977) has called fiction and metaphor models for the re-description of the world.

6. The meter of everyday English is typically trochaic, with the stress on the beginning of most words that have more than one syllable. So in English one says coff-ee, as compared with the French caf-é. In the sonnet that starts *Romeo and Juliet*, Shakespeare is careful to arrange most of the disyllabic words in the sonnet so that the stress falls in the accustomed place, but a reversal of the typical trochaic stress pattern of English comes with "bury" in line 8, in which (in an unaccustomed way) the meter prompts the stress on the second syllable.

   As Stephen Greenblatt (1980) has shown, Shakespeare probably learned the potentialities of iambic verse from seeing Christopher Marlowe's *Tamburlaine* (1587) when he arrived in London.

   The difference of iambic meter from ordinary English diction offers what Viktor Shklovsky (1917) calls defamiliarization: making language slightly strange. (I discuss defamilarization further in Chapter 3.)

7. Frank Kermode (2000) describes Shakespeare's use of "shadow" and "substance." With the Elizabethan meaning of shadow as reflection in a mirror, in *Measure of Measure* Shakespeare writes the line, "His glassy essence, like an angry ape" (2, 2, 875) to mean externally observable character. The idea of mirror also carries the connotation of that by which we can see ourselves.

8. It is often said that lyric poetry and prose fiction are very different but, as Patrick Hogan (2003) has shown, one can think of a lyric poem, such as a sonnet, as depicting a turning point in narrative in which an emotion, at the center, is projected into a metaphorical plane, where it can be explored intently. I shall therefore treat pieces of lyric poetry such as Shakespeare's Sonnet 27 as fiction.

   The turning points in a sonnet can embody the notion that Aristotle described in *Poetics* as *peripeteia*: "a shift of what is being undertaken to the opposite . . . in accordance with probability or necessity" (pp. 35–36). This can be a change of circumstance, understanding, or character, to something far different than the initial state.

Bill Benzon (2006) has argued that works of literature have structures that are potentially shared among all readers, and that perhaps are resonant with patternings of the brain. In an exchange with him on this topic, I suggested that the sonnet may have the following structure: 8 lines + 4 lines + 2 lines. Not only is this interestingly formal, it lends itself to both narrative and reflection. There is an exposition in the octave (long enough to be complete), a transformation (half its length because the exposition has established the essentials), and a conclusion (half the length of the transformation because it becomes an abstraction or generalization).

9. The idea of "*zealous*" in Sonnet 27, having the word "jealous" hiding behind it is Helen Vendler's (1997). Her commentary on Shakespeare's *Sonnets* is invaluable.

10. Turning points are important in fiction, and in the modern short story there is again the idea of a turning point. Frank O'Connor (1963) has argued that the modern short story (as opposed to tales and yarns) emerged only in the middle of the nineteenth century, with writers such as Nicolai Gogol and Ivan Turgenev.

11. The argument that fiction is about what is possible for us human beings, rather than merely about what has happened, was made by Aristotle in *Poetics*.

12. In his excellent introduction to the psychology of fiction, Jerome Bruner (1986) says: "We know precious little about the reader-in-the-text as a psychological process." Since then we have come to know more, and here I introduce some of what we now know about the reader-in-the-text, along with what we know about the writer-in-the-text. In this book Bruner points out that narrative is a distinct mode of thought and feeling about human intentions and the vicissitudes that these intentions meet.

Another important book on the psychology of fiction is Richard Gerrig's (1993). In it, he introduces an idea that is, perhaps, not very different from the idea of dream on which I focus here. Gerrig's term is transportation. Narrative, he says, transports us into a narrative world, in which we can become absorbed. Transported in this way, we experience distinctive states of attention, imagery, and emotion. In the vehicle of narrative, we travel some distance from our ordinary world, and leave behind some of its aspects. When we return, we may find we have been changed by our journey. I discuss Gerrig's idea of transportation further in Chapter 7.

13. Years after he had written "The art of fiction" (1884) in which he said a novel is a direct impression of life, Henry James came to agree more closely with Robert Louis Stevenson, and wrote "Life being all inclusion and confusion, and art being all discrimination and selection . . . life has no direct sense whatever for the subject and is capable, luckily for us, of nothing but splendid waste. Hence the opportunity for the sublime economy of art, which rescues, which saves, and hoards and "banks," investing and reinvesting these fruits of toil in

wondrous useful "works" and thus making up for us, desperate spendthrifts that we all naturally are, the most princely of incomes" (James, 1907).

14. I discuss Sigmund Freud's (1908) idea of fiction as derived from day-dreaming in Chapter 2. In terms of reader-response, psychoanalytic ideas of dream and phantasy have become influential; see for instance, Norman Holland's fine books of 1968 and 1975. Such ideas have also been influential in critical analysis of film; see for example Christian Metz (1982). I accept some of these ideas, but my psychological approach is based largely on theories and evidence from cognitive psychology and neuroscience.

15. *A midsummer night's dream* also includes a play-within-the-play, a model within the model.

16. We can say, I think, that, in Shakespeare's plays and poetry, the world-imitating aspect and the world-simulating aspect of *mimesis* correspond, respectively, to shadow and substance. Tony Nuttall (1983) has written persuasively that among Shakespeare's achievements was imitative representation of inner worlds.

17. I use the idea of "to make strange," which enables a reader or hearer to see something vividly. This is Viktor Shklovsky's (1917) idea, and I discuss it in more detail in Chapter 3.

18. Some years ago, members of the research group of Les Greenberg (a distinguished researcher on emotions in psychotherapy) and members of my psychology-of-fiction research group got together over a series of meetings to view and discuss video recordings from psychotherapeutic sessions, to see what value narrative analysis might have. One client I remember was very angry at a parent. Over many sessions, she was angry, angry, angry, and then angry, angry, angry – full of blame – until in one session came sadness, as she recognized her own involvement in the matters she was so angry about.

19. Robert Weimann (1985) has suggested that *Hamlet* can be read almost as a treatise on theatrical *mimesis*, with everyone giving performances and being spectators. Thus the ghost comes dramatically from another world and everyone is attentive, Claudius acts as if he is the legitimate successor to the old Hamlet, Hamlet acts as if he is mad, Polonius arranges for Hamlet to be observed as by an audience, and the play within the play as intended by Hamlet to display the truth amid the obfuscations of Claudius in order to test him publicly, and to let him see himself in the mirror of the play.

In *As you like it*, Shakespeare signals the model-making nature of theater by a change of scene from the court to a parallel world, the Forest of Arden. So, within the model (which is the play) there is embedded another model world (the Forest of Arden) in which Rosalind, dressed as a man, can speak about love to the man she loves in a way that convention usually forbids. In *Othello*, the idea is explored for its potential for social evil. Again the model world is signaled by a move: from Venice to Cyprus. What happens in Cyprus can be thought of as a different kind of play-within-a-play, one in which Othello is enjoined by Iago's directorial prompts to believe Desdemona is unfaithful.

20. Some have seen the speech by Prospero, which contains the phrase that is the title of this book, as a kind of apology for European colonialism. Among the things that Prospero says is "... the great globe itself/ Yea, all which it inherit, shall dissolve," But the world of colonialism did not dissolve. It had to be overthrown, and many of its substantive effects continue.

21. The German literary theorist August Wilhelm Schlegel (1849) wrote this: "theatrical as well as every other poetical illusion is a waking dream, to which we voluntarily surrender ourselves" (p. 246). The writer whom I regard as the greatest English novelist, George Eliot, also uses the idea. In a famous passage that begins Chapter 20 of *Middlemarch*, in which Dorothea beset by a procession of images of Rome, where she is on honeymoon, is seen weeping in confusion at what she has done in marrying the desiccated Mr Casaubon, we read: "But this stupendous fragmentariness [of the images] heightened the dreamlike strangeness of her bridal life."

22. An example of an extended allegory of religious and moral symbolism is *The Faerie Queene*: a long poem by Edmund Spenser (1596) about the Virtues, starting with Holiness in which St George slays the dragon. A word used in the King James Bible for allegory is "similitude." John Bunyan (1678) gives "Hosea, xii. 10. *I have used similitude*" as an epigraph to *The Pilgrim's progress*; a few words into the start of which we read: "As I slept I dreamed a dream ... I saw a man clothed in rags ... a book in his hand, and a great burden on his back."

23. I used the idea of simulation in my 1992 book *Best laid schemes*. As I explained there, the idea was suggested to me by Simon Garrod, who read a draft chapter of that book in which I was struggling to explain fictional narrative in terms such as depiction. Garrod said, "Why don't you use simulation?" I immediately, and gratefully, saw that this was the concept I needed. For a cognitive psychologist brought up through artificial intelligence, simulation was just right. I had not, at that time, connected the idea to that of simulation in theory-of-mind. Simulation in the theory-of-mind sense, as used for instance by Paul Harris (2000), has become influential, and this sense of simulation has, as it were, been taken. It was therefore suggested to me at a talk I gave that I should use the idea of emulation. But the concept of emulation has also been taken, by Josep Call and Michael Tomasello (1995) as a method of learning by a kind of imitation, and their idea (constructing an action on a different piece of hardware than the original one), is not what I want. So I shall stick with simulation.

The idea of simulation as I use it is also related to its use in philosophy of mind by Alvin Goldman, in cognitive psychology by Lawrence Barsalou (2008), and in story comprehension by Rolf Zwaan (2008).

24. My approach to reading and watching fiction as an enactment, although based on different considerations, is comparable to that of Wolfgang Iser (1974) and Norman Holland (1975).

25. Some art, of course, is politically engaged, and in general art might be thought of as embodying a political idea-in-the-large of understanding what it is to be human. But there is a difference between art (which is exploratory and offers a certain openness to the reader's or viewer's experience) and propaganda (which seeks to direct the minds of readers and viewers towards a predetermined end).

26. The experiments in which participants observed or read phrases relating to foot, hand, or mouth actions, while fMRI recordings were being made, was by Lisa Aziz-Zadeh *et al.* (2006).

27. The work-around using transcranial magnetic stimulation was by Giovanni Buccino *et al.* (2005).

28. Arthur Glenberg *et al.* (2008) found activations of pre-motor areas both as people read sentences about physical transfer of something away from the person, for instance "You give the papers to Marco," and also about abstract transfer for instance, "You delegate the responsibilities to Anna." These effects did not occur when transfers were in a direction towards the subject.

29. The regions of the core network include the medial aspects of the prefrontal, temporal and parietal lobes, the temporoparietal junction, as well as parts of the lateral prefrontal, temporal, and occipital cortices; see, for instance, Raymond Mar (2011) and Jennifer Summerfield, Demis Hassabis, and Eleanor Maguire (2010).

Chapter 2

1. Children's play and a play at the theater use the same word. In addition, fiction in England, which reached a summit in Shakespeare's plays, derived from plays staged on carts in the towns of medieval England, sponsored by the guilds, and drawing on both Biblical and populist sources.

2. In the quotation from Aristotle's *Poetics* on childhood origins of *mimesis,* I use the Greek term as it occurs four times in these lines. Gerald Else translates these four occurrences, respectively, as "imitating, imitative, imitation, imitation," but if we take heed of the double meaning of *mimesis,* this practice by Else and other translators diminishes the text. This is a systematic effect throughout the whole of Aristotle's *Poetics,* and it occurs throughout all the English translations of it that I have seen.

3. Emily Wyman *et al.* (2009) have shown that by the age of three children can keep the pretend-identity of an object, for instance a yellow elongated plastic block as a toothbrush in one pretend scenario separate from that of the same

object in a different pretend scenario in which it might, for instance, be a spoon.

4. In a way that is comparable to the one discussed by Sigmund Freud in his 1908 paper on creative writing and day dreaming, movies have come to be seen as dreams which are more logically connected than night-time dreams but which, in their enjoyable way, serve many of the same functions as day dreams, see e.g. Norman Holland (1968) and (2009).

5. A recent argument that art is an evolutionary adaptation is by Dennis Dutton (2009) for whom art's adaptive value includes acquisition of skills, creativity, making special, and imagining make-believe worlds, which contributed to our ancestors' fitness for survival. Dutton says that the ability to imagine states that do not exist has been very important for humankind. He infers, by reverse engineering, that stories provide three important features: valuable experience but without danger, sources of didactic information, and exploration of points-of-view of other minds.

6. It is thought that reptiles – a class of animals from which mammals have descended but which are not themselves very social – do not play at all. Julia Vettin and Dietmar Todt (2005) have shown close correspondences between human laughter and the play-sounds of macaques and chimpanzees during rough-and-tumble play, and tickling. Jaak Panksepp (2005) has described how laughing emerges naturally in babies, and is carried on as children play such games as chase, with the one being chased laughing more than the one doing the chasing. He reports that rats emit chirping sounds when they play and that, when humans tickle them so that they emit these sounds, the rats become bonded to these particular humans. He reports, too, that the sub-cortical brain systems activated during playful rat-chirping are the same as those activated in humans when they laugh. Panksepp's research has shown that social play is the very paradigm of enjoyment.

7. The division of play into three kinds is by Peter Smith (2005); symbolic play also involves play that includes roles, which I treat in a later section.

8. Jaak Panksepp (1998) has also shown that in animals the brain area that sub-serves play is different from the one that subserves exploration. We have to assume, I think, that in humans play and exploration become easily connected.

9. Jordan Peterson (1999) has pointed out that mythological stories often concern the balance between the known (that for which we have skills) and the unknown (which affords threats as well as opportunities). Though any particular society depends on its current skills and practices, the meta-problem of how societies are formed and develop generally seems to depend on our ability to play and explore, including our ability to create and understand stories. Thus the hero – a figure who can act as a model, and who recurs in the world's stories (someone like the Buddha or like Hercules) – is a fictionalized member of

society from before the time of living memory, who is an amalgam of practices that have been invented that include (recursively) the practice of exploratory invention. The human ability to form societies, each with its own culture, depends on *mimesis* in its most common meaning of imitation (which can include instruction). Imitation occurs in play, in the elaboration of the beliefs and skills which are nerves and sinews of any society, and also in the practices of exploration which include art.

10. An important article on pretend play and its relation to theory-of-mind was by Alan Leslie (1987).

11. An influential book on the philosophy of the arts is by Kendall Walton (1990) who argues that fiction is make-believe. If in a novel or at the cinema we are moved emotionally, he says the emotions we feel are pseudo-emotions, of the kind that children feel when they are playing. So, if we go to the cinema to watch a thriller and feel frightened, this is not real fear. If it were, we would run outside, because real fear has an outcome: a strong urge to escape. Instead we stay in our seats. In general, says Walton, the emotions we feel in fiction are not merely make-believe, they are only make-believe.

I think Walton has this exactly the wrong way round. Developmentally, as Harris (2000) has proposed, culture (including language, science, the arts) and abstraction grows from play and from the imagination. Walton offers an anti-developmental theory so that adult art, instead being a set of abstractions of increasing power and relevance, is regression to a supposed childhood state. Walton seems to have argued himself into a position that is opposed to abstraction. He defines emotion as having a certain kind of behavioral outcome. He then takes his own definition literally. Then he maintains: "I can't have been frightened by the thriller because I didn't run out of the cinema."

Walton's argument is a version of an ancient ambivalence (fascination plus scorn) towards poetry, that was expressed by Plato, who offered, in *The republic* books 2 – 3, and book 10, the first extended discussions of the concept of *mimesis*. Plato said that we need to remind ourselves that poetry is "childish" (608a). Although this is the center of what Walton later argued, it is surprising that he does not mention Plato. Nor does he mention Freud (1908) who also thought that fiction had aspects of regression to childhood play.

12. Literacy involves, of course, learning to read and, according to Stanislas Dehaene (2009) this in turn has involved neural mechanisms adapted to recognizing such features of the natural world as edges and corners to be put into service for recognizing letters, syllables, and hence words. From this recognition process, reading involves forming brain networks that connect to separate processes responsible for identifying sounds and identifying meanings.

13. Another explanation along lines similar to those of Paul Harris (2000) is by David Olson and me (2010). We argue that the question asked by Aleksandr Luria about the colour of the bears in Novaya Zemlya was in the genre of nar-

rative, whereas the answer that was expected was in the genre of logic. People are generally familiar with narrative, but it needs education to be inducted into logic, where one entertains possibilities on the basis of mere words.

14. There is, of course, nothing wrong with living in the here-and-now. For some it has become an ideal. A group in Amazonia, the Pirahã, have been described by Daniel Everett (2005) as living entirely in this way. Peter Gordon (2004) has found their system of counting is simply: one – two – many. Their story-creating skills are also undeveloped. The modern world, however, does require abstract thought, including arithmetical and narrative skills.

15. Many people have thought that fiction enables us to have many experiences in quick order. Lynn Hunt (2007) cites Denis Diderot as writing "In the space of a few hours I went through a great number of situations which the longest life can hardly offer across its entire duration" (pp. 55–56), as a result of reading a novel by Samuel Richardson.

16. Roman Jakobson (1956) pointed out that when brain damage affects speech, usually either the selection function or the combination function is affected, but less frequently both. A person with damage in one part of the brain makes mistakes in selecting words, while one with damage in a different part makes mistakes with combinations, with words for which parts go with which. You see something comparable, says Jakobson, in a test that is sometimes given to children. You can ask the child: what do you think of next when the word "hut" is said. One kind of response is based on selection (the metaphorical function), so that (says Jakobson) the child might say "cabin" or "palace." In the other kind of response based on combination (or the metonymic function), the child might mention associated features such as "thatch," or "poverty."

17. In a conversation, David Lodge told me that when he read the passage in which Roman Jakobson (1956) described the metaphoric and metonymic poles, it was a revelation. In 1977 he wrote a scholarly book about the distinction, and he based his novel *Nice work* (1988) on it. In the novel, the metaphoric is university-as-factory, and the metonymic is based on a university lecturer juxtaposed – in some parts of the novel very closely – with a factory owner. I have more to say on metonym in Chapter 5.

18. If someone explains how, for instance, a sewing machine works, one understands it by making a mental model of it. Perhaps this involves looking at a sewing machine, perhaps making diagrams, perhaps thinking of possible explanations, perhaps by discussing it with someone else, until one's model embodies the principles. This process was studied by Naomi Miyake (1986).

19. Only details of a small patch, about twice the diameter of one's thumbnail at arm's length at the point at which our eyes fixate, are available in high resolution to the visual system. About 50% of the optic nerve and 50% of the visual cortex are devoted to information from this patch. Everything else is available only at very low resolution. Vision thus is model-construction of a world of

objects arrayed in three dimensions, made by the visual system from a succession of fixations of small two-dimensional patches. If, between fixations, a large change is made in the visual field to one side of the fixation point, it is not noticed.

20. It was reading Kenneth Craik's (1943) book on mental models that suddenly enabled me, when I was an undergraduate, to make sense of psychology which, before then, had seemed a jumble of unrelated material. The theory of mental models has been the basis for the most important current approach to understanding thinking, by Phil Johnson-Laird, see his 1983 and 2007 books.

21. Cognitive psychologists such as Sam Glucksberg (2003) have conducted a good deal of research on how metaphors work in language.

22. In an extension of the work of George Lakoff and Mark Johnson(1980), Raymond Gibbs (1994) has proposed that processes that used to be considered figurative, such as metaphor and metonym, enter our mental lives in ways that are not merely ornamental. The very functions of the human mind, the way it works in everyday thinking and in its most impressive achievements is imaginative, and hence deeply poetic.

23. Patrick Hogan (2002) has argued persuasively that there are problems with Lakoff and Johnson's account of meaning-by-metaphor. He points out that "Smith's car is white" is intended to evoke a different domain of meaning than "The suspect is white." He compares this with an example discussed by George Lakoff and Mark Turner (1989) of a surgeon who comes out of an operating theater and says "We lost him." To understand this, according to their analysis, we map from the source domain of losing to the target domain of what happened in the operating theater. But, says Hogan, the source domain of losing does not help because its commonest experiential meanings are: losing something because it was mislaid or stolen, losing in a game, losing one's way, losing someone in a crowd, losing ten pounds on a diet. None of these accomplishes the task of understanding what happened in the operating theater. What happened was that the patient died. Instead (as with the white car and the white suspect) the speaker has a certain intention, and the hearer must search the range of meanings of losing to discover it.

24. The fMRI study on whether phrases such as "bite the bullet" activate areas of the brain associated with biting was by Lisa Aziz-Zadeh *et al.* (2006). Aziz-Zadeh and Antonio Damasio (2008) write that once a metaphor becomes conventionalized it no longer activates the brain's motor system. So let me see if I can make up a couple of sentences: "I'm going to hit the road," means "I'm going to leave." It does not invite cross-domain mapping. It is a figure of speech but not a figure of thought. It means "I'm going to leave," in much the same way as "I'm going to leave" means "I'm going to leave." One would not predict effects in any motor area involved with hitting, though one would predict activation of an area concerned with leaving a room. By contrast, "I'm going

to hit him with everything I've got," is a figure of speech and a figure of thought. It summons up conflict. If researchers used techniques of the kind employed by Aziz-Zadeh and her colleagues to make the comparison, I would predict that reading this sentence would have an effect comparable to that of watching a video of someone hitting someone else.

25. Gerard Steen (2008) has put the onus of metaphor on whether a speaker or writer intends metaphorical usage (this includes similes, which also map across domains). Working with data-bases of Dutch and English writings and transcriptions, Steen and his colleagues have found that with the most generous definitions of the metaphorical, only 13.5% of all units of language can be classed in this way. Some 99% of all metaphor in academic discourse, news discourse, fiction, and conversation, is conventional; that is to say is processed mentally not as cross-domain mapping but as categorization within a domain, for instance by the same processes of identification of meaning (perhaps like looking up the meanings of words in a mental dictionary) as those used for non-metaphorical terms. The issue, says Steen, is of how deliberate the writer or speaker is in inviting hearers or reader to map between domains. Here is an example that Steen used at a conference talk. If someone says "I've got to defend my thesis next week," Lakoff and Johnson would say this metaphor derives from fighting. But, says Steen, no such implication need exist. To defend means to attend an oral examination and answer questions. By contrast, if someone says "Football is war" this is a metaphor deliberately employed, and would initiate the cross domain mapping between football and intense fighting.

26. Rachel Giora (2007) describes what she calls the standard semantic view of metaphor, that first a literal interpretation is considered and then, if this seems inappropriate, a figurative alternative is considered. Metaphor thereby becomes subject to a special type of alternative processing. Giora explains that this has neurological implications, because literal meanings are thought to be processed quickly in the language regions of the left hemisphere, whereas metaphorical meanings are delayed and also involve the right hemisphere. She concludes that the view that metaphor requires special right hemispheric processing is not supported by the evidence. A concept that better explains the results concerns the unusualness of phrases or sentences, which can apply to literal as well as metaphorical expressions.

What Giora calls her "take-home message" is this:

> Reviewing the results on metaphor processing . . . it seems safe to conclude that metaphor *per se* is not unique. The brain is not sensitive to metaphoricity or literalness as such. Instead, it is sensitive to degrees of meaning salience, remoteness of semantic relationships, open-endedness, transparency of stimuli's meanings, and speakers' intention (regardless of contextual appropriateness) (p. 113).

27. The version of *The epic of Gilgamesh* that I cite is a translation by Andrew George (see the bibliography), but many other versions are available on the internet, e.g. http://www.aina.org/books/eog/eog.pdf

28. Johan Huizinga (1955) argued that culture is a form of play, which grows up alongside childhood play. He assumed an evolutionary basis, and also proposed that play is civilizing. He regards poetry as occurring within the playground of the mind, in a world that the mind creates for it. Erving Goffman (1961) can be seen as picking up where Huizinga left off.

29. Erving Goffman (1961) has insightfully allowed us to see into imaginary worlds such as play, and Goffman (1959) has also shown how the ordinary world depends on presentations of ourselves as if we were actors in the theater.

30. Ed Tan (2008) has offered an argument for why entertainment is enjoyable; he, too, proposes that fiction is based on play.

31. Ludwig Wittgenstein (1953) wrote that one cannot draw a dividing line round the idea of game, and say these activities are in, and those are out. "Can you give the boundary?" asks Wittgenstein, and he answers "No" (para 68). But we can nonetheless use the word "game" successfully. The fact that we can use words even though we can not necessarily define them is important, but one can come close to knowing what a game is by reading Goffman (1961).

32. Among modern commentators, the one who argues most strongly for thinking of characters and authors as friends is Wayne Booth (1988).

    Wendi Gardner and Megan Knowles (2008) investigated what makes people see favorite television characters as real people, and they also investigated how people saw equally familiar, but non-favorite, characters from the same shows. Favorite characters were more real to participants than non-favorites, and the sense of reality seemed to be determined by participants' liking for the characters. In a second study participants saw an image of their favorite or non-favorite character, and had to perform either a well practiced or a novel task. When they performed the well learned task in presence of the image of their favorite character they did better at it than in the presence of the image of a non-favorite character, and when they performed the novel task they did worse. These are exactly the effects of so-called social facilitation and inhibition that social psychologists have demonstrated with real people.

33. Simon Baron-Cohen *et al.* (2001) have argued that autism and Asberger's Syndrome, sufferers from which are neither interested in other people, nor good at understanding them, involve an inability to empathize, and a lack of theory-of-mind.

34. Michael Tomasello and his colleagues (Hermann *et al.*, 2007; Tomasello, 2008; Tomasello and Hermann, 2010) have gathered evidence for the idea that humans are distinguished from chimpanzees not by being more intelligent generally, but by being more socially intelligent: we know we are agents (able

to act in the world), and we know others are agents, too. Chimpanzees don't know this. These researchers call this the human cultural intelligence hypothesis, and argue that human communication is based on shared mutual knowledge.

35. The statistical method that Julie Comay (2008) used to find whether theory-of-mind as such had measurable effects on story-telling skill was hierarchical regression. This method is like plotting (on the y-axis of graphs) the outcome scores of all the participants in a study against each of the factors in turn (on the x-axis) which one thinks might affect the outcome.

   Thus Comay thought that age, language ability, and working memory might affect narrative skill. So, first imagine putting the measure of narrative skill on the y-axis and age on the x-axis of your graph. Then imagine drawing a straight line through average of the data points. This represents the effect of age on narrative skill. It is possible statistically to subtract out that effect. The term most frequently used, which I will also use, is to control for the effect. After one has done this subtraction, one can now look in turn, and subtract out, the contribution of each other variable on one's list. In this way Comay found that theory of mind affected story-telling ability, even when other possible variables (age, language skill, working memory) were controlled for, that is to say subtracted out.

36. Another contributor to early story-telling ability has been found by Gabriel Trionfi and Elaine Reese (2005) who studied five-and-a-half-year-old children. Half of these children had an imaginary friend, and some of these friends derived from fiction. When children who had such a friend were asked to retell a story, they told better stories that contained more descriptors, dialogue, and other story elements, than did children who were without such a friend. This difference occurred even though the vocabularies of children without an imaginary friend were as good as those with such a friend.

37. James Stiller and Robin Dunbar (2007) have found that the number of individuals in a person's innermost circle of friends is predicted by individual differences in their abilities at theory-of-mind. However, the number of people who the person has as frequent social partners is better explained by that person's performance on memory tasks; with the implication that for the frequent partners one needs to make detailed mental models.

38. The theory of imputation, by projecting some of what we know of ourselves onto others is by Raymond Nickerson (1999).

39. Daniel Hutto (2008) argues that many features attributed to theory-of-mind, derive from something simpler: an understanding expressed in folk psychological narratives (in fiction, in conversation, and elsewhere), that people act for reasons. To illustrate, Hutto gives us a little narrative.

   He recounts how he was going on a trip and asked his wife to arrange for his car to be serviced and kept in his local garage while he was away. He gave her the phone number of the garage and, as he says, "she kindly made the booking for me" (p. 18). Then, he says: "On the morning of my flight, she agreed to drive me to Heathrow after I had first dropped off my car at the garage. So, we set off in our separate cars and she took the lead, her trunk laden with my luggage" (p. 18). What happened next was that, instead of taking the turning to the garage as Hutto had expected, Mrs Hutto (may we call her that?) drove straight on. "I was at an utter loss to make any sense of her actions," he says, "even though I had a detailed knowledge of the circumstances as well as her history and character" (p. 19). Although Mrs Hutto had made the appointment for the car, she thought that the phone number that Hutto had given her was "the number of our old garage, in the next village" (p. 20). That was where she was going.

Hutto points out that no existing theory of theory-of-mind could "reliably have generated this explanation" (p. 20). His conclusion is that his wife was acting for a reason, although he did not guess what it was. And so, says Hutto:

> My claim is that our ability to make sense of intentional action in practice . . . rests on our knowing in general which details might be relevant and knowing how and when to make the appropriate adjustments in particular cases. Folk psychological narratives are uniquely well suited to fostering this kind of understanding, because they provide examples of people acting for reasons in appropriately rich settings (p. 35).

40. Among the many essays on Jane Austen's irony is one by Reuben Brower (1963) who concludes: "The triumph of *Pride and prejudice* is a rare one because it is so difficult to balance a purely ironic vision with a credible presentation of a man and woman undergoing a 'serious change of sentiment'" (p. 75).

In this book I generally use the idea of irony in its meaning of what is written being ambiguous and provisional, rather than in the sense that is sometimes discussed in literature as dramatic irony, which is when a reader knows something crucial to a character that the character does not know.

41. Jerome Bruner (2002) has spoken of this quality of the provisional in narrative in terms of subjunctivizing, making conclusions depend on circumstances, as compared with making predictions in the way one does in science.

42. The authorized text of *Pride and prejudice* is published by Oxford University Press, as cited in the bibliography. It can be found on the web at: http://www.gutenberg.org/files/1342/1342.txt

Chapter 3

1. We can take the Romantic era to have begun around 1750 in Continental Europe. Samuel Taylor Coleridge was among those who expounded its theory in England.

2. The best book I know to examine, psychologically, the Romantic idea of inspiration and show how it needs to be modified is by Daniel Perkins (1981).

3. An example of someone who talked about inspiration in her interview for *Paris Review* was Edna O'Brien: "I write in the morning," she said, "because one is nearer to the unconscious, the source of inspiration" (p. 356).

4. The theory that creativity involves stages of Preparation, Unconscious Incubation, Sudden Illumination, and Verification was by Graham Wallas (1926).

5. The philosopher who said that Darwin's idea was the best anyone ever had was Daniel Dennett (1995, p. 21).

6. Harold Gruber and Paul Barrett (1974) have followed, from extensive notebooks kept by Darwin, the steps in his thinking as he approached his theory of evolution. Gruber argues that these steps were similar to those by which each of us, in the course of our own cognitive development, progressed from simpler to more sophisticated theories of how the physical and social world work as discovered by Jean Piaget (see e.g., Piaget and Inhelder, 1969). In their understanding of quantity, for instance, children initially think that "more" means something that is spread out, so that there would be more pennies in a line of them that is longer than those in a line that is shorter. Only via intermediate stages do they reach a theory (understanding) that to know properly which of two sets of things has more in it, you need to count the things.

7. Valentine Cadieux has said to me that she wonders whether Donald Winnicott does not over-estimate the importance of creativity: what about people who are able to live in quiet contentment?

8. Mihaly Csikszentmihalyi used a method called experience sampling to find how people experienced different activities in their lives. One of his first studies using this method (Csikszentmihalyi and Reed Larson, 1984) was of how adolescents spend their time. In other studies Csikszentmihalyi supplemented the method with interviews, and the quotes in the paragraph that follow the point at which this note is inserted are from his 1996 book.

9. Although the task for a writer in science is to be persuasive, and in each work to strive for a single agreed meaning, the business of doing science is embedded in a social network in which everyone knows that conclusions are provisional, and that new evidence and better theories will be offered by others.

10. Joan Peskin, Greg Allen, and Rebecca Wells-Jopling (2010) have shown that instruction on symbolism was effective in enabling high-school students to see symbolic meanings in a fairly difficult poem that they read for the first time, whereas those who had poetry classes but without symbolic instruction were not able to see symbolic meanings in this poem. The students who had the symbolic instruction enjoyed the poem more.

11. The reader response movement is generally seen has having been started by Louise Rosenblatt (1938), with Norman Holland (1968) doing important early

work. A textbook of English influenced by the reader-response movement, quite different from the textbooks of the New Critics, is *Developing response to fiction*, by Robert Protherough (1983).

12. In his book on the psychology of fiction, Richard Gerrig (1993) makes Frederic Bartlett (1932) central, and uses this work to argue that we understand and remember fiction by means of the same cognitive processes that we used to understand and remember events in our lives. The understanding of fiction does not require any process that is special or distinctive. Brian Boyd (2009) also makes Bartlett's work an important element in his argument for how stories have had adaptational value in evolution.

13. A few people have a vastly more accurate memory than normal, but they tend to be disabled by this ability, see the classic in this field: Aleksandr Luria (1968).

14. The term "polysemous" meaning "with many meanings" is used as a descriptor of literary fiction by Jerome Bruner (1986). He says: "The prevailing view is that we must read and interpret in some multiple way if any 'literary' meaning is to be extracted from a text" (p. 5).

15. Kate Chopin's "The dream of an hour," was first published in *Vogue* magazine, and is sometimes called "The story of an hour." It is widely available on the internet, e.g. at http://www.vcu.edu/engweb/webtexts/hour/

16. The method of marking the margin when some significant mental event occurred during reading was invented by Steen Larsen and Uffe Seilman (1988), who asked people to read a story, and to mark the margin wherever memories occurred. I augmented this method by asking people to read a story and, when a memory occurred to write an M in the margin, and when an emotion occurred to write an E. After reading, participants were asked to go back and to note down, in a diary-like fashion, what their memories and emotions had been (see e.g. Oatley, 2002). Note, too, that in terms of the core brain network which, I described at the end of Chapter 1, and which I suggested underlies our ability to start up and maintain a simulation, the psychological process that overlap in this network include autobiographical memories, thoughts of future possibilities, and thoughts that might be understood as being based in one's own preoccupations.

17. The study with Elise Axelrad, on how personal memories enter into retellings of a story, is described in Oatley (2002).

18. The study by Seema Nundy and me, of how readers have different overall emotions when reading Russell Banks's story "Sarah Cole," and different modes of reasoning dependent on what emotion they experienced, is described in Oatley (2004). The differences in reasoning by backward chaining as compared with forward chaining, between readers made sad and readers made angry by the story, were statistically significant.

19. The terms *fabula* and *syuzhet* were introduced by Viktor Shklovsky (1919). Their usual English translations have become, respectively, "story" and "plot"

see Irena Makaryk (1993) in which we find the following, attributed to the Russian Formalist Boris Tomashevsky: "the story consists of a series of narrative motifs in their chronological sequence, whereas the plot represents these same motifs but in the specific order of occurrence to which they are assigned in the text" (p. 632). E. M. Forster (1927) reaches towards this distinction when he says: "'The king died and then the queen died,' is a story. 'The king died, and then the queen died of grief' is a plot" (p. 82).

20. Two principal groups were involved in Russian Formalism: one was the Moscow Linguistic Circle, whose most famous figure was Roman Jakobson, and the other was the OPAYAZ group in St Petersburg, led by Viktor Shklovsky. Willie van Peer has pointed out to me that they did not call themselves formalists (this was a term of abuse). A better term might be functionalists.

21. The terms "event structure" and "discourse structure" were introduced by Bill Brewer and Ed Lichtenstein (1981).

22. Even if, as I assert, the event structure of Shakespeare's plays is the least creative aspect of them, Brian Boyd has pointed out to me that the event structures of many of his adaptations is still brilliant.

23. In *Poetics*, Aristotle proposed that plot should have a beginning, middle, and end. The beginning is an introduction of a setting, characters, and their projects, from which things start. The middle can be thought of as starting with some striking event, vicissitude or complication that disturbs the state of affairs of the beginning, and which will be worked through in the story. The end will be a resolution of some kind. In *Hamlet*, the middle starts with the appearance of the ghost to Hamlet.

24. A good source of the Indic theory of poetics is Abhinavagupta (in his book Locana, translated by Daniel Ingalls *et al.*, 1990). Another theorist, whose work is also translated in Ingalls *et al.*'s book is Anandavardana. The verse discussed by Abhinavagupta, spoken by the young woman when a traveller visits her house, is from p. 98 of Ingalls *et al.*'s book.

25. I like to think of this idea of enactment as related to what Robin Collingwood, (1946) called "re-enactment." To understand history, said Collingwood, we have to re-enact it in ourselves, rather as if we were reading a historical novel. Taking the cue from Collingwood, we might go on to say that reading any novel requires an inner enactment.

26. In *Rhetoric*, Aristotle says that "variation from what is usual makes the language appear more stately . . . It is therefore well to give to everyday speech an unfamiliar air" (Book 3, part 2). Rachel Giora (2007) starts her paper with this quotation, and showed that linguistic metaphor as such requires no special processing in the brain, but is best discussed neurologically in terms of its unusualness (now generally called defamiliarization) together with a feeling of relevance. An implication of this effect was described by Longinus (50 BCE)

who argued that the best of such verbal forms were responsible for the occasional experience of literature as sublime.

In a recent account, Brian Boyd (2009) argues that the creative drawing of attention to a matter of shared relevance is very close to the center of art, to why art has been important in evolution, and to why it is important in culture. An artist makes something that will attract attention (as in defamiliarization). Someone looking at it or reading it pays attention, joining the artist to consider this object. The viewer or reader acquires something that engages his or her interest. The artist gains respect.

27. "Foregrounding" is a term that was used by members of the Prague Linguistic Circle, who took up some of the ideas of the Russian Formalists.

28. There are cultural differences in the effects of foregrounding: Willie van Peer, Frank Hakemulder and Sonia Zyngier (2007) tested, in several countries, a poem which consisted of eight lines of "I love you not" and a ninth line of "I love you notwithstanding." The foregrounding surprise of the ninth line was generally perceived as more beautiful than the first eight lines, but this effect was larger in some countries than in others.

In studies by David Miall and Don Kuiken (1994), by Frank Hakemulder (2004) and by Paul Sopcak (2007), foregrounded passages have been found to be read more slowly, to increase emotional engagement with the text, and sometimes to invoke emotional states immediately.

29. As Lev Vygotsky (1962) has pointed out, mind is not just a container for thoughts. It actually IS the thoughts, which usually have started, outside us, in our social world. They become our own as we internalize them, creatively expand them, and transform them within ourselves.

30. Compelling examples of how the associative processor works in the construction of mental models of others were found by Laurette Larocque and me (2006) in our study of diaries kept by people who had made joint errors, arrangements with someone else that went wrong, for instance this one: "One participant waited for a new colleague in one restaurant, while he sat for over an hour in a different location of the same chain of restaurants waiting for her. Our participant stated that the fact that he had 'stood her up' would be at the back of her mind the next time she had dealings with him. She said this although, by her own account, he had been no more at fault than she" (p. 258).

31. We can think of the intuitive-associative mind as working in the ways outlined by people like Geoffrey Hinton, as a neural network that operates in parallel and learns by changing the strengths of neural connections. For an article that explains this kind of associative process, and how it is affected by damage, see Geoffrey Hinton, D.C. Plaut and Tim Shallice (1993).

Another line of research is by people who work on reasoning, like Keith Stanovich (2004) who have found two kinds of mental processes. One works fast by intuitions and heuristics. The other works sequentially, and slowly. A recent book on how voting is affected unconsciously by intuitive-associative processes of mind, usually addressed by political narratives, is by Drew Westen (2007).

Miriam Faust, Ofra Barak, and Christine Chiarello (2006) have found that when we read words, the most direct meanings are processed fast by the language areas of the left hemisphere, but that then, more remote and unusual associations are made more slowly in the right hemisphere.

32. One way of thinking about Andy Clark's idea of the hybrid mind is that the mind runs on a processor of neurons that work in parallel. In its most basic operations it is associative; one piece of information is associated with another, and on a larger scale, one idea with another. But the same neural mechanisms can also operate sequentially, for instance to construct a model of the visual scene based on coordinating results of successive glances, or plan to do one thing after another. Verbal language is of this second kind, processing one word after another, to construct the meaning of an utterance. Philip Johnson-Laird (2006) has shown that in some ways the sequential processing associated with language is more powerful than associative processing. It can verbalize mental models, so that we can think verbally in such forms as syllogisms, and it can do such operations as recursion, which means that we can make model of models, or as Shakespeare did, embed models within models, plays within plays. Sequential processing enables syntax, which makes use of orderings of words in sentences. In humans, sequential processing has a restriction of working memory to about seven-plus-or-minus-two chunks of information. The experiences that derive from metaphor and cognitive blending seem to require the participation of sequential processing, working with language.

33. This scene of ascending a staircase is from my novel *Therefore choose* (2010), p. 37.

Chapter 4

1. "Character in fiction" was the title of an earlier version of Virginia Woolf's talk, and the 1924 essay from which I quote was retitled: "Mr Bennett and Mrs Brown."

2. In her saying "in or about December 1910 human character changed," Virginia Woolf (1924) was using hyperbole. There is inwardness in the writing of Augustine and Montaigne, in devotional writings and reflective poetry down the ages, and Shakespeare depicted inward soliloquies. Nonetheless Woolf points to a movement towards inwardness that occurred in literary prose fiction from, say, Katharine Mansfield and Gertrude Stein onwards.

3. Since 1993, Robin Dunbar has established what has become known as the social brain hypothesis: that the large expansion of the human brain (as compared

with those of our primates ancestors) occurred because the brain needs to contain models of more individuals, and more complex models of others, in social groups that became larger. It includes his early paper, Leslie Aiello and Dunbar (1993), the review article (Dunbar, 1993), and more recently Dunbar (2003) and (2004).

4. The *Rāmāyana* can be read in the version by David Farr (2007).

5. An exploration of how personality traits stay constant over time is by Paul Costa and Robert McRae (1988).

6. John Coie and Janis Kupersmidt (1983) found that once reputation is formed in a social group, the mental models of others which contain reputation, and the interactions that flow from these models, tend to persist. Their study was of ten-year-old boys who met in groups of four for a play session once a week for six weeks. Each group consisted of a boy who (in his school) was a leader, one who was average, one who was rejected, and one who was neglected. In half the groups the boys were from the same schools and knew each other previously. In the other half of the groups the boys were from different schools and did not know each other. During the first play group sessions all the boys were on their best behavior, and interactions did not predict how the boys would be later. But by the third session, the boys in the groups who did not know each other had established behavior patterns, reputations, and the responses they tended to elicit from other boys, which matched those that they had in the schools from which they came. The groups of boys who knew each other established these patterns, even more quickly, by the second session.

   John Doris (2002) has pointed out, the idea of character and of personality traits as dispositions that are unchanging and global, are unrealistic.

7. Brent Roberts and Daniel Mroczek (2008) have shown that personality does change in adulthood, in some of the kinds of ways depicted in fiction

8. Some authors, notably, Bernard Williams (1993) have argued against the idea that there was anything further to develop in literature beyond Homer. Brian Boyd (2009) gives an account of Homer's *Odysseus* in which he argues that the literary idea of character was already well developed in that work.

9. Patrick Hogan has pointed out to me that it is difficult to say if Dante was really the first to depict character in terms of people making choices in a modern way. One might better say that Dante is a striking representative of a tendency that is rare in earlier works, but became more pronounced and pervasive in the modern period.

10. A generation after Dante came Boccaccio (1353) whose *Decameron* was a set of stories told to each other by people who left Florence to flee the plague. These stories are earthly, indeed earthy: about clumsy cuckolds, merchants on the make, and abbesses looking for a bit on the side. The style is spare, without psychological analysis. The reader is invited, from his or her own experience,

to supply the psychology, and hence the emotions. A generation after Boccaccio came Geoffrey Chaucer (1395) who drew on the *Decameron*, but with softer tone.

11. See Stephen Greenblatt (1980) for an account of how shocking Shakespeare's *Richard III* would have been to audiences when it was first performed.

12. John Jones (1995) more or less catches Shakespeare in the act of turning general descriptions of people into tellingly detailed characters acting in specific ways, for instance, in his depiction of Lincoln, in the collaboratively written play, *Sir Thomas More*.

13. For historians it is important to know what evidence there might be that Cassius once saved Caesar's life as they swam across the River Tiber, and whether it was he who recruited Brutus in the plot to assassinate Caesar. For readers of fiction, it is perhaps more important to consider whether events and emotions of the kind Shakespeare depicts could throw light on what can happen between powerful and determined people.

14. Shakespeare's account of the unconscious comes 300 years before Freud (e.g. in his 1905 case history of Dora). Shakespeare's interest in what hovers on the edge of consciousness is seen in *The tempest*. Prospero and his daughter Miranda were banished, and shipwrecked on a distant island many years previously. Now Prospero asks Miranda to think back to before that time. Is there anything she can remember?

   Miranda. Tis far off And rather like a dream than an assurance That my remembrance warrants. Had I not Four or five women once that tended me?

   Prospero. Thou hadst, and more, Miranda. But how is it That this lives in thy mind? What seest thou else In the dark backward and abysm of time? If thou remember'st aught ere thou camest here (*The tempest*, 1, 2, 138)

15. Brian Boyd has pointed out to me that Shakespeare was not the earliest to delineate character from incidents of emotional significance; for instance in Homer's *Odyssey* we see something of the character of Odysseus in his encounter with the Cyclops. This is so, but it seems to me that Shakespeare makes the idea more explicit, and more general.

16. In a book that has become standard, Robert Scholes, James Phelan and Ronald Kellogg (2006) describe the history of character in narrative, from Homer to Joyce, and they include devices such as monologues that writers have used to depict inwardness.

17. As Ulric Neisser (1963) pointed out, although motivation has been central to psychology, there has been a failure to recognize that human beings typically have many motives. The place to see multiple motives at work is fiction.

18. The best way I know of thinking about becoming a particular kind of person in a particular kind of relationship derives from an idea of Karen Horney (1950). Imagine you have a boss who seeks attention and praise, who is generally accepting of those in an inner circle but is contemptuous to those outside

it. You really need this job. You become skilled at adapting to this person, praising him, keeping on his good side. Now imagine this is your mother.

19. Attachment has become the largest single topic in child social development. There is now a great deal of evidence on it, including on styles of attachment which, as Everett Waters *et al.* (2000) have shown, continue into adulthood to form the bases of later intimate relationships.

20. John Bowlby (1991), founder of attachment theory, has written an excellent biography of Charles Darwin, whose childhood involved a good deal of anxiety about illness, and was marked by his mother's death when Charles was eight. Bowlby writes of Darwin's life both as involving strong and lasting attachments to family and friends, a wonderful creativity, but also a series of anxiety attacks, episodes of depression, and psychosomatic symptoms, so that after he married he rarely left home except to seek cures.

21. This idea of life involving a series of phases, each with its own emotional challenge, is due to the psychoanalyst and biographer Erik Erikson (1959). If a challenge at one phase of life is not met and its lessons assimilated, it tends to reappear in a transformed way in later stages of life.

22. The film, *Three approaches to psychotherapy*, by Everett Shostrom (1966) is extraordinary in the vividness with which Carl Rogers, Albert Ellis, and Fritz Perls present themselves.

23. One fiction writer who has depicted first love and its formative effects is Frank O'Connor in "*My Oedipus complex.*"

24. In 2008 the newspapers reported that a man named as Josef F. kept his daughter in a cellar for years and raped her. It's hard for most of us to empathize with this man. The closest I know in fiction to this situation is in John Fowles's (1963) novel *The collector*.

    David Hume, said that: "a very violent effort is requisite to change our judgment of manners, and excite sentiments of approbation or blame, love or hatred, different from those to which the mind from long custom has been familiarized" (Hume 1965, §33). Hume goes on to say that generally a reader will not pervert his or her usual sentiments for a writer. In his discussion of this passage, Ronald de Sousa (2010) points out that if, while running a simulation of fiction, a reader were completely to abandon his or her attitudes, the point of the simulation would be lost, since then the reader would have lost all basis for his or her own feelings and opinions in the fictional situation. At the same time, as we will see from the discussion of intractable characters in the following section, we do seem to allow ourselves greater latitude in fiction than in ordinary life.

25. The paper in which the study of interviews from *Paris Review*, in which writers described their experience of characters going off in independent directions was by Maja Djikic, Keith Oatley and Jordan Peterson (2008).

26. Earlier in this chapter I described how children translate a mean action by another child into the attribution that the child IS mean. The tendency

continues in adulthood, in which people tend to explain others' behavior in terms of persisting traits of personality, but explain their own behavior in terms of circumstances. This has been described by Lee Ross (1977) as the fundamental attribution bias. The finding that writers discover their characters to be more affected by the circumstances they are in than by the writers' ideas of their personalities is an interesting variation of this attribution bias.

27. David Miall has pointed out to me that when teaching Edgar Allen Poe's tale "The Cask of Amontillado" he has found that perhaps half of the students claim empathy with Montresor, the narrator, who is witty, sardonic and clever, but behaves appallingly. Miall says that fiction often encourages us to suspend judgment of characters who may be very different from us, and can give permission to entertain ideas and feelings that we forbid ourselves in real life.

28. Edward Royzman and Paul Rozin (2006) have shown that we don't find it easy to feel sympathy for someone who is being successful unless we know that person well. We readily sympathize with a person who is in difficulties.

29. Tzvetan Todorov (1977) puts it very nicely: each work of detective fiction is actually based on two stories. One is of the crime being committed; the other is the story of the investigation. In his thoughtful lectures, Timothy Spurgin (2009) draws on Peter Brooks's *Reading for the plot*, to put it in a related way: he points out that we can think of Arthur Conan-Doyle's detective, Sherlock Holmes as an ideal reader. He reads the clues (the *syuzhet*) in order to reconstruct events, including the crime, as they occurred in chronological order (the *fabula*). In *Pride and prejudice*, we have something of this same structure, with the clues of Darcy's behavior in the present coming, in the course of Austen's presentation, to allow both the protagonist (Elizabeth Bennett) and the reader to understand Darcy in terms of the reconstruction of events in his past.

30. Art Graesser, Brent Olde and Bianca Klettke (2002) have argued that narratives always contain features of explanation because readers must understand why characters have acted in the way they did. P.D. James (2009) has made a similar point to the one I am making, in seeing Jane Austen as inventing a certain kind of detective story, though the example she chooses is not *Pride and Prejudice*, but *Emma*. "Here," says James, "the secret which is the mainspring of the action is the unrecognized relationships between the limited number of characters" (p. 6).

Chapter 5

1. The Kuleshov effect, in which the neutral face of an actor is juxtaposed with an emotionally salient object at which the actor is taken to have been looking, has been investigated experimentally by Dean Mobbs *et al.* (2006). They found that pairing an image of a neutral face with contexts of emotional movie clips

changed the way the faces were seen. They also found comparable effects of contexts with neuro-imaging.

2. Yon Barna (1973) says that Eisenstein was a close friend of Kuleshov, and in 1923, at the beginning of his career in film, he studied with Kuleshov for three months.

3. Fiction has been affected by technology. The technology of writing, introduced 5000 years ago, affected it profoundly. Since then, we have moved from entirely oral renditions – in pairs, in informal groups, and when professional story-tellers visited a village or town – to the idea of middle-class women sitting in comfortable armchairs in the English Home Counties, to read the newly published, and beautifully printed *Pride and prejudice*. Since then, the movies have arrived. More recently, the computer has offered video games which, in terms of the economic size of the industry, passed that of the movie industry in 2006. With this technology, the basis of fiction in pretend play, which I described in Chapter 2, has reasserted itself. Pretend play in video games in imagined worlds owes much to printed and filmic fiction.

4. The published version is by Stephan Schwan and Sermin Ildirar (2010).

5. Christine Nothelfer, Jordan DeLong and James Cutting (2009) measured the lengths of shots in digitized Hollywood films over 80 years. Their sample was of one film from each of three genres – drama, comedy, and action – from each of the years 1945, 1965, 1985, and 2005. They found that over the 60-year period the length of shots decreased in all genres from a mean of 13 seconds in the 1945 films, to 6.8 seconds in the 1965 films, to about 4 seconds in the 1985 and 2005 films.

6. The recognition of emotions by facial expressions has become one of the main findings of research on emotions. The most prominent researcher in this area is Paul Ekman (2003) who proposes that some emotional expressions are human universals that can be recognized all round the world, and also that less obvious aspects of facial expression can be picked up by those trained to recognize the movements of facial muscles so that, for instance, lying can be detected in fleeting facial expressions of anxiety. Ekman's ideas have made the unusual jump from the academic literature of psychology to the world of television soap opera in the series *Lie to me*, created by Samuel Baum (2009).

7. Interesting analyses of the emotions of fictional characters have been made for many years, for instance in Shakespeare's characters by A.C. Bradley (1904). It's surprising that analyses of audiences' emotions in Shakespeare has occurred only more recently, e.g. by Samuel L. Johnson (1952). Paying attention to readers' emotions was frowned on by the New Critics, Kurt Wimsatt and Monroe Beardsley (1954) in a famous paper in which they argued that it is a fallacy to confuse a poem, the real object of study, with its effects on the reader.

8. The study that showed that the same area of the brain was involved in both making and recognizing disgust was by Bruno Wicker *et al.* (2003). The area

was the anterior insula. This kind of conclusion is supported, too, by other research.

9. Hanah Chapman *et al.* (2009) found that the facial expression of disgust, which involves contracting the *levator labii* muscles, was made when tasting something bitter and also when being treated unfairly in a game.

10. Paula Niedenthal *et al.* (2009) had participants read concrete words that implied happiness (such as "smile"), disgust (such as "vomit"), anger (such as "fight"), and neutral words (such as "chair"), as electrical activity was recorded in participants' facial muscles. Participants who were asked to judge whether each word was associated with an emotion showed activation of the particular facial muscles that were involved in making the corresponding happy, disgusted, or angry, facial expressions (though not when neutral words were read), whereas participants who were asked to judge whether the word they saw was written in upper case or lower case letters showed no activation of the facial muscles. Preventing participants from making facial expressions by having them hold a pen in their mouths (using teeth and lips) resulted in less accurate judgments of whether the words indicated an emotion, and this suggested that the mirroring has a causal role in understanding emotions. The making of facial expressions as part of recognizing emotions, for which there is now much evidence, is discussed by Lawrence Barsalou (2008) as well as by Niedenthal *et al.* in terms of simulation, and of embodiment. Kathleen Bogart and David Matsumoto (2010), however, have shown recently that people with Moebius syndrome, whose faces are paralyzed, can still recognize facial expressions. The authors suggest that the brain is flexible, so that if one system does not work, there is an alternative method of recognition.

11. Wataru Sato and Sakiko Yoshikawa (2007) performed the study in which they unobtrusively recorded facial expression when people looked at happy or angry expressions. Francesco Foroni and Gün Semin (2009) recorded the activity of facial muscles and found that when readers encountered a verbal description of an emotional expression, such as "smile," they activated facial muscles for the corresponding emotional expression in themselves.

12. The description of empathy as having four parts, is by Frederique de Vignemont and Tania Singer (2006). There is energetic research on mirroring and its relation to empathy, see for instance Marco Iacoboni (2009). A study by Marco Tamietto *et al.* (2009) has, moreover, shown that two patients in whom cortical brain damage prevented them from consciously being able to see displays of faces or emotional actions, still exhibited facial expressions which mirrored the emotions implied by displays they were shown, indicating the existence of a non-cortical (perhaps evolutionarily old) pathway that subserves mirroring and empathy.

13. In the forefront of the argument that empathy is long established in the evolutionary history of primates is Frans de Waal (2004).

14. This quotation from Ludwig Wittgenstein, "We see emotion . . . We do not see facial contortions," is from a citation by Brian Boyd (2009) p. 134. In their apprenticeship, painters take a long time to learn to paint patterns of light and color to depict faces. In the same way, researchers on the anatomy of facial expressions took a long time to discriminate what muscles were used to express each kind of emotion, see for instance Paul Ekman (2003).

15. An article in which I proposed that empathetic recognition allows us to coordinate socially with others is Oatley (2009).

16. There is a substantial difference between the emotional significance of mental models that we build of another's character from observations or reports, and the larger power and significance of actions, or inactions, by another person that have affected us personally, for instance when we feel let down by someone or when we have accomplished some difficult task jointly with another. Evidence of this emotionally salient kind of effect in mental models can be found in the books by Muzafer and Carolyn Sherif (1953), and in studies by Oatley and Laurette Larocque (1995), and Larocque and Oatley (2006).

17. Valentine Cadieux (2008) has said that we choose non-fiction rather deliberately, because its topics are already of great prior interest, so we often feel moved by them. Cadieux suggests that in fiction one can also be moved by matters that were not salient to us beforehand.

18. The idea of emotions as relating events to concerns seems first to have been made by Aristotle, in *Rhetoric*. The form I give here is due to Nico Fridja (1986), and it is further expounded by Keith Oatley, Jennifer Jenkins and Dacher Keltner (2006).

19. In our first study using the method of asking people to mark Ms and Es in the margin of stories as they read them (the PhD thesis of Angela Biason, 1993), out of 59 high-school students who read a 4000-word story of adolescent identity by either Alice Munro or Carson McCullers, only two failed to mark an M or E in the margin (see my paper of 2002). Raymond Mar, Maja Djikic, and I (2011) discuss fresh emotions and emotional memories that occur while reading.

20. Identification in fiction used to be thought to be based on liking, and wanting to be like, a character. A paper by Keith Oatley and Mitra Gholamain (1997) contains a discussion of this. While identification certainly includes liking, I think the idea of identification as empathy (which often involves liking) improves on these older ideas.

21. This taking on of the goals of a character can occur even with a character we detest, as for instance occurs with Shakespeare's Richard III. This is a curious effect; the attraction to such characters seems difficult to understand.

22. The effects found by Tom Trabasso and Jennifer Chung (2004) closely reflect the effects, and the formula, outlined by Freud in his 1908 paper on daydreaming and fiction, which I discussed in Chapter 2.

I don't read German, so I apologize for having only read the abstract and heard the talk of the book by Fritz Breithaupt (2009) in which he argues that empathy often involves a scenario of one person witnessing two others in conflict. This is salient in the films used by Trabasso and Chung, in both of which there is an antagonist whose presence increases our empathy for the protagonist. In such three-person scenarios it is frequent for an empathizer simply to side with one rather than the other contestant. Breithaupt points out that this is a serious limitation of empathy, because it can become no better than siding with us against them. Henri Tajfel (e.g., 1982) showed that even the most trivial differences can induce (empathetic) preference and between-group discrimination. For instance in one of Tajfel's studies participants were told that they were in one group rather than the other by the toss of a coin. Once assigned to a group (their ingroup), participants made choices such as distribution of monetary rewards. They favored members of their ingroup (e.g. those for whom the coin came down as heads) and discriminated against members of their outgroup (e.g. those for whom the coin came down as tails). The minimal conditions needed to induce this kind of effect show that empathy can occur without thought or judgement. Whereas this may be fine for football, it can be disastrous in life.

23. In literary theory, an idea equivalent to "pattern of appraisal" was put by T. S. Eliot (1919) in which he says this:

> The only way of expressing emotion in the form of art is by finding an "objective correlative;" in other words a set of objects, a situation, a chain of events which shall be the formula for that particular emotion; such that when the external facts, which must terminate in sensory experience, are given, the emotion is immediately evoked (pp. 107–108).

> Eliot's idea is that an external pattern of events an "objective correlative" is communicated to the audience member or reader, by "a skillful accumulation of imagined sensory impressions" released by the words, so that there is a "complete adequacy of the external to the emotion" (p. 108). Eliot seems to be saying that the words that indicate the external events allow imagination of the sensory impression, which then causes the internal emotion. Recent psychological evidence, as have discussed in this book, suggests that it would be better to replace the idea of sensory impression by the idea of inner enactment.

24. Perhaps, as the philosopher of film, Nöel Carroll (1990) has argued, once an event that induces fear or anger is presented in a narrative, we long for, and enjoy, narrative closure.

There is not much research on people's expectations in engaging with a work of fiction, or on whether such expectations are fulfilled. One piece of research in our group was by Patricia Steckley and Laurette Larocque (1996) who made contact with people as they were about to rent a video film. Participants completed questionnaires that asked them to record their emotions when they selected a film, and then again after they had finished watching it. Participants avoided renting films that they expected would induce emotions they did not want to experience. Most people did not expect that watching the film they had rented would change their mood but a majority did experience such a change. Subjects' moods matched characters' moods if subjects identified with the circumstances of a character, or with what the character said or did. Enjoyment was based on the story and on the experience of emotions that viewers had expected. This was often enhanced by being shared with a friend or partner.

25. Abhinavagupta's commentary on *rasas* is given in Daniel Ingalls et al. (1990).

26. Elly Konijn (2000) has made a valuable study of the emotions of actors. The idea that the emotions of actors can derive, in the way that Konstantin Stanislavski recommended, from remembered experiences in their own lives, applies principally to rehearsal. During performances, actors' emotions are focussed more on being able to accomplish the performance well, and to make emotional contact with the audience.

27. Gerald Cupchik (2002) discusses the concept of psychical distance based on the proposal by Edward Bullough (1912).

28. Maja Djikic et al. (2009b) have found that people who mentally are heavily defended, and somewhat cut off, had stronger emotions than non-defended people when reading a story. The fiction form was able to circumvent their usual defences.

29. David Miall and Donald Kuiken (2002) also propose that fresh emotions of identification and sympathy occur when reading, alongside the possibility of self-modifying emotions that are drawn principally from memory.

An indication that different genres can prompt emotions in different ways has been found by Michelle Hilscher, Gerald Cupchik and Garry Leonard (2008), who asked people to watch films made in the 1940s or 1950s that were either melodramas or *films noirs*. They found that viewers of melodramas (as compared with *films noirs)* were more able to recognize characters' emotions, were more likely to identify with characters, and were more likely to experience personal memories. Overall, it is likely that different techniques and styles (in prose fiction and film) incline readers and viewers towards different modes of emotional experience.

30. Victor Nell (1988) asked participants to select a book they had not read, but knew they would like, and bring it into the laboratory. There, they had their electro-encephalogram (EEG) recorded while they read their chosen book. Nell found that readers who were engaged in the text entered a state of pleasurable high arousal, somewhat like a trance.

31. This paragraph on moving among a series of emotional states in the course of reading a literary work was prompted by David Miall (2008) who, in turn, relates the idea to aesthetic distance of the text.

32. Let us say that in a prose story, a paragraph is typically one idea, or one observation (the equivalent of a shot in a film), or one utterance of a character. Of course some writers write compound paragraphs that contain several ideas.

In metonymy, I think, three issues are closely related. One is that juxtaposition can produce defamiliarization (of the kind discussed in Chapter 3), which does not just draw attention but which potentially invites emotion. A second issue is that juxtaposition can suggest temporal sequence, contrast (which William Blake, 1793, called "Contraries" without which there is no progression), similarity, and many other kinds of relationship. The third issue, known as synecdoche, is to use just a part of a larger object. The part can be mentioned in a paragraph or put in a film shot, and it can serve as an invitation to imagine the whole of which it is usually part; it invites the reader or viewer to complete a juxtaposition. These three issues can work separately or together.

33. The most beautiful and densely packed metonymic lines I know are from near the end of *Hamlet* when Hamlet is dying. Horatio says:

Now cracks a noble heart. Good night, sweet prince,
And flights of angels sing thee to thy rest (*Hamlet,* 5, 2, 364–365).

In "Now cracks a noble heart," the heart stands for the substance of the whole person (a metonymic figure of synecdoche). "Good night, sweet prince" is another synecdoche, which suggests a sleep, but more importantly (as pointed out to me by Patrick Hogan) it is part of an attachment ritual, and suggests the idea of attachment. In death, attachment is finally severed. "Sings" stands for a whole ceremonial. More important yet, the scene moves us, I think, because the death of this one particular person – albeit an imaginary one – stands for the vulnerability of us all, and so with the second line, "And flights of angels . . ." the words seem unutterably sad, and our consciousness expands to include all humankind, everyone to whom the phrase "Good-night" has ever been said, including ourselves.

34. This letter is in James Baldwin's (1963) *The fire next time.* An inscription in my copy shows it was given to me on my 25th birthday, in 1964. I think I read it at that time. I had received a somewhat sheltered upbringing in England, a rather white England. The passage was defamiliarizing for me in a striking way that I have remembered ever since. The title of Baldwin's book is taken from a verse he gives as an epigraph: "God gave Noah the rainbow sign, / No more water, the fire next time!" This profound and moving metaphor reminds us that unless we human beings become more considerate to each other and of our world, there will be disaster.

35. The idea that gaps in the text prompt the reader's judgement and imagination is discussed by Wolfgang Iser (1974). The extension of the idea to gaps between images is discussed by Scott McCloud (1993).

The juxtaposition of one pattern with another is described by Mark Turner (2008):

> *Conceptual integration,* also called "blending," is a *basic mental operation* that works on *conceptual arrays* to produce *conceptual integration networks.* Certain conceptual arrays provide *inputs* to the network. Selective projection from the input conceptual arrays and from the relations between them carries elements and relations to a *blended conceptual array* that often has *emergent structure* of its own (p. 13).

In double scope blending two arrays may each affect the other. Clashes may occur, from which wholly new properties may emerge. Although Turner discussed double scope blending in relation to metaphor, it seems to me to work better for metonymy.

36. This lovely phrase about readers adding the subjective elements of a story comes from a letter from Anton Chekhov to Aleksei Suvorin of 1 April, 1890; Yarmolinsky, 1973, p. 395).

37. For a while I thought of making a classification of metonymic effects: causality and other kinds of temporal succession, similarity by means of a common higher-level theme (which is close to metaphor), contrast, emotion of one element seeping into another element with which it is juxtaposed, and so on. The most important of these is the first: causality, because in narrative temporal succession is used to represent actions as caused by goals (or reasons), outcomes as caused by actions, emotions as caused by outcomes. Such causal structures in narrative plots have been explained by Tom Trabasso and Paul van den Broek (1985). But I realized that the possibilities of metonymic effects are infinite, because the range of possible associations between one experience and another, for individuals and for groups, is infinite.

    The Surrealists became interested in arbitrary juxtapositions as ways of exploring the unconscious. In their game, Exquisite Cadaver, one person writes a word and folds over the paper so that the next person can't see it, then the next person writes another word, and so on, to create a sentence, for instance within the frame "The *adjective noun verb* the *adjective noun*" which, in an early instance of the game, famously produced "The exquisite cadaver will drink the new wine." This game is related to the childhood game Broken Telephone in which a child whispers something to the next in a row, who whispers it to the next, and so on, until a result quite different from the first message is announced by the last child in the sequence. It is also related to the method of Serial Reproduction used by Frederic Bartlett (1932) as discussed in Chapter 3.

38. Jordan Peterson has discussed with me how, in psychotherapy, patients often have areas of experience that are not connected to each other. Sometimes, by saying something, a therapist can enable them to make a connection.

39. David Lodge (1977) proposes that metonymy is essential to prose fiction and the movies, whereas metaphor seems more native to lyric poetry and theatre. One can see what Lodge means. But perhaps what has occurred with prose fiction and films is that metonymy has now attracted more attention. As one

thinks about it in the way that Roman Jakobson (1956) suggests, the language of prose-writing and film-making requires both selection and combination. This is true from the smaller end of the scale (words and image-parts) to the larger end of the scale (scenes and schemas). At each point in the scale, the poles of language give rise respectively to possibilities of metaphor, and of metonymy.

40. Jaak Panksepp (2005) has made a persuasive case that in mammalian evolution, emotion was the earliest form of consciousness, and remains its core.

41. There is not much psychological work on why we often feel moved to tears by works of art. Ed Tan and Nico Fridja (1999) argue that this occurs when we sense we are in the presence of something bigger than ourselves.

Chapter 6

1. I am grateful to Andrew George for letting me have his translation of this first verse of *The epic of Gilgamesh*. The verse was incomplete at the time of his Penguin translation, in 1999, but fresh evidence has shown its completion.

2. The newspaper magnate Randolph Hearst became famous for having stories for his papers fabricated to suit his political opinions. As Martin Lee and Norman Solomon (1990) put it, Hearst "routinely invented sensational stories, faked interviews, ran phony pictures and distorted real events."

3. Interesting research on readers' construction of scenes has been conducted by Rolf Zwaan (2008).

4. There are hundreds of books and articles on how to write fiction. Some are very good, and some are written by distinguished practitioners. All agree that dialogue is tremendously important. I have sampled a lot of these books. Sol Stein's (1999) is, I think, among the best. (Stein, by the way, was James Baldwin's editor.)

5. Notice, in the passage from the first chapter of Jane Austen's *Pride and prejudice,* how quotation marks indicate direct speech. Notice, too, how each utterance is its own paragraph. Notice, also, how, to enable the reader to keep track of who is speaking, the author offers little tags such as "replied his wife." Punctuation is a set of conventions, the full set of which was introduced not long before Jane Austen used it. Compare Austen's punctuation with that of Samuel Richardson's *Pamela* (of the previous century) cited in Chapter 7. The term "punctuation" comes from *punctus,* a point, originally meaning a point at which to draw breath when reading aloud M.B. Parkes (1992). The purpose of punctuation is to give the reader cues as to how to interpret what he or she is reading. In medieval Europe, it was probable that most readers were monks. What they read often had no punctuation marks, and sometimes not even gaps between the words. This was presumably acceptable to them because they knew

what they were reading. The monastic theory of reading was to read aloud, and listen to what one heard oneself saying. In the modern period, silent reading of material that was new to the reader, who expected to make sense of it in the first encounter, began after the invention of printing and with the gradual spread of education in literacy. It is this kind of reading that punctuation assists.

6. In his prefaces, Henry James discussed the importance of point-of-view, and points out the defects of fiction in which points of view become muddled. Percy Lubbock (1926) a friend of James, continued the discussion of this topic. Here, I discuss just the most common points of view in narrative fiction.

7. Anton Chekhov's "The lady with the little dog" was published in 1899. (Its title in translation is sometimes "The lady with the lapdog" or "The lady with the toy dog.") The version of the story I cite in this book is in the bibliography; this is good, but even better is Richard Pevear and Larissa Volokhonsky's, in their (2000) *Anton Chekhov: Stories.* New York: Bantam. On the internet you easily can find other translations, e.g. at http://chekhov2.tripod.com/197.htm

8. A useful review article of the concept of expertise is by Anders Ericsson and Andreas Lehmann (1999). A magazine article is by Philip Ross (2006), and a book based on biographies of people becoming expert in different domains (including one of Virginia Woolf) is by Howard Gardner (1997). The approximate time taken to attain expertise, 10000 hours, working in the domain of interest is about three hours a day for ten years is about the amount of time most children spend in school classrooms during their lives. Ten hours a day for three years is about the time undergraduates might be expected to spend in a university degree. For real accomplishment, the time has to be spent in problem solving, and in acquiring knowledge and procedures in a particular domain. Coaching is often an important component.

9. Expertise in writing has parallels in reading. Joan Peskin (1998) compared novices (students who had taken courses in poetry in their final two years at high school and undergraduates in English studies in their first two years of university) with experts (advanced PhD students in a Department of English), and asked them to read two poems (from the sixteenth and seventeenth centuries) that were new to them. Novices tended to concentrate on interpreting words and phrases, but found the sense of the whole poem elusive. This worked against their enjoyment. By contrast, experts could handle large-scale structures of each poem, pick up allusions, and think about the meaning of whole poems.

10. Stanislas Dehaene (2009) calls short-term working memory a "conscious neuronal workspace," that has arisen as "vast system of cortical connections, [which] allows for the flexible arrangement of mental objects for novel purposes" (p. 301), not only in conscious thought, but in the explorations of art.

11. N. Ann Chenowth and John Hayes (2003) have found that interfering with short-term memory interferes with fluency of writing. When novices write, they tend mainly to be prompted by their capacity-limited short-term memory of their previous sentence, rather than by any overall plan; see also Thierry Olive (2004).

12. The researcher who established more knowledge of a topic made for greater fluency of writing about it is Ronald Kellogg (1994) and (2001).

13. Various means can be used to investigate unconscious sources in works of literature. These include what authors say about themselves in interviews, computational methods (called corpus stylistics) for searching bodies of authors's works. Maja Djikic, Keith Oatley and Jordan Peterson (2006) analyzed interviews of famous writers of fiction and of famous physicists. We found more preoccupation with negative emotions among the writers, than among the physicists.

14. Shakespeare's dog imagery was remarked in 1935 by Caroline Spurgeon.

15. As compared with the limited storage capacity of stort-term memory, long term memory seems to have almost unlimited capacity. It is the set of memories, meanings, and schematic understandings we have, of the kind that were studied by Frederic Bartlett (1932). Anders Ericsson and Walter Kintsch (1995) have studied the comprehension of text and found that experts develop what they called a long-term working memory. Useful discussions of this concept in relation to writing are by Deborah McCutchen (2000), and by Lucille Chanquoy and Denis Almargot (2002).

Chapter 7

1. Frank Hakemulder has pointed out to me that in Plato's dialogues characters speak much as they do in fiction, that is to say, in ways that stem from their personality, from plausibility, and from circumstance.

2. The idea that the essence of fiction is of selves in the social world, or of intentions and their vicissitudes, is I think, correct, but the category has untidy boundaries. The conventional definition of fiction excludes, for instance, memoir and biography, which can also be about these matters. Recent biographies of relationships by Hazel Rowley (2006) Katie Roiphe (2007) and Janet Malcolm (2007) have had all the characteristics that I am writing about, as does a memoir of growing up in Germany in the 20s and 30s by Sebastian Haffner (2002). By contrast, certain kinds of science fiction are more about technology than about the social world.

3. Eric Havelock (1963) and Jack Goody and Ian Watt (1963) argued that being able to read and write had a completely transformative effect on the mind, of enabling abstract thought. The strong form of this idea was refuted by the

experiment of Sylvia Scribner and Michael Cole (1981), who found that being able to think in abstractions was not an effect of learning to read and write as such, but an effect of education of the kind that is acquired in school. An excellent history of these movements is to be found in David Olson (1994).

4. Taxi-drivers in London have to pass a test (called "the knowledge") on how to get from anywhere to anywhere else in the town in order to obtain a license to drive a taxi. Eleanor Maguire *et al.* (2003) studied London taxi-drivers and found that in them the hippocampus was larger than that of non-taxi-drivers, and that its size was associated with the number of years spent taxi-driving.

5. The question of brain areas of skills of understanding the social world, which are involved in fiction, has been reviewed by Raymond Mar (2004), and by Nathan Spreng, Raymond Mar and Alice Kim (2009), and by Mar (2010).

6. Dolf Zillmann (1991) has argued that film and television involve super-normal representations of emotions, across a range far wider than we would encounter in daily-life. This over exposure might be expected to increase empathy.

7. The first study in which we showed an effect of reading fiction on social abilities was by Raymond Mar, Keith Oatley, Jacob Hirsh, Jennifer dela Paz and Jordan Peterson (2006).

8. The Mind-in-the-Eyes test is by Simon Baron-Cohen *et al.* (2001).

9. The second study in which we showed an effect of reading fiction on social abilities was by Raymond Mar, Keith Oatley and Jordan Peterson (2009). We used a standard personality test for the so-called Big Five traits: Extraversion, Neuroticism, Openness, Agreeableness, and Conscientiousness. (The trait of being interested in, and getting on well with others in social interaction, is Agreeableness.) We also gave our participants a test of Fantasy, which indicated their tendency to be drawn into imaginative narratives.

Among our findings in this study was a replication of findings from many studies that women read more fiction than men, for instance, in their 2008 survey entitled *Reading on the rise* (2009). In 2008, in partnership with the US Census Bureau, the National Endowment for the Arts did interviews, primarily by telephone, with 18 000 Americans of 18 and over (with an 82% response rate), and asked: "During the last 12 months, did you read any a) plays; b) poetry; or c) novels or short stories?" Counting literary reading as a positive response to any category (a, b, or c), 41.9% of men were found to have read some literature as compared with 58% of women. (The total proportion of the adult US population found to have read some literature in the 2008 survey was 50.2%, a rise since the previous survey in 2002, when the proportion was 46.7%.)

10. Somewhat at odds with Mar *et al.*'s finding that adult readers of fiction were generally more sociable than others is the finding by Mihaly Csikszentmihalyi and Jeremy Hunter (2003) that school children who spent more time pleasure

reading spent less time with friends, and that although being with friends was associated with being more happy generally, pleasure reading was not. This result may, however, be confined to children; 59% of the sample were in Grades 6 and 8, and the rest in Grades 10 and 12.

11. The study of social intelligence in students of the humanities and the sciences was done by Willie van Peer's PhD student Eirini Tsiknaki (see van Peer 2008a). This study would bear repetition with controls such as general intelligence, and amount of fictional and non-fictional reading.

12. Some support for Willie van Peer's (2008a) conclusion that teaching of literature takes the humanity out of the humanities is the finding by Angela Biason (1993) in her PhD thesis that a measure of emotional engagement in high-school students as they read two literary short stories had an inverse correlation with the students' expected marks in English. We interpreted this finding in terms of priority being given to technical proficiency rather than personal involvement in assessment of high-school English.

13. The question arises as to whether, if fiction helps social understanding, writers of fiction should be especially understanding of others and themselves. The much-replicated research by James Pennebaker (1997), in which writing about emotional problems has been found to have therapeutic properties, seems to support this hypothesis. Maja Djikic, Keith Oatley and Jordan Peterson (2006) have shown that writers of fiction tend to write about emotional preoccupations, particularly negative ones. It may be that some writers increase their understanding, but writers are not known generally for attainment of states of contentment or social decency. Although this question has not been well researched, it seems most likely that many writers of fiction do write from a position of struggle with their emotional lives. Perhaps many of them start from a position that is rather far out on this spectrum. So although they may make gains for themselves, they don't necessarily do all that well as compared with the non-writing population.

14. The paper on changes in personality as a function of reading Anton Chekhov's "The lady with the little dog," or a non-fiction-styled version was by Maja Djikic, Keith Oatley, Sara Zoeterman and Jordan Peterson (2009a). Personality was measured in terms of the Big Five personality traits: Extraversion, Neuroticism, Openness, Agreeableness, and Conscientiousness.

15. Frank Hakemulder (2000) did a study that was a forerunner of the study by Djikic et al. (2009a). He had people read a short story which was either by Ann Beattie or by Anton Chekhov. Both stories had a female protagonist who had an adulterous affair. Hakemulder changed the stories somewhat so that they were presented either from the point of view of the protagonist or not, and with either a happy or a sad ending. For the Beattie story, though not the Chekhov story, he found a shift in perception in male (but not female) readers so that those who read the version that was from the point of view of the

protagonist became more like her in their attitudes. He discusses his result in terms of Hazel Markus and Paula Nurius's (1986) theory of possible selves.

16. Marc Sestir and Melanie Green (2010) have found that identification with characters in film clips induces changes in viewers, tending to make them feel themselves, at least temporarily, to be more like the characters they have watched.

17. An important contributor to theory of mind is the amount of talk children experience from their mother, or other caregiver, about people's mental states, that is to say about wanting, thinking, and feeling. Ted Ruffman et al. (2002) investigated the relation between the content of mothers' talk and their children's theory-of-mind at three time points over a year. At each time point, mothers were asked to describe some pictures to their child. At each point, the amount of mothers' talk about mental states predicted children's later theory-of-mind understanding, and this held even when children's age and language ability were controlled for.

Kimberly Wright Cassidy et al. (1998) asked parents of preschool children to note down, over a one-week period, the names of books they read to their young children, or that the children read themselves. These books were analyzed for mental state talk: 78% of the books contained internal state language, 34% contained characters believing something that turned out to be false, and 43% contained descriptors of personality. So, not just mothers' talk but children's books induct them into thinking about people's minds.

In another study, Jennifer Dyer et al (2000) analyzed 90 books for three- to four-year-olds and five- to six-year-olds, and found that references to mental states such as thinking, wanting, and feeling occurred approximately every three sentences.

18. Juan Adrian et al. (2005) asked mothers to read four picture-books to their four-year-old and five-year-old children, and talk to them about the pictures and stories. The frequency of parents reading picture story-books at home, and the frequency of mother's use of mental state terms in the picture books she read to her children in the laboratory were both significantly associated with children's abilities at theory-of-mind tasks (after controlling for such factors as age and IQ).

Dorit Aram and Sigalit Aviram (2009) found that it was mothers' skill in choosing books to read to their pre-school children that was most closely related their children's empathy and social development.

19. See also, Peter Dixon and Marisa Bortolussi, 2004.

20. In a scathing article, Jerome Stolnitz (1991) argued that art – though long – has only short-term effects. Greek drama is regarded as powerful but, Stolnitz says, "There is no evidence that Aristophanes shortened the Peloponnesian War by so much as a day" (p. 200). Stolnitz argues that effects of art simply do not appear in history. Except, as Frank Hakemulder has pointed out to me, that

they do. For instance as Lynn Hunt (2007) has shown, the forwarding of human rights has been affected a good deal by literary art.

21. Steiner is correct in seeing the crisis of World War II not just as German, but as one of civilization generally. Willie van Peer, however, said to me that Steiner had no evidence for his assertion that camp workers at Auschwitz were educated in the arts, or read Goethe and Rilke. To think more deeply on this issue, I re-read Christopher Browning's (1992) *Ordinary men,* on Battalion 101 of the German Order Police, who formed killing squads in Poland, of whom more is known than of Auschwitz workers. Most of Browning's research was based on judicial interrogations of 125 of the 486 men in the battalion. At least some of the battalion's 11 officers reached high school education. The rank and file, recruited mostly from the working-class in Hamburg, average age 39. Apart from vocational training, almost none had education beyond age 15. In 1942, two and a half years after recruitment, it became their job to massacre Jews in towns and villages in Poland. Browning compares them with those of Philip Zimbardo's (2007) Stanford Prison Experiment, in which men were recruited from an advertisement in a local California newspaper and assigned to be guards in a simulated prison (an equal number were randomly assigned to be prisoners). Among both the Order Police and the guards in the prison simulation, some 80% acted as their roles required, and a substantial proportion enjoyed their newfound power and became brutal. (In the prison experiment, about a third of the guards constantly invented new forms of cruelty and harassment.) Some 10% to 20% of the Order Police battalion refused to take part in shootings. Comparably, two of the eleven guards in the prison simulation behaved with consideration to the prisoners. Among the 70 volunteers for the prison simulation, those with psychiatric disorders, or histories of crime or drugs were excluded, and 24 were chosen for inclusion in the study: the most stable and psychologically healthy, all college students. Zimbardo was unable to predict from initial personality testing which of these would behave in particular ways. The epidemiological evidence is that some 5.8% of men (in the American population) have the psychiatric disorder of anti-social personality, victims generally of genetic vulnerability and abusive parenting, disposed towards life-long interpersonal violence (see e.g. Oatley, Keltner and Jenkins, 2006). But among ordinary men, it's not known why some become brutal when put in positions of power. There is no empirical evidence of how experience of literature affects people who enter societal roles such as the police that require coercion and force.

22. Among recent historical accounts of reasons for Germany's adoption of Nazism, the best I know is Richard Evans (2004). Already in 1939, the journalist Sebastian Haffner (1940) had perceived that core Nazis were not so much proponents of a political program, but men of a certain personality type (which today we would call anti-social personality disorder).

23. Martha Nussbaum (1994) discusses the question of betterment as seen by Greek philosophical schools that started with Plato and Aristotle. These schools included the Epicureans and Stoics, who believed that philosophy, in which reading was central, was not principally about conceptual understanding. It was about how to become a better person, about medicine for the soul.

24. The experiment in which it was shown that fiction can induce people to believe things that are untrue was by Deborah Prentice, Richard Gerrig and Daniel Bailis (1997).

25. The literature on possible effects of violence and of sexuality in the media is huge, and this is not the place to review it. Recent articles are by Paul Boxer *et al.* (2009) on effects on adolescents of media violence, and Deborah Fisher *et al.* (2009) on effects on adolescents of televised sexuality. Although there are questions as to how conclusive these bodies of research are, there is cause for concern that some forms of fiction may have harmful effects.

26. Brian Boyd has suggested to me that my list of four potentially beneficial social themes is too limiting and suggests, in addition, that literature can enable us to reflect more deeply on the ultimate issues, invite us to perceive the natural world better, to move more swiftly in imagination, to shift from image to image or tone to tone in ways that are not only social. Though these suggestions are interesting, my point is that, at bottom, fictional literature is social.

27. Literature was important in ending slavery in the West. A significant book was the 1789 autobiography Oludah Equiano who was taken from Africa, and shipped to the New World as a slave. He travelled widely, acquired a good education, bought his freedom and settled in England. In a literary prose that was fully equal to that of Dr Samuel Johnson, his autobiography is a moving story of how slaves were treated. His book was extremely popular, and became a powerful stimulus in Britain for the abolition of the slave trade. In the United States, of course, Harriet Beecher Stowe's novel of 1852, *Uncle Tom's cabin*, was credited with comparable effects in the abolition of slavery.

28. This effect of a mirror in enabling Gomov to see himself as others see him, can be Related back to Hamlet's idea (discussed in Chapter 1) of the play within the play in *Hamlet* as able to hold up a mirror to Claudius so that he could see his shadow (reflection), to see himself as others saw him.

29. Does the effect of transportation into a story happen only when the material is new? Melanie Green *et al.* (2008) asked this question in a study in which they recruited people who came out of a cinema after seeing a *Harry Potter* film or a *Lord of the rings* film. Those who had read the book from which the movie was adapted reported stronger effects of transportation into the story world. This may have occurred because those who had read the books were more likely to have been fans of Harry Potter or the denizens of Tolkien's world, so the researchers also did an experiment: participants came into the laboratory on two occasions on each of which they were exposed to the same events, in text

or video form. Reading the story segment following by watching the movie version of the same events produced the strongest transportation effect. Watching the same movie clip twice showed the lowest transportation (Watching followed by reading, and reading followed by reading produced no change of transportation between the two sessions). Perhaps reading enables more reflection to occur, so that if one then watches a movie of the same events, one is primed to notice more and different things, and engage in them more intensely.

30. Sonya Dal Cin *et al.* (2004) have confirmed that transportation is effective in persuading people to adopt beliefs. In experimental studies she has found that portrayals of smoking in movies influenced beliefs and evaluations of smoking and, in a longitudinal cohort study, that teenagers who had been exposed to characters smoking in films were more likely themselves to smoke.

A study of how preferences can be induced in children by reading has been made by Jeanne Tsai *et al.* (2007). In different cultures emotional states are valued in different ways. Tsai and her colleagues found that whereas for European American preschoolers excited and happy states were valued, pre-school children in Taiwan preferred states that were calm. They found, too, that this same preference was reflected in children's picture-books. In USA, pictures in story-books more frequently exhibited excited expressions and activities, than did pictures in Taiwanese story-books. These researchers also found that exposing children to stories that were either exciting or calm changed their preferences towards excited or calm states, and that this effect occurred for both American and Taiwanese children.

31. Amber Reinhart and Thomas Feeley (2007) have conducted meta-analyses of studies that compare persuasion by narrative with persuasion by presenting statistical evidence. Their abstract states that: "A random-effects meta-analysis of 22 studies was conducted comparing narrative messages to statistical messages. When the outcome measures were explored independently, narrative messages, compared to statistical messages, were significantly more persuasive for attitudes, $r = .099, p = .015$."

32. In social psychology, the just-world theory is the belief that the world is just. Marcus Appel (2008) measured beliefs of television viewers in the just world theory and in its opposite the frightening world theory, and also asked about daily hours of television viewing in 19 different genres that included non-fiction programs such as news, and four kinds of fictional programs. He found that the general amount of television watching predicted the strength of people's beliefs that the world is frightening. This is understandable since much television, particularly the news, shows victims of violence, disease, and disaster. But he found, too, that people who spent more time watching television of fictional genres had significantly stronger beliefs in the idea of a just world. Frank Kermode (1966) has argued that fiction is one of the ways in which we strive to make meaningful sense of the world, and the idea of justice, as

depicted for instance in many television stories of detection, legal argument, and judgment, offers this kind of meaning-making.

Does this indicate that televised fiction gives a falsely optimistic view of the world, of the kind advocated by Dr Pangloss in Voltaire's *Candide* (1759)? It may sometimes do so. But if we consider two kinds of television – news reporting and fiction – perhaps the one serves to elicit our empathy for those afflicted by harrowing events in a way that is far more vivid and widely publicized now than a hundred years ago, while the other offers us models of how we might think about cruelty, arbitrariness, and injustice.

33. Among empirical studies related to the idea that literature promotes sympathy is that of Willie van Peer and Pander Maat (1996) who found effects on readers' sympathy for different characters in a short story about a marital argument as a function of the point of view from which the story was written.

34. Frank Hakemulder's PhD thesis is published in book form (2000). In one of his studies, Hakemulder found decreased tolerance for current norms in students who read a fiction piece with instructions to think themselves into the situation of the female protagonist of the fictional story as they read, as compared with those asked to read the story without these instructions but asked to mark the structure of the text with a pencil.

    In a field experiment on a similar issue, Betsy Paluck (2009) studied effects of exposure of children in communities in Rwanda to two kinds of radio soap opera: one on health, one aimed at reducing prejudice. As compared with those who heard the health programs, those who heard the programs designed to reduce prejudice changed their perceptions and behavior towards more respect for intermarriage, more empathy, and more cooperation.

35. Forum Theatre is a kind of drama developed by Augusto Bola, the intention of which was to promote awareness of relations between oppressors and the oppressed, as well as the possibilities of avoiding deleterious consequences.

Chapter 8

1. Bernard Rimé (2009) has done a series of studies in which he asked people, at the end of each day, to record in a diary structured like a questionnaire, any emotions they experienced during the day. He asked them to say, also, whether they had shared these emotions in conversation with anyone else. He found that about 90% of emotions that were salient enough to be remembered had also been shared with one or more other people.

2. A good account of the Western canon of literature is given by Harold Bloom (1994). Importantly, there are empirical questions of what literature is better than others, and *The quality of literature,* edited by Willie van Peer (2008) contains discussions of them.

3. The famous textbooks of the movement of New Criticism were by Cleanth Brooks and Robert Penn Warren (1938) and (1959).

4. The phrase by Bill Benzon on how texts work in the mind and brain appeared in *On Fiction*, appears in the *On Fiction*, Jan 2009 http://www.onfiction.ca/2009/01/on-interpretation.html

5. Zazie Todd selected 30 contemporary novels and convened three discussions (on three separate novels) in seven groups each of seven or eight people recruited from newsletter and newspaper articles. She analyzed the transcripts of the resulting 21 discussions, each of which was slightly less than an hour long.

6. There is a book on *Changing lives through literature* by Jean Trounstine and Robert Waxler (2005). Personal accounts are also given by Trounstine (2000) and by Waxler (2000). An evaluation of the project has been made by Roger Jarjoura and Susan Krumholz (1998) on 72 young, male, repeat offenders who were on probation. In a Program Group, 32 of these men took the Changing Lives Through Literature program (in four eight-person classes, which included the literature seminars, and other input). In a Comparison Group 40 of these men with comparable criminal records did not take the program. During the study period six of the men in the Program Group (18.75%) committed further offences while 18 in the Comparison Group (45%) did so. Although this result is encouraging, the report contains no statistical analyses, and there is ambiguity about the active ingredients of the program.

7. Susan Neuman's (1996) finding that the language of children improves when parents read stories to them, suggests that movements like Literature for Life are likely to help the development of literacy. Hence a culture of literacy spreads not only to the young women who attend the reading circles, but also to their children.

8. Joan Swann and Daniel Allington (2009) give examples of how literary discussion and the management of relationships occur together in reading groups.

9. In her study of reading groups, Zazie Todd (2008) found that participants used the plot as a way of anchoring their discussions.

10. Zazie Todd (2008) found some evidence for what David Miall and Donald Kuiken (2002) call self-modifying feelings, in which emotional memories occur and, as a result of reading, readers change how they experience the memories' implications.

11. In his commentary on "The lady with the little dog," Timothy Spurgin (2009) recommends that, as readers, we monitor our feelings as we progress through the story. He suggests that at the beginning we read that Gomov has been frequently unfaithful to his wife, and is therefore a flawed and shallow character. We might wonder, therefore whether he will have yet another affair – which he does – and we may ask what will be different about this one? Might it be that he will be the one who is dumped? Spurgin suggests that in parallel with

the emotional growth of Gomov in coming to feel for Anna, we readers experience a growth in being able to feel for him. In his lectures, Spurgin comes also,
to conclusions about parallels between literary characters and ourselves when
we read, as in this Chekhov story, and about the partnership of writer and
reader, which are similar to those I reach in this book.

Bibliography

In the text I have avoided including dates in citations, but I have sometimes identified the researchers. References can be found from that identification or from the notes.

Adrian, J.E., Clemente, R.A., Villanueva, L., and Rieffe, C. (2005). Parent-child picture-book reading, mother's mental state language, and children's theory of mind. *Journal of Child Language, 32*, 673–686.

Aesop. (600–564 BCE). *The complete fables* (O. Temple and R. Temple, Trans.). London: Penguin (current edition 1998).

Aiello, L.C., and Dunbar, R.I.M. (1993). Neocortex size, group size, and the evolution of language. *Current Anthropology, 34*, 184–193.

Ainsworth, M.D.S., Blehar, M.C., Waters, E., and Wall, S. (1978). *Patterns of attachment: A psychological study of the strange situation*. Hillsdale, NJ: Erlbaum.

Anonymous. (1000–1500). *Arabian nights' entertainments* (H. Weber, Trans.). Oxford: Oxford University Press (current edition 1995).

Anonymous. (1700 BCE). *The epic of Gilgamesh: The Babylonian Epic Poem and other texts in Akkadian and Sumerian* (A. George, Trans.). London: Penguin (current edition 2000).

Appel, M. (2008). Fictional narratives cultivate just-world beliefs. *Journal of Communication, 58*, 62–83.

Apuleius. (160–180). *The transformations of Lucius, or The golden ass* (R. Graves, Trans.). Harmondsworth, Middlesex: Penguin (current edition 1950).

Aram, D., and Aviram, S. (2009). Mothers' storybook reading and kindergartners' socioemotional and literacy development. *Reading Psychology, 30*, 175–194.

Aristotle. (c. 350 BCE). *Rhetoric*. In W.R. Roberts (Ed.), *Aristotle: Rhetoric and Poetics* (pp. 3–218). New York: Random House (current edition 1954).

Such Stuff as Dreams: The Psychology of Fiction, First Edition. K. Oatley.
© 2011 K. Oatley. Published 2011 by John Wiley & Sons, Ltd.

Aristotle. (c. 350 BCE). *Poetics* (G.E. Else, Trans.). Ann Arbor, MI: University of Michigan Press (current edition 1970).

Auerbach, E. (1953). *Mimesis: The representation of reality in Western literature* (W.R. Trask, Trans.). Princeton, NJ: Princeton University Press.

Augustine. (c. 401). *The confessions* (G. Wills, Trans.). New York: Penguin (current edition 2006).

Austen, J. (1813). *Pride and prejudice*. London: Dent (current edition 1906).

Axelrad, E. (1993). *Repeated recall as a measure of subjective response to literature*. MA thesis, University of Toronto.

Aziz-Zadeh, L., and Damasio, A.R. (2008). Embodied semantics for actions: Findings from functional brain imaging. *Journal of Physiology – Paris, 102*, 35–39.

Aziz-Zadeh, L., Wilson, S.M., Rizzolatti, G., and Iacoboni, M. (2006). Congruent embodied representations for visually presented actions and linguistic phrases describing actions. *Current Biology, 16*, 1818–1823.

Baldwin, J. (1963). Down at the cross: Letter from a region in my mind. In *The fire next time* (pp. 23–112). London: Michael Joseph.

Baron-Cohen, S., Wheelwright, S., Hill, J., Raste, Y., and Plumb, I. (2001). The "Reading the Mind in the Eyes" Test revised version: A study with normal adults, and adults with Asperger's syndrome or high-functioning autism. *Journal of Child Psychology and Psychiatry, 42*, 241–251.

Barna, Y. (1973). *Eisenstein: The growth of a cinematic genius*. Boston: Little Brown.

Barthes, R. (1975). *S / Z* (R. Miller, Trans.). London: Cape.

Bartlett, F.C. (1932). *Remembering: A study in experimental and social psychology*. Cambridge: Cambridge University Press.

Barsalou, L.W. (2008). Grounded cognition. *Annual Review of Psychology, 59*, 617–645.

Baum, S. (Creator and writer). (2009). *Lie to me*. Fox Broadcasting Company, USA.

Bayard, P. (2007). *How to talk about books you haven't read* (J. Mehlman, Trans.). London: Bloomsbury.

Benzon, W. (2006). Literary morphology: Nine propositions in a naturalist theory of form. *PsyArt: An Online Journal for the Psychological Study of the Arts*, http://www.clas.ufl.edu/ipsa/journal/2006_benzon01.shtml.

Bergman, I. (Director). (1982). *Fanny and Alexander*. Sweden.

Biason, A. (1993). *Emotional responses of high-school students to short stories*. PhD thesis, University of Toronto.

Blake, W. (1793). The marriage of heaven and hell. In M. Plowman (Ed.), *Blake's poems and prophecies* (pp. 42–55). London: Dent Everyman's Library.

Bloom, H. (1994). *The western canon: The books and school of the ages*. New York: Harcourt Brace.

Boccaccio, G. (1353). *The decameron* (G.H. McWilliam, Trans.). Harmondsworth: Penguin (current edition 1972).

Bogart, K.R., and Matsumoto, D. (2010). Facial mimicry is not necessary to recognize emotion: Facial expression recognition by people with Moebius syndrome. *Social Neuroscience*, 5, 241–251.

Bohannan, L. (1966). Shakespeare in the bush. *Natural History, Aug / Sept*, 1–6.

Booth, W.C. (1988). *The company we keep: An ethics of fiction*. Berkeley, CA: University of California Press.

Bortolussi, M., and Dixon, P. (2003). *Psychonarratology: Foundations for the empirical study of literary response*. New York: Cambridge University Press.

Bouzouggar, A., Barton, N., Vanhaeren, M., *et al.* (2007). 82,000-year-old shell beads from North Africa and implications for the origins of modern human behavior. *Proceedings of the National Academy of Sciences of the USA*, 104, 9964–9969.

Bowlby, J. (1951). *Child care and the growth of love*. Harmondsworth: Penguin.

Bowlby, J. (1991). *Charles Darwin: A new life*. New York: Norton.

Boxer, P., Huesmann, L.R., Bushman, B.J., O'Brien, M., and Moceri, D. (2009). The role of violent media preference in cumulative developmental risk for violence and general aggression. *Journal of Youth and Adolescence*, 38, 417–428.

Boyd, B. (2009). *On the origin of stories*. Cambridge, MA: Harvard University Press.

Bradley, A.C. (1904). *Shakespearian tragedy: Lectures on Hamlet, Othello, King Lear, and Macbeth*. London: Penguin (current edition 1991).

Breithaupt, F. (2009). *Kulturen der Empathie (Cultures of Empathy)*. Frankfurt: Suhrkamp Verlag.

Brewer, W.F., and Lichtenstein, E.H. (1981). Event schemas, story schemas and story grammars. In J. Long and A. Baddeley (Eds.), *Attention and performance 9* (pp. 363–379). Hillsdale, NJ: Erlbaum.

Brooks, C., and Warren, R.P. (1938). *Understanding poetry: An anthology for college students*. New York: Holt.

Brooks, C., and Warren, R.P. (1959). *Understanding fiction, second edition*. New York: Appleton-Century-Crofts.

Brooks, P. (1984). *Reading for the plot: Design and intention in narrative*. Cambridge, MA: Harvard University Press.

Brower, R.A. (1963). Light, bright, and sparkling: Irony and fiction in *Pride and prejudice*. In I. Watt (Ed.), *Jane Austen: A collection of critical essays* (pp. 62–75). Englewood Cliff, NJ: Prentice Hall.

Browning, C.R. (1992). *Ordinary men: Reserve Police Battalion 101 and the final solution in Poland*. New York: HarperCollins.

Bruner, J. (1986). *Actual minds, possible worlds*. Cambridge, MA: Harvard University Press.

Bruner, J.S. (2002). *Making stories: Law, literature, life*. New York: Farrar, Straus and Giroux.

Buccino, G., Riggio, L., Melli, G., *et al.* (2005). Listening to action-related sentences modulates the activity of the motor system: A combined TMS and behavioral study. *Cognitive Brain Research, 24,* 355–363.

Buckner, R.L., and Carroll, D.C. (2007). Self-projection and the brain. *Trends in Cognitive Sciences, 11,* 49–57.

Bullough, E. (1912). Psychical distance as a factor in art and an aesthetic principle. *British Journal of Psychology, 5,* 87–118.

Bunyan, J. (1678). *The pilgrim's progress.* Oxford: Oxford University Press (current edition 1984).

Burton, R. (1621). *The anatomy of melancholy: What it is, with all the kinds, causes, symptomes, prognostickes and several cures of it.* Oxford, Modern edition, London, Dent (current edition 1932).

Cadieux, K.V. (2008). Intractable characters as personality extensions. In *OnFiction.* http://www.onfiction.ca/2008/09/intractable-characters-as-personality.html.

Call, J., and Tomasello, M. (1995). Use of social information in the problem solving of orangutans (Pongo pygmaeus). and human children (Homo sapiens). *Journal of Comparative Psychology, 109,* 308–320.

Carroll, N. (1990). *The philosophy of horror or Paradoxes of the heart.* New York: Routledge.

Cassidy, K.W., Ball, L.V., Rourke, M.T., *et al.* (1998). Theory of mind concepts in children's literature. *Applied Psycholinguistics, 19,* 463–470.

Chanquoy, L., and Alamargot, D. (2002). Working memory and writing: Evolution of models and assessment of research/Mémoire de travail et rédaction de textes: évolution des modèles et bilan des premiers travaux. *L'année Psychologique, 102,* 363–398.

Chapman, H.A., Kim, D.A., Susskind, J.M., and Anderson, A.K. (2009). In bad taste: Evidence for the oral origins of moral disgust. *Science, 323,* 1222–1226.

Chaucer, G. (c. 1395). *The Canterbury tales* (N. Coghill, Trans.). Harmondsworth: Penguin (current edition 1951).

Chekhov, A. (1899). The lady with the toy dog, *in Anton Chekhov: Five great short stories.* New York: Dover (current edition 1990).

Chenowth, N.A., and Hayes, J.R. (2003). The inner voice in writing. *Written Communication, 20,* 99–118.

Chesterton, G.K. (1927). The secret of Flambeau, in *The secret of Father Brown* (pp. 170–176). Harmondsworth: Penguin (current edition 1974).

Chopin, K. (1894). The dream of an hour. In P. Knights (Ed.), *Kate Chopin: The awakening and other stories* (pp. 259–261). Oxford: Oxford University Press (current edition 2000).

Clark, A. (2006a). Language, embodiment, and the cognitive niche. *Trends in Cognitive Sciences, 10,* 370–374.

Clark, A. (2006b). Material symbols. *Philosophical Psychology, 19,* 291–307.

Coie, J.D., and Kupersmidt, J.D. (1983). A behavioral analysis of emerging social status in boys' groups. *Child Development, 54,* 1400–1416.

Coleridge, S.T. (1794–1820). *Coleridge's notebooks: a selection* (Ed. S. Perry). Oxford: Oxford University Press.

Coleridge, S.T. (1816). Kubla Khan in *The portable Coleridge* (pp. 156–158). Harmondsworth: Penguin (current edition 1977).

Collingwood, R.G. (1938). *The principles of art.* Oxford: Oxford University Press.

Collingwood, R.G. (1946). *The idea of history.* Oxford: Oxford University Press.

Comay, J. (2008). *Individual differences in narrative perspective-taking and theory of mind.* PhD thesis, University of Toronto.

Conan-Doyle, A. (1894). The Musgrave ritual, in *The Penguin complete adventures of Sherlock Holmes* (pp. 386–397). London: Penguin (current edition 1981).

Cooley, C.H. (1902). *Human nature and the social order.* New York: Scribner.

Costa, P.T., and McCrae, R.R. (1988). Personality in adulthood: A six-year longitudinal study of self reports and spouse ratings on the NEO Personality Inventory. *Journal of Personality and Social Psychology, 54,* 853–863.

Craik, K.J.W. (1943). *The nature of explanation.* Cambridge: Cambridge University Press.

Csikszentmihalyi, M. (1996). *Creativity: Flow and the psychology of discovery and invention.* New York: Harper Collins.

Csikszentmilalyi, M., and Hunter, J. (2003). Happiness in everyday life: The uses of experience sampling. *Journal of Happiness Studies, 4,* 185–199.

Csikszentmihalyi, M., and Larsen, R. (1984). *Being adolescent: Conflict and growth in the teenage years.* New York: Basic Books.

Cupchik, G.C. (2002). The evolution of psychical distance as an aesthetic concept. *Culture and Psychology, 8,* 155–187.

Cupchik, G.C., Oatley, K., and Vorderer, P. (1998). Emotional effects of reading excerpts from short stories by James Joyce. *Poetics, 25,* 363–377.

Dal Cin, S., Zanna, M.P., and Fong, G.T. (2004). Narrative persuasion and overcoming resistance. In E.S. Knowles and J.A. Linn (Eds.), *Resistance and persuasion* (pp. 175–191). Mahwah, NJ: Erlbaum.

Dante Alighieri. (1292–1295). *La vita nuova* (with facing English translation by Dino Cervigni and Edward Vasta.). Notre Dame, IN: University of Notre Dame Press (current publication 1995).

Darwin, C. (1839). *The voyage of the Beagle.* London: Dent (current edition 1906).

Darwin, C. (1859). *On the origin of species by means of natural selection.* London: Murray.

Darwin, C. (1872). *The expression of the emotions in man and animals (second edition, of 1889).* London: Murray.

De Biasi, P.-M. (2002). Flaubert: The labor of writing. In A.-M. Christin (Ed.), *A history of writing* (pp. 340–341). Paris: Flammarion.

De Groot, A. (1978). *Thought and choice in chess.* The Hague: Mouton.

Debray Genette, R. (2004). Flaubert's "A simple heart," or how to make an ending: A study of manuscripts. In J. Deppman, D. Ferrer and M. Groden (Eds.), *Genetic criticism: Texts and avant-textes* (pp. 69–95). Philadelphia: University of Pennsylvania Press.

Dehaene, S. (2009). *Reading in the brain: The science and evolution of a human invention.* New York: Viking.

DeLoache, J. (1987). Rapid change in symbolic functioning in young children. *Science, 238,* 1556–1557.

Dennett, D. (1995). *Darwin's dangerous idea: Evolution and the meaning of life.* New York: Simon and Schuster.

De Sousa, R. (2009). The mind's Bermuda Triangle: Philosophy of emotions and empirical science. In P. Goldie (Ed.), *Oxford Companion to Philosophy of Emotions.* Oxford: Oxford University Press.

De Vignemont, F., and Singer, T. (2006). The empathetic brain: How, when, and why. *Trends in Cognitive Sciences, 10,* 435–441.

De Waal, F. (2004). On the possiblity of animal empathy. In N.H. Frijda, A.S.R. Manstead and A. Fischer (Eds.), *Feelings and emotions: The Amsterdam Symposium* (pp. 381–401). New York: Cambridge University Press.

De Waal, F. (2009). *The age of empathy: Nature's lesson's for a kinder society.* Toronto: McClelland and Stewart.

Dixon, P., and Bortolussi, M. (2004). Methods and evidence in psychonarratology and the theory of the narrator: Reply to Diengott. *Narrative, 12,* 317–325.

Djikic, M., Oatley, K., and Peterson, J. (2006). The bitter-sweet labor of emoting: The linguistic comparison of writers and physicists. *Creativity Research Journal, 18,* 191–197.

Djikic, M., Oatley, K., Zoeterman, S., and Peterson, J.B. (2009a). On being moved by art: How reading fiction transforms the self. *Creativity Research Journal, 21,* 24–29.

Djikic, M., Oatley, K., Zoeterman, S., and Peterson, J.B. (2009b). Defenceless against art? Impact of reading fiction emotion in avoidantly attached individuals. *Journal of Research in Personality, 43,* 14–17.

Donne, J. (1615–1631). *The sermons of John Donne, Volume 8.* (Eds. G.R. Potter and E.M. Simpson), Berkeley: University of California Press (current edition, 1960).

Donne, J. (1633). Holy sonnet VII. In J. Hayward (Ed.), *Donne: Complete verse and selected prose* (pp. 282). London: Nonsuch Press (current edition 1978).

Doody, M.A. (1997). *The true story of the novel.* London: HarperCollins.

Doris, J. (2002). *Lack of character: Personality and moral behavior.* Cambridge: Cambridge University Press.

Dunbar, R.I.M. (1993). Coevolution of neocortical size, group size, and language in humans. *Behavioral and Brain Sciences, 16,* 681–735.

Dunbar, R.I.M. (2003). The social brain: mind, language, and society in evolutionary perspective. *Annual Review of Anthropology, 32,* 163–181.

Dunbar, R.I.M. (2004). *The human story: A new history of mankind's evolution*. London: Faber.

Dunn, J. (2004). *Children's friendships: The beginnings of intimacy*. Oxford: Blackwell.

Dutton, D. (2009). *The art instinct: Beauty, pleasure, and human evolution*. London: Bloomsbury.

Dyer, J.R., Shatz, M., and Wellman, H.M. (2000). Young children's storybooks as a source of mental state information. *Child Development, 15,* 17–37.

Eisenstein, S. (Director). (1925). *The battleship Potemkin*. Russia.

Ekman, P. (2003). *Emotions revealed: Recognizing faces and feelings to improve communication*. New York: Holt.

Ekman, P., and O'Sullivan, M. (1991). Who can catch a liar? *American Psychologist, 46,* 913–920.

Eliot, G. (1856). The natural history of German life: Riehl. In, *The works of George Eliot. Standard Edition: Essays*. (pp. 188–236). Edinburgh: Blackwood. (This edition, 1883).

Eliot, T.S. (1919). Hamlet. In J. Hayward (Ed.), *T.S. Eliot: Selected prose* (pp. 104–109). Harmondsworth: Penguin.

Eng, A. (2002). *Learning and processing non-fiction genre*. PhD thesis, University of Toronto.

Equiano, O. (1789). *The interesting narrative of the life of Oludah Equiano or Gustavus Vassa, the African, written by himself*. New York: Norton (current edition 2001).

Erasmus, D. (1508). *Praise of folly* (R.M. Adams, Ed. and Trans.). New York: Norton (current edition 1989).

Ericsson, K.A. (1990). Theoretical issues in the study of exceptional performance. In K.J. Gilhooly, M.T.J. Keane, R.H. Logie and G. Erdos (Eds.), *Lines of thinking: Reflections on the psychology of thought, Vol 2. Skills, emotion, creative processes, individual differences and teaching thinking* (pp. 5–28). Chichester: Wiley.

Ericsson, K.A., and Kintsch, W. (1995). Long term working memory. *Psychological Review, 102,* 211–245.

Ericsson, K.A., and Lehmann, A.C. (1999). Expertise. In M.A. Runco and S.R. Pritzker (Eds.), *Encyclopaedia of Creativity, Volume 1* (pp. 695–706). San Diego: Academic Press.

Erikson, E.H. (1959). Identity and the life cycle. *Psychological Issues, 1,* 1–171.

Evans, R.J. (2004). *The coming of the Third Reich*. New York: Penguin.

Evans, R.J. (2005). *The Third Reich in power, 1933–1939*. New York: Penguin.

Everett, D.L. (2005). Cultural constraints on grammar and cognition in Pirahã: Another look at the design features of human language. *Current Anthropology, 46,* 621–646.

Farr, D. (2007). *Rāmāyana: A dramatic retelling of the great Indian epic*. London: Faber and Faber.

Faust, M., Barak, O., and Chiarello, C. (2006). The effects of multiple script priming on word recognition by the two cerebral hemispheres: Implications for discourse processing. *Brain and Language, 99,* 2478–2257.

Fernyhough, C. (2008). *The baby in the mirror: A child's world from birth to three.* London: Granta.

Fielding, H. (1749). *The history of Tom Jones.* London: Penguin (current edition 1985).

Fisher, D.A., Hill, D.L., Grube, J.W., Bersamin, M.M., Walker, S., and Gruber, E.L. (2009). Televised sexual content and parental mediation: Influences on adolescent sexuality. *Media Psychology, 12,* 121–147.

Fister, B. (2005). Reading as a contact sport: Online book groups and the social dimensions of reading. *Reference and User Services Quarterly, 44,* 303–309.

Flaubert, G. (1857). *Madame Bovary.* (M. Marmur, Trans.). New York: New American Library (current edition 1964).

Flerx, V.C., Fidler, D.S., and Rogers, R.W. (1976). Sex role stereotypes: Developmental aspects and early intervention. *Child Development, 47,* 998–1007.

Flower, L.S., Schriver, K.A., Carey, L., Haas, C., and Hayes, J.R. (1989). *Planning in writing: The cognition of a constructive process.* Berkeley, CA: Center for the Study of Writing, Technical Report No.34.

Foroni, F., and Semin, G. (2009). Language that puts you in touch with your bodily feelings: The multimodal responsiveness of affective expressions. *Psychological Science, 20,* 974–980.

Forster, E.M. (1927). *Aspects of the novel.* London: Edward Arnold.

Fowles, J. (1963). *The collector.* London: Jonathan Cape.

Freud, S. (1905). Fragment of an analysis of a case of hysteria (Dora). (A. Tyson, Trans.). In J. Strachey and A. Richards (Eds.), *The Pelican Freud Library, Vol 8:* (pp. 29–164). London: Penguin (current edition 1979).

Freud, S. (1908). Creative writers and day-dreaming. In A. Dickson (Ed.), *Pelican Freud Library, Vol. 14.* (pp. 130–141). London: Penguin (current edition 1985).

Frijda, N.H. (1986). *The emotions.* Cambridge: Cambridge University Press.

Gardner, H. (1997). *Extraordinary minds: Portraits of exceptional individuals and an examination of our extraordinariness.* New York: Basic Books.

Gardner, W.L., and Knowles, M.L. (2008). Love makes you real: Favorite television characters are perceived as "real" in a social facilitation paradigm. *Social Cognition, 26,* 156–168.

Gerrig, R.J. (1993). *Experiencing narrative worlds: On the psychological activities of reading.* New Haven, CT: Yale University Press.

Gholamain, M. (1999). *The attachment and personality dynamics of reader response.* PhD thesis, University of Toronto.

Gibbs, R.W. (1994). *The poetics of mind: Figurative thought, language, and understanding.* New York: Cambridge University Press.

Giora, R. (2007). Is metaphor special? *Brain and Language, 100,* 111–114.

Glenberg, A.M., Satao, M., Cattaneo, L., Riggio, L., Palumbo, D., and Buccino, G. (2008). Processing abstract language modulates motor system activity. *Quarterly Journal of Experimental Psychology*, *61*, 905–919.

Glucksberg, S. (2003). The psycholinguistics of metaphor. *Trends in Cognitive Sciences*, *7*, 92–96.

Gogol, N. (1842). The overcoat (C. Garnett, Trans.). *The overcoat and other stories*(pp. 3–51). London: Chatto and Windus (current edition 1923).

Goffman, E. (1959). *The presentation of self in everyday life*. New York: Doubleday.

Goffman, E. (1961). Fun in games, in *Encounters: Two studies in the sociology of interaction* (pp. 15–81). Indianapolis, IN: Bobbs-Merrill.

Goldman, A. (2009). Two routes to empathy: Insights from cognitive neuroscience. In A. Coplan and P. Goldie (Eds.), *Empathy: Philosophical and psychological perspectives*. New York: Oxford University Press.

Gombrich, E.H. (1960). *Art and illusion*. London: Phaidon.

Goody, J. (1987). *The interface between the oral and the written*. Cambridge: Cambridge University Press.

Goody, J., and Watt, I. (1963). The consequences of literacy. *Comparative Studies in Society and History*, *5* (pp. 27–68 (reprinted in Goody, J. 1968, *Literacy in traditional societies*, New York: Cambridge University Press)

Gordon, P. (2004). Numerical cognition without words: Evidence from Amazonia. *Science*, *306*, 496–499.

Graesser, A.C., Olde, B., and Klettke, B. (2002). How does the mind construct and represent stories. In M.C. Green, J.J. Strange and T.C. Brock (Eds.), *Narrative impact: Social and cognitive foundations* (pp. 229–262). Mahwah, NJ: Erlbaum.

Green, M.C. (2004). Transportation into narrative worlds: The role of prior knowledge and perceived realism. *Discourse Processes*, *38*, 247–266.

Green, M.C., and Brock, T.C. (2000). The role of transportation in the persuasiveness of public narratives. *Journal of Personality and Social Psychology*, *79*, 702–721.

Green, M.C., Kass, S., Carrey, J., Herzig, B., Feeney, R., and Sabini, J. (2008). Transportation across media: Repeated exposure to text and film. *Media Psychology*, *11*, 512–539.

Greenblatt, S. (1980). *Renaissance self-fashioning*. Chicago: University of Chicago Press.

Greenblatt, S. (2004). *Will in the world: How Shakespeare became Shakespeare*. New York: Norton.

Greene, G. (2005). *The third man and The fallen idol*. London: Vintage.

Grice, H.P. (1975). Logic and conversation. In P. Cole and J.L. Morgan (Eds.), *Syntax and semantics, 3. Speech acts*. New York: Academic Press.

Gruber, H.E., and Barrett, P.H. (1974). *Darwin on man: A psychological study of scientific creativity, together with Darwin's early and unpublished notebooks*. New York: Dutton.

Haffner, S. (1940). *Germany Jekyll and Hyde: A contemporary account of Nazi Germany*. London: Secker and Warburg (reissued, 2008, Abacus)

Haffner, S. (2002). *Defying Hitler: A memoir*. New York: Picador.

Hakemulder, J.F. (2000). *The moral laboratory: Experiments examining the effects of reading literature on social perception and moral self-concept*. Amsterdam: Benjamin.

Hakemulder, J.F. (2004). Foregrounding and its effects on reader's perception. *Discourse Processes, 38*, 193–208.

Hakemulder, J.F. (2008). Imagining what could happen: Taking the role of a character on social cognition. In S. Zyngier, M. Bortolussi, A. Chesnokova and J. Auracher (Eds.), *Directions in empirical literary studies: In honor of Willie van Peer* (pp. 139–153). Amsterdam: Benjamins.

Halliwell, S. (2002). *The aesthetics of mimesis: Ancient texts and modern problems*. Princeton, NJ: Princeton University Press.

Harding, D.W. (1940). Regulated hatred: An aspect of the work of Jane Austen. *Scrutiny, 8*, 346–362.

Hardy, T. (1984). *The life and works of Thomas Hardy* (Ed. M. Millgate). London: Macmillan.

Harris, P.L. (2000). *The work of the imagination*. Oxford: Blackwell.

Hartley, J., and Turvey, S. (2001). *Reading groups*. Oxford: Oxford University Press.

Havelock, E.A. (1963). *Preface to Plato*. Cambridge, MA: Harvard University Press.

Hayes, J.R., and Flower, L.S. (1986). Writing research and the writer. *American Psychologist, 41*, 1106–1113.

Heider, F. (1958). *The psychology of interpersonal relations*. New York: Wiley.

Heider, F., and Simmel, M.A. (1944). An experimental study of apparent behavior. *American Journal of Psychology, 57*, 243–259.

Hermann, E., Call, J., Hernandez-Lloreda, M.V., Hare, B., and Tomasello, M. (2007). Humans have evolved specialized skills of social cognition: The cultural intelligence hypothesis. *Science, 317*, 1360–1366.

Hilscher, M.C., Cupchik, G.C., and Leonard, G. (2008). Melodrama and film noir on today's big screen: How modern audiences experience yesterday's classics. *Psychology of Aesthetics, Creativity, and the Arts, 2*, 203–212.

Hinton, G.E., Plaut, D.C., and Shallice, T. (1993). Simulating brain damage. *Scientific American* (October).

Hitchcock, A. (Director). (1958). *Vertigo*. USA.

Hogan, P.C. (2002). A minimal lexicalist/constituent transfer account of metaphor. *Style (Dekalb, III), 36*, 484–502.

Hogan, P.C. (2003). *The mind and its stories: Narrative universals and human emotion*. Cambridge: Cambridge University Press.

Hogan, P.C. (2009). *Understanding nationalism: On narrative, cognitive science, and identity*. Columbus, OH: Ohio State University Press.

Holland, N.N. (1968). *The dynamics of literary response.* New York: Columbia University Press.

Holland, N.N. (1975). *Five readers reading.* New Haven: Yale University Press.

Holland, N.N. (2009). *Literature and the brain.* Gainesville, FL: PsyArt Foundation.

Homer (c. 850 BCE). *The Iliad* (ed. and trans. M. Hammond). Harmondsworth: Penguin (current edition 1987).

Homer (c. 830 BCE). *The Odyssey* (R. Fagles, Ed. and Trans.). Harmondsworth: Penguin (current edition 1999).

Horney, K. (1950). *Neurosis and human growth: The struggle towards self realization.* New York: Norton.

Huizinga, J. (1955). *Homo ludens: A study of the play-element in culture.* Boston: Beacon.

Hume, D. (1965). Of the standard of taste. In J.W. Lenz (Ed.), *David Hume: Of the standard of taste and other essays,* §33. Indianapolis, In: Bobbs Merrill.

Hunt, L. (2007). *Inventing human rights.* New York: Norton.

Hutto, D.D. (2008). *Folk psychological narratives: The sociocultural basis of understanding reasons.* Cambridge, MA: MIT Press.

Iacoboni, M. (2009). Imitation, empathy, and mirror neurons. *Annual Review of Psychology, 60,* 653–670.

Ildirar, S. (2008). *Do film illiterates understand basic cinematographic principles?* Paper presented at the 29th International Congress of Psychology, Berlin, July 20–25.

Ingalls, D.H.H., Masson, J.M., and Patwardhan, M.V. (1990). *The Dhvanyaloka of Anandavardana with the Locana of Abhinavagupta.* Cambridge, MA: Harvard University Press.

Iser, W. (1974). *The implied reader: Patterns of communication in prose fiction from Bunyan to Beckett.* Baltimore: Johns Hopkins University Press.

Jakobson, R. (1956). Two aspects of language and two types of aphasic disturbance. In R. Jakobson and M. Halle (Eds.), *Fundamentals of language* (pp. 53–83). 'S-Gravenhage: Mouton.

Jakobson, R. (1960). Linguistics and poetics. In D. Lodge (Ed.), *Modern criticism and theory* (pp. 32–57). London: Longman (current edition 1988).

James, H. (1884). The art of fiction. *Longman's Magazine, September,* Reprinted in *The Portable Henry James* (Ed. M.D. Zabel). New York: Viking, (pp. 1391–1418). (current edition 1951).

James, H. (1907). Preface to The spoils of Peynton. Retrieved 1 October 2009: http://www.henryjames.org.uk/prefaces/text10.htm

James, P.D. (2009). *Talking about detective fiction.* New York: Knopf.

Jarjoura, G.R., and Krumholz, S.T. (1998). Combining bibliotherapy and positive role modeling as an alternative to incarceration. *Journal of Offender Rehabilitation, 28,* 127–139.

Jenkins, J.M., and Astington, J.W. (2000). Theory of mind and social behavior: Causal models tested in a longitudinal study. *Merrill-Palmer Quarterly*, *46*, 203–220.

Johnson, S.F. (1952). The regeneration of Hamlet: A reply to E.M.W. Tillyard with a counter-proposal. *Shakespeare Quarterly*, *3*, 187–207.

Johnson-Laird, P.N. (1983). *Mental models: Towards a cognitive science of language, inference, and consciousness*. Cambridge: Cambridge University Press.

Johnson-Laird, P.N. (2006). *How we reason*. Oxford: Oxford University Press.

Jones, J. (1995). *Shakespeare at work*. Oxford: Clarendon Press.

Joyce, J. (1914). Clay. In J. Joyce (Ed.), *Dubliners*. London: Penguin (currrent edition 1976).

Joyce, J. (1922). *Ulysses*. London: Penguin and Bodley Head (current edition 1986).

Kafka, F. (1916). Metamorphosis, in *Metamorphosis and other stories*. London: Penguin (current edition 1961).

Keats, J. (1816–20). *Selected poems and letters of Keats* (Ed. D. Bush). New York: Houghton Mifflin (current edition 1959).

Kellogg, R.T. (1994). *The psychology of writing*. New York: Oxford University Press.

Kellogg, R.T. (2001). Long-term working memory in text production. *Memory and Cognition*, *29*, 43–52.

Kermode, F. (1966). *The sense of an ending: Studies in the theory of fiction*. Oxford: Oxford University Press.

Kermode, F. (2000). *Shakespeare's language*. London: Allen Lane.

Kierkegaard, S. (1846). *Concluding unscientific postscript* (D.F. Swenson and W. Lowrie, Trans.). Princeton, NJ: Princeton University Press (current edition 1968).

Konijn, E. (2000). *Acting emotions: Shaping emotions on stage*. Amsterdam: Amsterdam University Press.

Lakoff, G., and Johnson, M. (1980). *Metaphors we live by*. Chicago: Chicago University Press.

Lakoff, G., and Turner, M. (1989). *More cool than reason: A field guide to poetic metaphor*. Cambridge: Cambridge University Press.

Lancashire, I. (2010). *Forgetful muses*. Toronto: University of Toronto Press.

Langer, S.K. (1988). *Mind: An essay on human feeling (abridged edition)*. Baltimore, MD: Johns Hopkins University Press.

Larocque, L., and Oatley, K. (2006). Joint plans, emotions, and relationships: A diary study of errors. *Journal of Cultural and Evolutionary Psychology*, *3–4*, 246–265.

Larsen, S.F., and Seilman, U. (1988). Personal meanings while reading literature. *Text*, *8*, 411–429.

Leavis, F.R. (1948). *The great tradition*. London: Chatto and Windus.

Lee, M.A., and Solomon, N. (1990). *Unreliable sources: A guide to detecting bias in news media*. New York: Carol Publishing Group.

Leslie, A.M. (1987). Pretence and representation: The orgins of "theory of mind." *Psychological Review*, *94*, 412–426.

Lessing, D. (1962). *The golden notebook*. London: Michael Joseph.

Lodge, D. (1975). *Changing places*. London: Secker and Warburg.

Lodge, D. (1977). *The modes of modern writing: Metaphor, metonymy, and the typology of modern fiction*. Ithaca, NY: Cornell University Press.

Lodge, D. (1988). *Nice work*. London: Secker and Warburg.

Lodge, D. (2001). *Thinks*. London: Secker and Warburg.

Lodge, D. (2002). Consciousness and the novel. In D. Lodge (Ed.), *Consciousness and the novel* (pp. 1–91). Cambridge, MA: Harvard University Press.

Long, E. (1986). Women, reading, and cultural authority: Some implications of the audience perspective in cultural studies. *American Quarterly*, *38*, 591–612.

Longinus. (1st Century CE). On the sublime. In T.S. Dorsch (Ed.), *Aristotle, Horace, Longinus: Classical literary criticism*. Harmondsworth: Penguin (current edition 1965).

Lorenz, K. (1935). Der Kumpan in der Umwelt des Vogels (Companionship in bird life: Fellow members of the species as releasers of social behavior). (C. Schiller, Trans.). In C. Schiller (Ed.), (pp. 83–128). London: Methuen (current publication 1957).

Lubbock, P. (1926). *The craft of fiction*. London: Cape.

Luria, A.R. (1968). *The mind of a mnemonist: A little book about a vast memory* (L. Solotaroff, Trans.). New York: Basic Books.

Luria, A.R. (1976). *Cognitive development: Its cultural and social foundations*. Cambridge, MA: Harvard University Press.

Magai, C., and Haviland-Jones, J. (2002). *The hidden genius of emotion: Lifespan transformations of personality*. New York: Cambridge University Press.

Maguire, E.A., Spiers, H., Good, C.D., *et al.* (2003). Navigation expertise and the human hippocampus: A structural brain imaging analysis. *Hippocampus*, *13*, 250–259.

Makaryk, I.R. (Ed.) (1993). *Encyclopaedia of contemporary literary theory: Approaches, scholars, terms*. Toronto: University of Toronto Press.

Malcolm, J. (2002). *Reading Chekhov: A critical journey*. New York: Random House.

Malcolm, J. (2007). *Two lives*. New Haven, CT: Yale University Press.

Malthus, T.R. (1798). *An essay on the principle of population*. Harmonsworth: Penguin (current edition 1976).

Mar, R.A. (2004). The neuropsychology of narrative: Story comprehension, story production and their interrelation. *Neuropsychologia*, *42*, 1414–1434.

Mar, R.A. (2007). *Simulation-based theories of narrative comprehension: Evidence and implications*. PhD thesis. University of Toronto.

Mar, R.A. (2011). The neural bases of social cognition and story comprehension. *Annual Review of Psychology*, *62*, 102–234.

Mar, R.A., Oatley, K., Hirsh, J., dela Paz, J., and Peterson, J.B. (2006). Bookworms versus nerds: Exposure to fiction versus non-fiction, divergent associations with social ability, and the simulation of fictional social worlds. *Journal of Research in Personality*, 40, 694–712.

Mar, R.A., Oatley, K., and Peterson, J.B. (2009). Exploring the link between reading fiction and empathy: Ruling out individual differences and examining outcomes. *Communications The European Journal of Communication*, 34, 407–428.

Mar, R.A., Tackett, J.L., and Moore, C. (2010). Exposure to media and theory-of-mind development in preschoolers. *Cognitive Development*, 25, 69–78.

Mar, R.A., Oatley, K., Djikic, M., and Mullin, J. (2011). Emotion and narrative fiction: Interactive influences before, during and after reading. *Cognition and Emotion*, in press.

Markus, H.R., and Nurius, P. (1986). Possible selves. *American Psychologist*, 41, 954–969.

Marlowe, C. (1587). Tamburlaine the Great. In E. Thomas (Ed.), *The plays of Christopher Marlowe* (pp. 1–119). London: Dent Everyman's Library (current edition 1931).

Mazzocco, P.M., Green, M.C., Sasota, J.A., and Jones, N.W. (2010). This story is not for everyone: Transportability and narrative persuasion. *Social Psychology and Personality Science*, 4, 361–368.

McCloud, S. (1993). *Understanding comics: The invisible art*. New York: HarperCollins.

McCutchen, D. (2000). Knowledge, processing, and working memory: Implications for a theory of writing. *Educational Psychologist*, 35, 13–23.

Metz, C. (1982). *The imaginary signifier: Psychoanalysis and the cinema* (C. Britton, Trans.). Bloomington, IN: Indiana University Press.

Miall, D.S. (2008). Foregrounding and feeling in narrative. In S. Zyngier, M. Bortolussi, A. Chesnokova and J. Auracher (Eds.), *Directions in empirical literary studies: In honor of Willie van Peer* (pp. 89–102). Amsterdam: Benjamins.

Miall, D.S. (2009). On interpretation. In *OnFiction*. http://www.onfiction. ca/2009/01/on-interpretation.html

Miall, D.S., and Kuiken, D. (1994). Foregrounding, defamiliarization, and affect: Response to literary stories. *Poetics*, 22, 389–407.

Miall, D.S., and Kuiken, D. (2002). A feeling for fiction: Becoming what we behold. *Poetics*, 30, 221–241.

Mithen, S. (1996). *The prehistory of the mind: The cognitive origins of art and science*. London: Thames and Hudson.

Miyake, N. (1986). Constructive interaction and the iterative process of understanding. *Cognitive Science*, 10, 151–177.

Mobbs, D., Wieskopf, N., Lau, H.C., Featherstone, E., Dolan, R.J., and Frith, C. (2006). The Kuleshov effect: The influence of contextual framing on emotional attributions. *Social, Cognitive, and Affective Neuroscience, 1,* 95–106.

Musil, R. (1942). *The man without qualities* (E. Wilkins and E. Kaiser, Trans.). London: Secker and Warburg (current edition 1979).

National Endowment for the Arts (2009). *Reading on the rise: A new chapter in American literacy.* Washington, DC: National Endowment for the Arts.

Neisser, U. (1963). The imitation of the man by machine. *Science, 139,* 193–197.

Nell, V. (1988). *Lost in a book: The psychology of reading for pleasure.* Newhaven, CT: Yale University Press.

Neuman, S.B. (1996). Children engaging in storybook reading: The influence of access to print resources, opportunity, and parental interaction. *Early Childhood Research Quarterly, 11,* 495–513.

Nickerson, R. (1999). How we know – and sometimes misjudge – what others know: Imputing one's own knowledge to others. *Psychological Bulletin, 125,* 737–759.

Niedenthal, P.M., Winckielman, P., Mondillon, L., and Vermeulen, N. (2009). Embodiment of emotion concepts. *Journal of Personality and Social Psychology, 96,* 1120–1136.

Nothelfer, C.E., DeLong, J.E., and Cutting, J.E. (2009). Shot structure in Hollywood film. *Indiana Undergraduate Journal of Cognitive Science, 4,* 103–113.

Nundy, S. (1996). *Effects of emotion on human inference.* PhD thesis, University of Toronto.

Nussbaum, M.C. (1986). *The fragility of goodness: Luck and ethics in Greek tragedy and philosophy.* Cambridge: Cambridge University Press.

Nussbaum, M.C. (1994). *The therapy of desire: Theory and practice in Hellenistic ethics.* Princeton, NJ: Princeton University Press.

Nussbaum, M.C. (1995). *Poetic justice: The literary imagination and public life.* Boston: Beacon.

Nuttall, A.D. (1983). *A new mimesis: Shakespeare and the representation of reality.* London: Methuen.

Oatley, K. (1992). *Best laid schemes: The psychology of emotions.* New York, NY: Cambridge University Press.

Oatley, K. (2002). Emotions and the story worlds of fiction. In M.C. Green, J.J. Strange and T.C. Brock (Eds.), *Narrative impact: Social and cognitive foundations* (pp. 39–69). Mahwah, NJ: Erlbaum.

Oatley, K. (2004). From the emotions of conversation to the passions of fiction. In N.H. Frijda, A.S.R. Manstead and A. Fischer (Eds.), *Feelings and Emotions: The Amsterdam Symposium* (pp. 98–115). New York: Cambridge University Press.

Oatley, K. (2009). Communications to self and others: Emotional experience and its skills. *Emotion Review, 1,* 206–213.

Oatley, K. (2010). *Therefore choose*. Fredericton: Goose Lane Editions.

Oatley, K., and Duncan, E. (1994). The experience of emotions in everyday life. *Cognition and Emotion, 8,* 369–381.

Oatley, K., and Gholamain, M. (1997). Emotions and identification: Connections between readers and fiction. In M. Hjort and S. Laver (Eds.), *Emotion and the arts* (pp. 163–281). New York: Oxford University Press.

Oatley, K., Keltner, D., and Jenkins, J.M. (2006). *Understanding emotions, second edition*. Malden, MA: Blackwell.

Oatley, K., and Larocque, L. (1995). Everyday concepts of emotions following every-other-day errors in joint plans. In J. Russell, J.-M. Fernandez-Dols, A.S.R. Manstead and J. Wellenkamp (Eds.), *Everyday conceptions of Emotions: An introduction to the psychology, anthropology, and linguistics of emotion. NATO ASI Series D 81* (pp. 145–165). Dordrecht: Kluwer.

Oatley, K., Mar, R.A., and Djikic, M. (2011 in press). The psychology of fiction: Present and future. In I. Jaen and J. Simon (Eds.), *The Cognition of Literature*. New Haven, CT: Yale University Press.

Oatley, K., and Olson, D.R. (2010). Cues to the imagination in memoir, science, and fiction. *Review of General Psychology, 14,* 56–64.

Oatley, K., and Yuill, N. (1985). Perception of personal and inter-personal action in a cartoon film. *British Journal of Social Psychology, 24,* 115–124.

O'Brien, E. (1989). Interview with Edna O'Brien. In G. Plimpton (Ed.), *Women writers at work: The Paris Review interviews* (pp. 337–359). Harmondsworth: Penguin.

O'Connor, F. (1933). "My Oedipus complex." In *My Oedipus Complex, and other stories*. (pp. 20–31). Harmondsworth: Penguin (current edition, 1963).

O'Connor, F. (1963). *The lonely voice*. New York: World Publishing Co (reprinted 2004, Melville House).

Olive, T. (2004). Working memory in writing: Empirical evidence from the dual-task technique. *European Psychologist, 9,* 32–42.

Olson, D.R. (1994). *The world on paper*. New York: Cambridge University Press.

Olson, D.R. (2010). Narrative, cognition, and rationality. In J.P. Gee and M. Handford (Eds.), *Routledge handbook of discourse analysis*. London: Routledge.

OnFiction On-line magazine on the psychology of fiction http://www.onfiction.ca/

Paluck, E.L. (2009). Reducing intergroup prejudice and conflict using the media: A field experiment in Rwanda. *Journal of Personality and Social Psychology, 96,* 574–587.

Panksepp, J. (1998). *Affective neuroscience: The foundations of human and animal emotions*. Oxford: Oxford University Press.

Panksepp, J. (2005). Beyond a joke: From animal laughter to human joy. *Science, 308,* 62–63.

Panksepp, J. (2005). Affective consciousness: Core emotional feelings in animals and humans. *Consciousness and Cognition, 14,* 30–80.

Parkes, M.B. (1992). *Pause and effect: An introduction to the history of punctuation in the West*. Aldershot: Ashgate.

Pennebaker, J.W. (1997). Writing about emotional experiences as a therapeutic process. *Psychological Science, 8*, 162–166.

Peskin, J. (1998). Constructing meaning when reading poetry: An expert-novice study. *Cognition and Instruction, 16*, 235–263.

Peskin, J., and Astington, J.W. (2004). The effects of adding metacognitive language to story texts. *Cognitive Development, 19*, 253–273.

Peskin, J., Allen, G., and Wells-Jopling, R. (2010). The "Educated Imagination:"Applying instructional research to the teaching of symbolic interpretation of poetry. *Journal of Adolescent and Adult Literacy, 53*, 498–507.

Perkins, D.N. (1981). *The mind's best work*. Cambridge, MA: Harvard University Press.

Peterson, J. (1999). *Maps of meaning: The architecture of belief*. London: Routledge.

Piaget, J., and Inhelder, B. (1969). *The psychology of the child*. London: Routledge and Kegan Paul.

Plato. (375 BCE). *The republic*. Harmondsworth, Middlesex: Penguin (current edition 1955).

Plutarch. (c. 100). Brutus. In I. Scott-Kilvert (Ed.), *Plutarch: Makers of Rome* (pp. 223–270). Harmondsworth: Penguin (current edition 1965).

Plutarch. (c. 100). Ceasar. In R. Warner (Ed.), *Plutarch: Fall of the Roman Republic* (pp. 243–310). Harmondsworth: Penguin (current edition 1958).

Poe, E.A. (1841). The murders in the rue Morgue. In D. Galloway (Ed.), *Edgar Allan Poe: Selected writings* (pp. 189–224). Harmondsworth: Penguin (current edition 1967).

Poe, E.A. (1846). The cask of Amontillado. In D. Galloway (Ed.), *Edgar Allan Poe: Selected writings* (pp. 360–366). Harmondsworth: Penguin (current edition 1967).

Porter, E. (Director). (1903). *The great train robbery*. USA.

Powell, B. (2002). *Writing and the origins of Greek literature*. Cambridge: Cambridge University Press.

Prentice, D., Gerrig, R.J., and Bailis, D.S. (1997). What readers bring to the processing of fictional texts. *Psychonomic Bulletin and Review, 4*, 416–420.

Proust, M. (1905). *Sur la lecture*: Mozambook http://www.bullesdozer.com/mediatheque/ebook/Proust/Sur%20la%20lecture.pdf (current edition 2001).

Proust, M. (1913–1927). *À la recherche du temps perdu*, Vols. I–VIII. Paris: Gallimard (current editions 1954–1987).

Protherough, R. (1983). *Developing response to fiction*. Milton Keynes: Open University Press.

Reinhart, A., and Feeley, T.H. (2007). Comparing the persuasive effects of narrative versus statistical messages: A meta-analytic review. Paper presented at the National Communication Association 93rd Annual Convention.

Richards, I.A. (1929). *Practical criticism: A study of literary judgement*. London: Routledge and Kegan Paul.

Richardson, S. (1740). *Pamela*. Oxford: Oxford University Press (current edition 2001).

Ricoeur, P. (1977). *The rule of metaphor: Multi disciplinary studies in the creation of meaning in language*. Toronto: University of Toronto Press.

Rimé, B. (2009). Emotion elicits social sharing of emotion: Theory and empirical review. *Emotion Review, 1*, 60–85.

Roberts, B.W., and Mroczek, D. (2008). Personality trait change in adulthood. *Current Directions in Psychological Science, 17*, 31–35.

Roiphe, K. (2007). *Uncommon arrangements: Seven portraits of married life in London literary circles, 1910–1939*. New York: Virago.

Rosenblatt, L. (1938). *Literature as exploration*. New York: Noble and Noble.

Ross, L. (1977). The intuitive psychologist and his shortcomings: Distortions in the attribution process. In L. Berkowitz (Ed.), *Advances in experimental social psychology, Vol 10*. New York: Academic Press.

Ross, P.E. (2006). The expert mind. *Scientific American, 295*(2), 64–71.

Rowley, H. (2006). *Tête-à-Tête: Simone de Beauvoir and Jean-Paul Sartre*. New York: Harper Perennial.

Royzman, E.B., and Rozin, P. (2006). Limits of synhedonia: The differential role of prior emotional attachment in sympathy and sympathetic joy. *Emotion, 6*, 82–93.

Ruffman, T., Slade, L., and Crowe, E. (2002). The relation between children's and mothers' mental state language and theory-of-mind understanding. *Child Development, 73*, 734–751.

Sato, W., and Yoshikawa, S. (2007). Spontaneous facial mimicry in response to dynamic facial expressions. *Cognition, 104*, 1–18.

Satterfield, T., Slovik, S., and Gregory, R. (2000). Narrative valuation in a policy judgment context. *Ecological Economics, 34*, 315–331.

Scarry, E. (1999). *Dreaming by the book*. Princeton, NJ: Princeton University Press.

Schacter, D., Addis, D.R., and Buckner, R.L. (2007). Remembering the past to imagine the future: The prospective brain. *Nature Reviews: Neuroscience, 8*, 657–661.

Scheff, T.J. (1979). *Catharsis in healing, ritual, and drama*. Berkeley: University of California Press.

Schlegel, A.W. (1849). *A course of lectures on dramatic art and literature* (J. Black, Trans.). London: Bohn.

Scholes, R., Phelan, J., and Kellogg, R.T. (2006). *The nature of narrative, revised and expanded*. New York: Oxford University Press.

Schwan, S., and Ildirar, S. (2010). Watching film for the first time: How adult viewers interpret perceptual discontinuities in film. *Psychological Science, 21*, 970–976.

Scribner, S., and Cole, M. (1981). *The psychology of literacy*. Cambridge, MA: Harvard University Press.

Sestir, M., and Green, M.C. (2010). You are who you watch: Identification and transportation effects on temporary self-concept. *Social Influence*, 5/4, 272–288.

Shakespeare, W. (1623). Open Source Shakespeare http://www. opensourceshakespeare.org/ (citations and line numbers are from this work). also: *The Norton Shakespeare* (Ed. S. Greenblatt). New York: Norton (modern edition, 1997).

Shelley, P.B. (1819). A defence of poetry. In C. Norman (Ed.), *Poets on poetry* (pp. 180–211). New York: Free Press. (current edition 1962).

Sherif, M., and Sherif, C.W. (1953). *Groups in harmony and in tension*. New York: Harper and Row.

Sherif, M., and Sherif, C.W. (1979). Research on intergroup relations. In W.G. Austin and S. Worchel (Eds.), *The social psychology of intergroup relations*. Monterey, CA: Brooks Cole.

Shklovsky, V. (1917). Art as technique (L.T. Lemon and M.J. Reis, Trans.). In D. Lodge (Ed.), *Modern criticism and theory* (pp. 16–30). London: Longman (current edition 1988).

Shklovsky, V. (1919). On the connection between devices of *Syuzhet* construction and general stylistic devices. In S. Bann and J.E. Bowlt (Eds.), *Russian formalism: A collection of articles and texts in translation* (pp. 48–71). Edinburgh: Scottish Academic Press (current edition 1973)

Shostrom, E.L.P. (Producer). (1966). *Three approaches to psychotherapy*. Santa Ana, CA: Psychological Films.

Simenon, G. (1977). Interview with Georges Simenon. In M. Cowley (Ed.), *Writers at work* (pp. 143–160). Harmondsworth: Penguin.

Simmons, W.K., Reddish, M., Bellgowan, P.S.F., and Martin, A. (2010). The selectivity and functional connectivity of the anterior temporal lobes. *Cerebral Cortex*, 20, 813–825.

Smith, A. (1759). *The theory of moral sentiments*. Oxford: Oxford University Press (currrent edition 1976).

Smith, P.K. (2005). Play: Types and functions in human development. In B.J. Ellis and D.F. Bjorkland (Eds.), *Origins of the social mind: Evolutionary psychology and child development* (pp. 271–291). New York: Guilford.

Sopcak, P. (2007). "Creation from nothing:" A foregrounding study of James Joyce's drafts for *Ulysses*. *Language and Literature*, 16, 183–196.

Southam, B. (2001). *Jane Austen's literary manuscripts: A study of the novelist's development through the surviving papers*. Revised edition. London: Athlone Press.

Speer, N.K., Reynolds, J.R., Swallow, K., and Zacks, J.M. (2009). Reading stories activates neural representations of visual and motor experience. *Psychological Science*, 20, 989–999.

Spenser, E. (1596). *The Faerie Queene*. Harmondsworth, Middlesex: Penguin (current edition 1987).

Spreng, N.R., Mar, R.A., and Kim, A.S.N. (2009). The common neural basis of autobiographical memory, prospection, navigation, theory of mind, and the default mode: A quantitative meta-analysis. *Journal of Cognitive Neuroscience, 21*, 489–510.

Spurgin, T. (2009). *The art of reading*. Chantilly, VA: The Teaching Company.

Stanislavski, C. (1936). *An actor prepares* (E.R. Habgood, Trans.). New York: Routledge.

Stanovich, K.E. (2004). *The robot's rebellion: Finding meaning in the age of Darwin*. Chicago: University of Chicago Press.

Stanovich, K.E., West, R.F., and Harrison, M.R. (1995). Knowledge growth and maintenance across the life span: The role of print exposure. *Developmental Psychology, 31*, 811–826.

Steckley, P., and Larocque, L. (1996). Horror, action or romance? Emotional bases for the enjoyment of home entertainment videos. Paper presented at the Ninth Conference of the International Society for Research on Emotions, Toronto.

Steen, G. (2008). The paradox of metaphor: Why we need a three-dimensional model of metaphor. *Metaphor and Symbol, 23*, 213–241.

Stein, S. (1999). *How to grow a novel: The most common mistakes writers make and how to overcome them*. New York: St Martin's.

Steiner, G. (1967). *Language and silence: Essays 1958–1966*. London: Faber.

Stevenson, R.L. (1883). *Treasure Island*. New York: Simon and Schuster (current edition 2000).

Stevenson, R.L. (1884). A humble remonstrance. *Longman's Magazine, December*, Reprinted in *R.L. Stevenson Essays and Poems*, (Ed. C. Harman). London: Dent Everyman's Library (pp. 1179–1188) (current edition 1992).

Stevenson, R.L. (1888). A chapter on dreams. *Scribner's Magazine, January*, Reprinted in *R.L. Stevenson Essays and Poems* (Ed. C. Harman). London: Dent Everyman's Library (pp. 1189–1199) (current edition 1992)

Stiller, J., and Dunbar, R.I.M. (2007). Perspective-taking and memory capacity predict social network size. *Social Networks, 29*, 93–104.

Stock, B. (2007). *Ethics through literature: Ascetic and aesthetic reading in Western culture*. Lebanon, NH: University Press of New England.

Stolnitz, J. (1991). On the historical triviality of art. *British Journal of Aesthetics, 31*, 195–202.

Stowe, H.B. (1851). *Uncle Tom's cabin, or Life among the lowly*. Harmondsworth: Penguin (current edition 1981).

Summerfield, J.J., Hassabis, D., and Maguire, E.A. (2010). Differential engagement of brain regions within a 'core' network during scene construction. *Neuropsychologia, 48*, 1501–1509.

Swann, J., and Allington, D. (2009). Reading groups and the language of literary texts: A case study in social reading. *Language and Literature, 18,* 247–264.

Tajfel, H. (1982). Social psychology of intergroup relations. *Annual Review of Psychology, 33,* 1–39.

Tamietto, M., Castelli, L., Vighetti, S., Perozzo, P., Geminiani, G., Weiskrantz, L., *et al.* (2009). Unseen facial and bodily expressions trigger fast emotional reactions. *Proceedings of the National Academy of Sciences of the USA, online version.*

Tan, E. (2008). Entertainment is emotion: The functional architecture of the entertainment experience. *Media Psychology, 11,* 28–51.

Tan, E. (1996). *Emotion and the structure of narrative film: Film as an emotion machine.* Mahwah, NJ: Erlbaum.

Tan, E., and Frijda, N.H. (1999). Sentiment in film viewing. In C. Plantinga and G.M. Smith (Eds.), *Passionate views: Film, cognition, and emotion* (pp. 48–64). Baltimore, MD: Johns Hopkins University Press.

The golden notebook project. http://thegoldennotebook.org/

Thomson, K. (2000). Literature for all of us. In E. Slezak (Ed.), *The book group book: A thoughtful guide to forming and enjoying a book discussion group.* Third edition. (pp. 173–179). Chicago: Chicago Review Press.

Todd, Z. (2008). Talking about books: A reading group study. *Psychology of Aesthetics, Creativity, and the Arts, 2,* 256–263.

Todorov, T. (1977). The typology of detective fiction (R. Howard, Trans.). *The poetics of prose* (pp. 42–52). Ithaca, NY: Cornell University Press.

Tolstoy, L. (1877). *Anna Karenina* (R. Pevear and L. Volokonsky, Trans.). London: Penguin (current edition 2000).

Tolstoy, L. (1885). Strider (*Kholstomer*). In R. Wilks and P. Foore (Eds. and Trans.), *Leo Tolstoy: Master and man, and other stories* (pp. 67–107). London: Penguin (current edition 2005).

Tomasello, M. (2008). *Origins of human communication.* Cambridge, MA: MIT Press.

Tomasello, M., and Hermann, E. (2010). Ape and human cognition: What's the difference. *Psychological Science, 19,* 3–8.

Trabasso, T., and Chung, J. (2004, January 23). *Empathy: Tracking characters and monitoring their concerns in film.* Paper presented at the Winter Text Conference, Jackson Hole.

Trabasso, T., and Van Den Broek, P. (1985). Causal thinking and the representation of narrative events. *Journal of Memory and Language, 24,* 612–630.

Trionfi, G., and Reese, E. (2005). A good story: Children with imaginary companions create richer narratives. *Child Development, 80,* 1301–1313.

Trounstine, J.R. (2000). Throw the book at them. In E. Slezak (Ed.), *The book group book: A thoughtful guide to forming and enjoying a book discussion group, third edition* (pp. 79–86). Chicago: Chicago Review Press.

Trounstine, J.R., and Waxler, R. (2005). *Finding a voice: The practice of changing lives through literature*. Ann Arbor, MI: University of Michigan Press.

Tsai, J.L., Louie, J.Y., Chen, E.E., and Uchida, Y. (2007). Learning what feelings to desire: Socialization of ideal affect through children's storybooks. *Personality and Social Psychology Bulletin, 33*, 17–30.

Turgenev, I. (1852). *Sketches from a hunter's album* (R. Freeborn, Trans.). London: Penguin (current edition 1990).

Turner, M. (1996). *The literary mind: The origins of thought and language*. New York: Oxford University Press.

Turner, M. (2008). Frame blending. In R.R. Favretti (Ed.), *Frames, corpora, and knowledge representation* (pp. 13–32). Bologna: Bononia University Press.

Van Peer, W. (1986). *Sylistics and psychology: Investigations of foregrounding*. London: Croom Helm.

Van Peer, W. (2008a). The inhumanity of the humanities. In J. Auracher and W. Van Peer (Eds.). *New beginnings in literary studies* (pp. 1–22). Newcastle: Cambridge Scholars Publishing.

Van Peer, W. (Ed.). (2008b). *The quality of literature: Linguistic studies in literary evaluation*. Amsterdam: Benjamins.

Van Peer, W., and Maat, H.P. (1996). Perspectivation and sympathy: Effects of narrative point of view. In R.J. Kreuz and M.S. MacNealy (Eds.), *Empirical approaches to literature and aesthetics. Advances in discourse processes, Vol. 52*. (pp. 143–154). Westport, CT: Ablex.

Van Peer, W., Zyngier, S., and Hakemulder, J.F. (2007). Foregrounding, past, present, and future. In D.L. Hoover and S. Lattig (Eds.), *Stylistics: Prospect and retrospect* (pp. 1–22). Amsterdam: Rodopi.

Vendler, H. (1997). *The art of Shakespeare's sonnets*. Cambridge, MA: Harvard University Press.

Verboord, M., and van Rees, K. (2009). Literary education curriculum and institutional contexts: Textbook content and teachers' textbook usage in Dutch literary education, 1968–2000. *Poetics, 37*, 74–97.

Vettin, J., and Todt, D. (2005). Human laughter, social play, and play vocalizations of non-human primates: An evolutionary approach. *Behaviour, 142*, 217–240.

Voltaire. (1759). *Candide and other stories* (R. Pearson, Trans.). New York: Knopf (current edition 1992).

Vygotsky, L. (1962). *Thought and language* (E.H.G. Vakar, Trans.). Cambridge, MA: MIT Press.

Wallas, G. (1926). *The art of thought*. London: Cape.

Walton, K.L. (1990). *Mimesis as make-believe: On the foundations of the representational arts*. Cambridge, MA: Harvard University Press.

Waters, E., Merrick, S., Treboux, D., Crowell, J., and Albersheim, L. (2000). Attachment security in infancy and early adulthood: a twenty-year longitudinal study. *Child Development, 71,* 684–689.

Waxler, R. (2000). A journey down the river. In E. Slezak (Ed.), *The book group book: A thoughtful guide to forming and enjoying a book discussion group, third edition* (pp. 87–92). Chicago: Chicago Review Press.

Weimann, R. (1985). Mimesis in *Hamlet.* In P. Parker and G. Hartman (Eds.), *Shakespeare and the question of theory.* London: Methuen.

Wells-Jopling, R. (2009). Distancing ourselves from fiction. In *OnFiction.* http://www.onfiction.ca/2009/10/distancing-ourselves-from-fiction.html.

Westen, D. (2007). *The political brain: The role of emotion in deciding the fate of the nation.* New York: Public Affairs Books.

Wicker, B., Keysers, C., Plailly, J., Royet, J.-P., Gallese, V., and Rizzolatti, G. (2003). Both of us disgusted in *my* insula: The common neural basis of seeing and feeling disgust. *Neuron, 40,* 655–664.

Williams, B. (1993). *Shame and necessity.* Berkeley, CA: University of California Press.

Williams, T. (2004). The writing process: scenarios, sketches and rough drafts. In T. Unwin (Ed.), *The Cambridge companion to Flaubert* (pp. 165–179). Cambridge: Cambridge University Press.

Wimmer, H., and Perner, J. (1983). Beliefs about beliefs: Representation and constraining function of wrong beliefs in young children's understanding of deception. *Cognition, 13,* 103–128.

Wimsatt, K.W., and Beardsley, M. (1954). The affective fallacy. In K.W. Wimsatt (Ed.), *The verbal icon: Studies in the meaning of poetry* (pp. 21). Lexington, KY: University of Kentucky Press.

Winnicott, D.W. (1971). *Playing and reality.* London: Tavistock.

Winston, A. (1992). Sweetness and light: Psychological aesthetics and sentimental art. In G.C. Cupchik and J. Laszlo (Eds.), *Emerging visions of the aesthetic process: Psychology, semiology, and philosophy* (pp. 118–136). New York: Cambridge University Press.

Winston, A., and Cupchik, G.C. (1992). The evaluation of high art and popular art by naive and experienced viewers. *Visual Arts Research, 18,* 1–14.

Wittgenstein, L. (1953). *Philosophical investigations.* Oxford: Blackwell.

Wolfe, T. (1975a). The new journalism. In T. Wolfe and E.W. Johnson (Eds.), *The new journalism* (pp. 13–68). London: Picador.

Wolfe, T. (1975b). Radical chic. In T. Wolfe and E.W. Johnson (Eds.), *The new journalism* (pp. 413–422 (extract from article originally published in the magazine *New York*)). London: Picador.

Woolf, V. (1924). Mr Bennett and Mrs Brown. *In Collected essays. Vol 1* (pp. 319–337). London: Chatto and Windus (currrent edition 1966).

Woolf, V. (1925). *Mrs Dalloway*. London: Hogarth Press.

Woolf, V. (1925). Jane Austen, in *Collected essays, Vol 1* (pp. 144–154). London: Chatto and Windus (current edition 1966).

Wyman, E., Rakoczy, H., and Tomasello, M. (2009). Young children understand multiple pretend identities in their object play. *British Journal of Developmental Psychology, 27*, 385–404.

Yarmolinsky, A. (Ed.). (1973). *Letters of Anton Chekhov*. New York: Viking.

Zillmann, D. (1991). Empathy: Affect from bearing witness to the emotions of others. In J. Bryant and D. Zillmann (Eds.), *Responding to the screen: Reception and reaction processes* (pp. 135–167). Hillsdale, NJ: Erlbaum.

Zimbardo, P.G. (2007). *The Lucifer effect: Understanding how good people turn evil.* New York: Random House.

Zunshine, L. (2006). *Why we read fiction: Theory of mind and the novel.* Columbus, OH: Ohio State University Press.

Zwaan, R. (2008). Time in language, situation models, and mental simulations. *Language Learning, 58*, 13–26.

Name Index

Such Stuff as Dreams: The Psychology of Fiction, First Edition. K. Oatley.
© 2011 K. Oatley. Published 2011 by John Wiley & Sons, Ltd.

Subject Index